Roland Legrand

Astrology for a better life

A complete and practical course to teach yourself astrology

Roland at a seminar in France in 2013

The Sphinx
Drawing by Roland

Introduction

Welcome to a better life with astrology!

Before we start, I need to remind you to make sure you understand every lesson in this book. It is essential that you follow the simple rules described below to ensure the best results from your study of astrology.

1 - Do not continue to lesson B before you are sure to have understood the context of Lesson A.

2 - Do the requested exercises. They are meant to help you progress and master this wonderful science.

3 - Do not hesitate to go back on any chapter or lesson to freshen up your memory and to verify your acquired knowledge.

4 - Practise, practise, and practise again! Astrology is like learning to play music. Practice is the key to mastering the instrument.

Read each lesson as many times as necessary to understand everything thoroughly before you continue to the next one. There are numerous important steps to follow before you can cast and analyse a birth chart correctly. This course is designed to provide you with the fundamentals of astrology. If you are dedicated, you will derive great benefits from this most fascinating subject. Before you start, though, here is one simple rule to remember:

Take your time!
Make sure you understand A before going on to B

I have often been asked, during private consultations or social meetings, why I had chosen astrology out of all the sciences, and how I had gone about getting the books and other information needed for its 'difficult study'…

Before I go on any further, I would like to emphasise the fact that the study of astrology is NOT difficult! **Anyone, anywhere and for any reason at all can decide to learn astrology.** The only important thing is to proceed in an orderly way and NOT try to absorb it all in one big gulp like some medicine or magic potion…

If you have decided to take this course, it is evidence that you are already interested in the subject. If I have decided to teach astrology, it is to guide those who might find it difficult to organise a self-taught course of study.

I know how hard and frustrating it can be to look for material to work from. The first choice is vital because it is the reaction to such a choice that is going to motivate progress and success in this fascinating science.

The present work is, therefore, dedicated to everyone. That is why I want it to be clear and simple but still intellectually stimulating and rewarding to all. Whatever your educational background, I think that the subject of each lesson can be absorbed and comprehended by you in an easy and entertaining manner. *Because the study of astrology IS entertaining!*

Astrologers are not 'hermits' wearing beautiful white beards and living in some hidden and secret cave somewhere in far-off Tibet. NOT AT ALL! It is because Astrology is a lively subject that those who study it can take full advantage of their lives.

Instead of worrying over absurd or frustrating problems, you will be able to live up to your expectations, in full control of your everyday actions and thoughts.

BE POSITIVE AND ALL THINGS BECOME POSSIBLE...

When I turned to astrology, I could have just as well consulted a clairvoyant, a numerologist, a psychoanalyst, or an astrologer. Psychologically I felt that something was missing in my life. To the eyes of those around me it all seemed very trivial but, deep inside I knew the volcano was beginning to awaken.

To be just a number or a ghost is the same in our society. If you do not have something that makes you special, nobody knows you even exist. You are alone, lost in the crowd... Tomorrow you may disappear and only very few people will take notice of it. And yet, you ARE somebody... There is a whole universe within yourself; a universe just as rich and interesting as that of the 'greatest' people.

That is how I felt when I met astrology by pure coincidence. But was it really a coincidence? The mysterious power of the planets became an understandable influence that I could almost control. It helped me solve many personal problems and made me feel I could move mountains...

I became a professional astrologer, but you do not need such an objective to learn astrology. It should be taught in schools, just like history, geography, or mathematics. Everyone has learned mathematics to some extent, but how many have become mathematicians?

Some people are passionate lovers of art, history, or geography. They have extensive knowledge and possess a fabulous collection of books and fascinating stories to tell. They are considered amateurs, but they often know more than the so-called professionals because they have learned only for their wellbeing, for their own pleasure and personal enrichment. How many amateur astronomers study the skies every night, using all sorts of sophisticated instruments? The information they collect often helps the professionals themselves.

How many amateur astronomers study the skies every night...

Even if you do not want to become a master mind, The Queen's or President's private Astrologer, or the secret adviser of some head of government, you can learn astrology for many good reasons. And yet, your personal studies and approach will contribute in some way to the progress of this science. And, why not, you may even one day, decide to become a professional astrologer!

I would be proud and happy to have guided your first steps.

Putting aside the idea of becoming a professional astrologer, you will find there are a thousand good reasons to learn astrology and each one of your reasons is one of the good reasons that made me decide to teach you.

On completing the present course, you will derive enormous profit from your acquired knowledge. Be it for others or for yourself, Astrology can give an answer to all your questions.

You will become the centre of attraction at social gatherings or family reunions. You will be able to converse with people of all walks of life, of all educational backgrounds and cultures, because astrology interests EVERYBODY, whatever one may say.

Everyone on Earth has, at least once in his life, looked up into a starry summer night sky in search of an answer to the question of existence. Since man is man, since he has been given the power to think, he has acquired the desire to create. It is such a desire that has made his mind turn to the mysteries of life and to God…

This is an incredibly old story. Astrology is not a science that was invented, discovered, or created in one day. No one has come out of a laboratory screaming: '*Eureka! I've got it all!*'

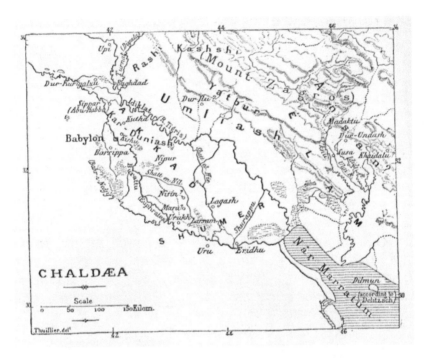

Truly we do not really know when it began, but we are sure that as far back as historical and archaeological research goes, some trace of astrology can be found as well as the influence it had on the course of history and the development of civilisations.

Numerous famous figures throughout the centuries of our present civilisation have taken part in the study of cosmic influences. In Chaldea, in Egypt and later in Greece, every scientist was, above all, an astrologer.

ARISTOTLE, for example, wrote this about astrology: '*This world is linked in a vital way to the movements of the world above. Any power in this world is governed by such movements.*'

DANTE also considered cosmic influences very seriously. He wrote this:

'The planets are the primary causes to your actions but you have been given a light that enables you to distinguish between good and evil, and a free will that after battling against the influence of the planets, will eventually triumph if it is well directed.'

Closer to us, **KEPLER** the great mathematician, admitted that *'twenty years of studies had convinced his rebel mind that Astrology was real.'*

The famous German author, **GOETHE** was not ignorant of this science either. In one of his books, *'Poetry and Truth'*, he wrote: *'I was born in Frankfort Am Main (Germany) on the 28th of August 1749 at Midday precisely. The constellations were happy, the Sun was in Virgo, Jupiter, and Venus in good aspect with it; Mercury was favourable, Saturn and Mars were neutral. Only the Moon, full on that day, exercised its power of restriction on me, holding up my birth until its planetary time had passed. The good aspects, highly appreciated by astrologers later on, are probably the reason why I stayed alive, because the ignorance of the nurse made everyone believe I was born dead and it is only after great effort that I finally saw the light.'*

As for **HONORÉ DE BALZAC** famous French writer of the romantic 19th century, was certain that *'astrology is an immense science that has ruled the greatest minds of this world'*.

The eminent psychoanalyst, **_CARL JUNG,_** at first very sceptical, later wrote:

'If poorly informed and educated people have been able until recently to laugh about Astrology, considering it as a so-called science of the past, that same Astrology, rising from the depth of people's souls, is presenting itself again at the doors of our universities that it had left for over three centuries.'

Closer to us again, **_HENRY MILLER_** the unconventional genius, writer of revolutionary books and novels based on his own life, said this, in an article for a French magazine called _'L'ASTROLOGUE'_, in its number-16 issue: _'Astrology speaks of Man in its entirety and I estimate that this is essential. It considers Man as a complete being. It shows that there are rhythms in nature and that every living thing participates to such rhythms.'_

In 1973, in his fascinating book called _'SUPERNATURE'_, **_LYALL WATSON,_** professor in biology in the U.S. gave had a scientific approach to astrology. Among other things, he wrote this:

'Astrology represents an equation of which the positions of the planets are variables. Such moving positions around a fixed point are scientifically predictable and combine to form a unique system of conditions capable of influencing whatever happens around this fixed point on Earth.'

Later in his books he added:

'I think Astrology was born out of an innate consciousness of cosmic powers that influence man to have certain ideas and, as much as each Astrologer has brought his own personal and particular contribution and could only trust this small fraction of the whole structure, the final product got a natural and well-balanced shape and aspect.'

To end this short list of experts' opinions, the **SUNDAY SUN**, in Brisbane (Australia) before it closed down in 1992, published on the 19th of December 1982, an article titled:

'ASTROLOGY: NOW IT'S RESPECTABLE!'

And it went on:

'One third of the western world believes in it already, but for the rest of us, sceptics, here is momentous news... Astrology may not be nonsense after all. After centuries of being dismissed as pie in the sky by serious scientists, the stargazing business has been declared respectable by two eminent British Psychologists.'

You will find a scan of this article on the following page.

Astrology: Now it's respectable

From BILL MELLOR in London

One third of the Western world's population believes it already, but for the rest of us sceptics here is momentous news ... Astrology may not be nonsense after all.

After centuries of being dismissed as pie in the sky by serious scientists; the star-gazing business has been declared respectable by two eminent British psychologists.

Or at least one branch of astrology has.

Called cosmobiology, it argues that people born when certain planets are in two "critical sectors" of their passage through the sky often distinguish themselves in various walks of life.

And statistics meticulously gleaned in Europe and America over 20 years provide the following dramatic and partially-persuasive evidence:

● Champion sportsmen are more likely to be born when Mars is either beginning its rise or just past the mid-point of its daily journey.

● The most eminent doctors and scientists tend to have been born when either Mars or Saturn is in those same positions.

● Many military top brass and war heroes really are under the influence of the god of war, Mars, or Jupiter.

● Leading actors and artists usually avoid being born under Saturn.

● And musicians tend not to be born under Mars.

These findings are the result of research on more than 16,000 famous people by a French husband-and-wife team, Michel and Francoise Gauquelin. For years, their work has been dismissed by many scientists as the usual astrological mumbo jumbo.

Science backs zodiac study

Approval

Now, however, it has been given the seal of approval by the eminent London University professors Hans Eysenck and D.J.B. Nias in a new book, *Astrology: Science or Superstition.*

Neither the authors nor the Gauquelins are quite sure how or why the position of planets influences people's characters and destinies. But they do come up with one fanciful theory — that a genetic characteristic may make a child "choose" to be born when a particular planet has just risen or culminated.

In this mysterious process, the planets are somehow acting as "celestial midwives," they suggest.

Incredible?

Yes, but surely the evidence they offer requires some explanation.

The Gauquelins divide the passage of the planets across the sky into 12 sectors, roughly similar to the traditional astrological houses. As the time the planets spend in each quarter is the same, the chance of anyone being born in the two critical sectors is one in six — or 16.66 per cent. Yet a study of 1,553 champion athletes in Europe and America showed 22 per cent were born when Mars was passing through these sectors.

And in an even more e group, 20 Olympic medalists, the figure 'o 35 per cent. The highest-ranking military men and war heroes killed or maimed on the battlefield also produced a Mars or Jupiter factor of well over 20 per cent.

Musicians, meanwhile, tended to avoid Mars. However, military musicians fell roughly halfway between the soldiers and the musicians!

Similarly, Saturn attracted doctors and scientists while avoiding actors and artists.

Michel Gauquelin is not an astrologer. He is a scientist who studied psychology and statistics at the Sorbonne.

Unlike many researchers in the field, he set out to objectively test traditional astrological claims — such as that death occurs more frequently under Saturn — and one by one he found them wanting.

Once, in a mischievous moment, he sent the birth times of 10 convicted murderers to a mail order firm that promised "to reveal your character and destiny in return for your birth data and a cheque."

Inconclusive

None of the character studies the firm sent him showed any hint of criminal tendencies or penal destiny.

However, when he got round to testing the exact time of birth of famous people, he discovered the apparent connection with some — though not all planets.

Not all the Gauquelins' results are consistent with traditional astrology. For instance, Venus and Mercury do not figure in their charts of musicians and artists, as would have been predicted by most astrologers.

And the furthest planets, Uranus, Neptune and Pluto have no significance to the Gauquelins at all.

But, with the acceptance of some of their work, the omens might at last be boding well for astrologers in their search for respectability.

*Published in Britain by Maurice Temple Smith of London

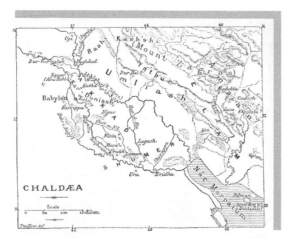

CHALDÆA

To come back to the history of astrology, experts have often tried to find its proper origin, going back more than twenty-six thousand years BC where they could trace the first Zodiac reproductions.

Modern archaeology does not yet allow experts to verify Pline and Cicero's appreciation of around 480,000 years! It has even been said that extraterrestrial people could have transmitted to Man their science of the cosmic influences, far superior to ours.

What we know for sure is that in the times of the Roman Empire, occultism was widely spread, and astrology had an important part in it. Astrologers were called '**Chaldeans**', which made one suppose that the origin of their science was Chaldea.

'It all started in SUMER' says French historian *Jacques Sadoul. T*he Sumerian civilisation developed between the *TIGRE* and the EUPHRATES rivers running down from the **CAUCASUS MOUNTAINS.** The **AKKADIANS, BABYLONIANS** and **ASSYRIANS** followed, and then came the **CHALDEANS.**

From 700 BC, the Assyrian Empire extended its influence to Egypt, conquered by **ESARHADDON King of NINIVE** in 671 BC. Over 16 years of occupation made foreign cultural exchange important and astrology must have come out of the Egyptian temples where it had been kept for centuries. All this also happened under King **ASHURBANIPAL** (son of Esarhaddon) the best known of all Kings of NINIVE.

Around 500 BC, Chaldeans appeared in **MESOPOTAMIA**, rapidly spreading their knowledge of astrology to the entire Mediterranean Gulf. In those days, astrologers were consulted for all the affairs of the kingdom. The astrologer-priest was a counsellor, a sort of medium between Heaven and Earth, between God and Man.

From its unfathomable origins until today, astrology has travelled its long journey through time, receiving all sorts of intellectual, mystical, and religious influences. Sometimes brought to the first rank of all sciences, sometimes refuted, it comes to us today, rich of its passed experiences to serve Man at all levels and in all areas of life.

Astrology should not be reserved to a privileged few. You must not think that only the great and famous can have access to it. Despite my name (Legrand), I am neither great nor famous... However, without considering the help given to those who have trusted me when consulting me for astrological analyses, I can confidently say that astrology is a fourth dimension, a new optic of life and a definite power, giving access to the joys of living and to happiness.

Professional or sentimental success is assured through the

inner discovery of personal potential and talents often buried under prejudice and wrong education. Sexual, emotional, artistic, mystical, intellectual needs or any other needs can be understood, accepted, and blended harmoniously within everyday life. It is the perfect reunion of body and soul.

Forget your complexes, remorse, frustrations, and other problems of that kind! Knowing **WHO *YOU ARE***, you will know ***HOW TO BEHAVE.*** The possibilities of astrology are infinite.

In addition to knowing yourself better, it teaches you how to behave with others. It gives you the ability to understand the ones you love as much as those you do not like so much…

It is a friend science, a confidant, a kind of godly witch to whom you can ask thousands of questions, who can fulfil your dreams, and eventually accomplish miracles…

Very quickly the study of astrology becomes a second nature because it seems that everything is linked to it. You will meet someone and start to guess their Sun Sign. Watching their hands, their attitude, their eyes, their movements, and their overall expression, you will come to precise conclusions.

You will observe people continuously, without even noticing it, but you will notice more and more about them. And this will only be a start…

Astrology goes far beyond a simple knowledge about the twelve zodiac signs. To say that someone was born under such or such sign does not allow for a proper analysis. This is vague. One must also consider, besides the DATE OF BIRTH, the TIME and PLACE of that birth. Such information enables the astrologer to draw what is commonly called a '***BIRTH CHART' or 'HOROSCOPE…'***

Lesson 1

Drawing a birth chart

In this lesson, you will learn about the drawing of a birth chart.

What is what?

- On the **BLANK CHART provided on the following page there are spaces that need to be filled by ABLAS students. You don't have to do that from this book, of course.**

There are spaces for the NAME, the **DATE OF BIRTH,** the **TIME OF BIRTH** and the **PLACE OF BIRTH.**

- Next, there is a space for the **GMT OF BIRTH** (Greenwich Mean Time according to **MERIDIAN ZERO,** starting point of all geographical and astrological calculations).

- From the above comes the **EXACT TIME OF BIRTH** or **'SOLAR TIME'** of birth, usually different from the **'LOCAL TIME' of birth.**

- The next step is to indicate the **EXACT SIDEREAL TIME (EST).** We will come back to this important point later…

The empty space below, reserved for **'REMARKS'** is reserved to any commentary about the BIRTH CHART in question.

Far down below, on the left side, it is interesting to write the date the drawing is done. This allows chronological classification of charts as well as the observation of one's own progress in astrology.

Four blank charts are printed on the following pages. They will be useful to learn how to draw the elements that make up a birth chart.

ASTROLOGICAL BIRTH CHART

Name: _____ Date of Birth: _____
Local time of birth: _____ Place of birth: _____
GMT of birth: ___ Exact time of birth: _____ TSE* of Birth: _____

Remark: *TSE or EST = Exact Sidereal Time

ASTROLOGICAL BIRTH CHART

Name: _____ Date of Birth: _____
Local time of birth: _____ Place of birth: _____
GMT of birth: __ Exact time of birth: _____ TSE* of Birth: _____

Remark: *TSE or EST = Exact Sidereal Time

ASTROLOGICAL BIRTH CHART

Name: _____ Date of Birth: _____
Local time of birth: _____ Place of birth: _____
GMT of birth: __ Exact time of birth: _____ TSE* of Birth: _____

Remark: *TSE or EST = Exact Sidereal Time

ASTROLOGICAL BIRTH CHART

Name: _____ Date of Birth: _____
Local time of birth: _____ Place of birth: _____
GMT of birth: __ Exact time of birth: ____ TSE* of Birth: _____

Remark: *TSE or EST = Exact Sidereal Time

On the drawing of the **BLANK CHART, the space outside the zodiac ring is used to place the SYMBOLS OF THE PLANETS and the cusps of the HOUSES.**

The **CIRCULAR SECTION or RING** is divided into 12 equal parts and is used to place the **SYMBOLS OF THE TWELVE ZODIAC SIGNS** _COUNTERCLOCKWISE._

The **INNER CIRCULAR SECTION** is used to trace the **'ASPECT LINES'** (various angles separating planets and other important elements around the chart). Aspects will be studied in future lessons.

WHAT IS WHAT?

Firstly, you must learn to draw and quickly recognise the different symbols of the signs and of the planets. Practise until you are confident about recognising each one of them.

NOW, draw these SYMBOLS on the BLANK CHART. Copy from your completed BIRTH CHART if you have it.

If not, you can work it out on this website:

https://www.astrotheme.com/horoscope_chart_sign_asc endant.php

ASTROLOGICAL BIRTH CHART

Name: _Smith_ Date of Birth: _June_
Local time of birth: _m_ Place of birth: _m_
GMT of birth: _m_ Exact time of birth: _m_ TSE* of Birth: _m_

Remark: *TSE or EST = Exact Sidereal Time

This is just an example

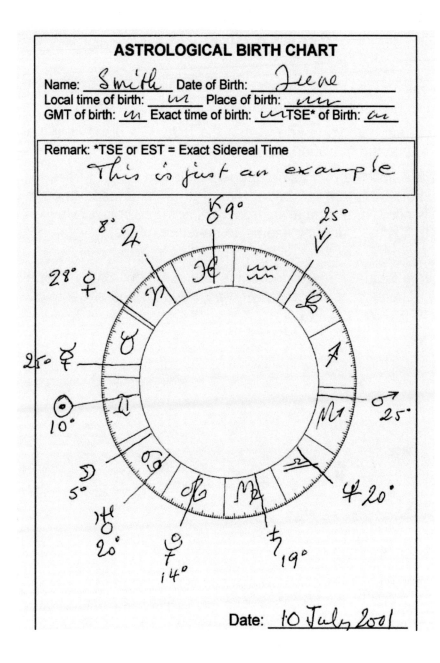

Date: _10 July 2001_

WHAT IS A ZODIAC SIGN?

A zodiac sign is determined by the alignment of the Sun with that sign on the day of birth.

Of course, everyone knows that the **SUN IS FIXED**, it is the Earth that turns around it in one year.

In the same manner as someone sitting in a moving train, for example, may get the impression that what he sees through the window is moving away from him, from our point of view on Earth it is the Sun that 'seems' to travel, from east to west, not us…

Have a look at the drawing of the zodiac below. Study it for a few minutes to understand what happens on an astronomical point of view…

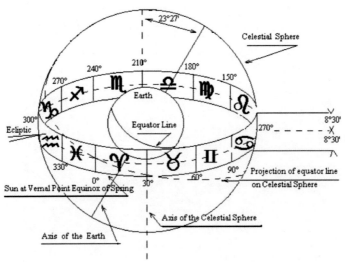

The zodiac is the celestial strip divided by the ecliptic and surrounding the Earth. Within its limits, the Sun, the Moon, and the planets seem to travel around us. The width of the zodiac strip is 17°, therefore 8° 30′ on either side of the ecliptic's dividing line.

The *ECLIPTIC* is the apparent path of the Sun around the earth in one year.

The axis of the Earth is slightly tilted from the plan of the ecliptic. The meeting point between the ecliptic and the equator line is called 'Vernal point' or 'Gamma point' or 'Degree zero'. It is from the vernal point that the zodiac runs, **counterclockwise** (anticlockwise).

The zodiac is made up of twelve sections called 'signs'. Each sign corresponds to an area of 30° around the circle of the zodiac and of the revolution of the Sun, therefore to approximately one month (because the Sun travels approximately one degree around the zodiac every day). Spring in the northern hemisphere begins on the 21st of March. The first sign, Aries, begins on this day and ends when the Sun has travelled the 30° allocated to this sign. Then the second sign begins, on the 20th of April, almost one month later.

The ZODIAC is the celestial strip between the limits of which the planets move around the Sun. (*See the drawing below*).

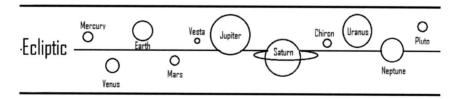

The orbit of Mercury and of the other planets will never vary outside the limits of the ZODIAC STRIP. Their path is linked to their speed of rotation, their distance from the Sun and its magnetic attraction.

It is that same orbit that has been divided into 12 sections that were named after the corresponding constellations.

The constellations are **Aries, Taurus, Gemini, Cancer, Leo, Virgo, Libra, Scorpio, Sagittarius, Capricorn, Aquarius, and Pisces.**

Ancient Astronomers gave various names to the different stars and constellations.

When the Sun transited within one of these cosmic spaces, astrologers got to associate its name to the moment of the year during which such transit occurred.

There is a phenomenon called *'equinoctial precession'*. According to this law of physics, the zodiac signs and the constellations are today out of alignment.

Once every 2600 years, approximately, the difference becomes one constellation, therefore one zodiac sign.

Astrology detractors use this evidence to refute any scientific value to this science. They are wrong…

What we must consider is the presence of the Sun within the *'Celestial Sphere'* at such or such time of the year according to the Earth. Such a position corresponds to certain events that tend to repeat themselves regularly (once a year) whatever name is given to the 'cosmic space' where the Sun seems to be transiting. The *seasons* are a good example of such phenomenon.

The planets travel around the Sun at different speeds and distances, but always within the limits of the zodiac, a 17° wide cosmic highway formed by the Sun's magnetic field.

The names of the signs have been given according to the names of the constellations, but the misalignment of signs and constellations does not change the moment of spring or any other season's arrival. The same principle applies to the symbolic meanings of the zodiac signs.

BACK TO THE CHART...

Each ZODIAC SIGN corresponds to a section of 30 degrees of arc around the circle. Each one of these sections corresponds to a certain period of the year.

The first section, from degree zero to degree thirty (0° - 30°) corresponds to the beginning of spring in the Northern Hemisphere of the Earth and to the beginning of autumn on the Southern Hemisphere. The sign 'ARIES' belongs to this section. Two thousand six hundred years ago, the constellation of ARIES gave it its name.

'ARIES' begins on the 21st of March (first day of spring in the north and first day of autumn in the south). It ends on the 20th of April. Therefore, to say that someone was born under the sign of ARIES means that the Sun was transiting in that ZODIAC section at the time.[1]

In some countries (like Australia), the seasons begin on the first day of the month. They are not in line with the equinox and solstice days…

There are two equinoxes, the first one on the 21st of March, the second one on the 23rd of September. There are two solstices, the first one on the 21st of June, the second one on the 21st of December.

Apart from the Sun and its obvious and vital influence on all

---

[1] During leap years of 366 days, Aries begins one day earlier, on March 20th and the following signs too.

living creatures on our planet, the Moon, Mercury, Venus, Mars, Jupiter, Saturn, Uranus, Neptune, and Pluto also influence our biological structure through their radiation reaching the Earth. That is without considering the *Ascendant, the other Houses, and the aspects!*

Important note:

There are two more celestial bodies taken into consideration in the present course:

Vesta and Chiron.

You will learn all about them in the following lessons.

WHAT IS THE ASCENDANT?

The **day of your birth** determines your **zodiac sign** (also called SOLAR SIGN) as we have just seen…

The *time of your birth* determines your *Ascendant.*

The *ASCENDANT or HOUSE I (1)* corresponds to the moment of the day of your birth when the SUN rose above the horizon to 'get up', if I may say…

According to your personal time of birth, it is the zodiac sign that rose above the horizon that influences you, just like your Sun sign or *zodiac sign.*

SOME OF YOU MAY ASK:

'HOW COULD THE SUN BE IN ONE SIGN TO DETERMINE MY ZODIAC SIGN, WHILE ANOTHER SIGN DETERMINES MY ASCENDANT?'

The *SUN SIGN* is determined according to a time lapse of 365 days. The Earth turns around the SUN as well as around itself on an invisible axis. One complete turn around the SUN in one year and one complete turn on itself in one day.

That implies two different visions of the celestial vault: one according to a slow movement (the orbit of the Earth around the Sun in one year) and one according to a fast movement (the rotation of the Earth on its axis in 24 hours).

Imagine a fair's carousel made up of long arms on the end of which are fast turning cabins where passengers could seat to get their fun while the long arms supporting the cabins would turn slowly around the carousel's main axis.

Any person sitting in one of the cabins anywhere on the wide circle made by the long supporting arm can also have a quick vision of the entire circle during the fast revolution of the cabin on itself.

These two aspects of the same vision explain the point of view of the *SUN SIGN* (slow motion) and of the *RISING SIGN or ASCENDANT* (fast motion).

That second sign, the *ASCENDANT, in partnership with the SUN SIGN,* creates a character duality that goes far beyond the simple study of the *ZODIAC SIGNS.* Instead of the 12 zodiac-sign possibilities, we obtain 12 times more, therefore 144 different associations of signs.

In the next lesson, we will study the twelve zodiac signs and their astrological and psychological correspondence. You will also learn how to classify them into various groups and qualities.

Lesson 2

FIRST STEP ANALYSIS

In this lesson you will learn about the twelve signs of the zodiac and discover their individual potential and influence on human nature.

THE SUN SIGN

The Sun sign of a person is the most important single factor in interpreting a birth chart. It indicates the way a person expresses basic energy potential and creative drives to grow and develop as an individual. This is determined by the position of the SUN in the SIGNS according to the date of birth, as we have seen earlier on.

The **"sign potential"** gives the planets their **"colour"**. To know that **Mercury** represents the **intellectual principle** of life (as you will learn in Lesson 3) is not enough. The astrologer needs to know **how** this principle is used by the native concerned. The **sign** in which the planet is found, then, provides valuable information to further the analysis of the chart.

"THE PLANETS IN THE SIGNS" are the subject of LESSONS N° 3, 4 and 5. Right now refer to the rapid description of each sign to improve your knowledge of the zodiac. Try to memorise them as much as you can. They will be particularly useful to speed up your progress in astrology when you deal with more complicated tuition in due time…

* * * * * * * * * * * * * * * * * * *

Note that since 1998 I use two asteroids to enhance my astrological interpretations. They are Vesta and Chiron.

Vesta orbits in the asteroid belt between Mars and Jupiter. It is a small object, but unlike other larger asteroids, Vesta is visible from the Earth with the naked eye.

Chiron orbits between Saturn and Uranus. According to astronomers, it is a comet residue locked by the strong energy fields of the two giant planets.

In 1998, I had a revelation while astral travelling (a practice I began to study in 1976) that I should use **Vesta in relation to Libra and Chiron in relation to Virgo**.

I made all sorts of tests to verify in many charts of people I know, and it instantly made sense. I have been using Vesta and Chiron in all my readings successfully since.

That is why I include them in my teaching.

Aries

Aries is the first sign of the zodiac. It is known to be an "aggressive sign" ruled by Mars. Its key phrase is: "I am."

Creativity, energy, and enthusiasm go with this sign. Arians like to initiate new activities all the time to keep themselves occupied until the novelty wears off... They have a strong drive and need for action in many ways.

Aries is not an intellectual sign; it is rather an impulsive and an impatient sign. Thought before action is not common to Arians, but it would certainly enable them to accomplish much more in life.

It is a competitive sign and Arians seek to be first in whatever they do...

Taurus

Taurus is the second sign of the zodiac. It is ruled by Venus. Its key phrase is "I have".

Taurus is the sign of purposeful determination and power. As an "earth" sign, it gives materialistic and down-to-earth needs and desires in life. Taureans are usually practical and efficient.

They are fond of the good things of life and enjoy food, drink, and love, sometimes excessively. Comfort, personal satisfactions, and pleasures are also characteristic of the needs of this sign. The need for money is always linked with what it can buy. Taurus is a generous sign with a highly developed need for love. The rulership of Venus gives Taureans appreciation for beauty in all forms. Material security is important to this sign and can motivate or lead the entire life of the native.

Gemini

Gemini is the third sign of the zodiac. It is ruled by Mercury. Its key phrase is "I think".

Gemini people have good intellectual and communicating abilities. The spoken and written forms of expression are important to them. Reading can also give them great pleasure, but the subject must not be too "heavy" or too long because Gemini people like to change. It is a versatile but sometimes superficial sign. Nervousness and lack of self-discipline is characteristic of this sign. Gemini is not a materialistic sign. Money is appreciated only for the freedom it can give them. Nonconformists, Gemini people often rebel against the status quo, breaking rules and doing all sorts of things to remain different at all cost.

Cancer

Cancer is the fourth sign of the zodiac. It is ruled by the Moon. Its key phrase is "I feel".

It is a sensitive and emotional sign, favouring the feminine, rather than the masculine principle of life, closely related to home environment and family.

Cancer people have a well-developed sense of responsibility but are also capable of childish weaknesses. They are moody and quite unpredictable, but diplomatic and tenacious.

Children born under this sign are very affectionate and sensitive, rather quiet, and always willing to be helpful. Cancer is a sign linked with the past, therefore, those born under it are often keen lovers of history.

Leo

Leo is the fifth sign of the zodiac. It is ruled by the Sun. Its key phrase is "I will".

Leo is the sign of generosity and mobility of heart. It represents the desire for expression to exteriorise the inner principle. The Sun is the ruler of Leo, giving it warmth and light. The Sun is the benefactor of all living things. It is the centre around which the planets turn. Leos, then, need to be in the spotlight. They need to be the centre of attraction. The sign Leo rules the heart. Therefore, Leo-born people tend to exaggerate their sorrow and often take things too seriously for their own good. They are certainly very "touchy" and easily offended. Leo is a domineering sign, with a good sense of justice and a philosophical view of life.

Virgo

Virgo is the sixth sign of the zodiac. It is ruled by Chiron. Its key phrase is "I analyse".

Virgo is the working sign. The urge to learn, conferred by Mercury, has materialistic goals rather than purely intellectual as for Gemini. Virgos are meticulous people, especially in their work, giving sometimes too much attention to details and always striving to keep things in good order. In its best form, Virgo is the sign of efficiency and brilliance, but it can also make the native narrow minded through excessive specialisation. Virgo is the sign of the analyst who looks at the world through a magnifying glass or a microscope. A tendency to criticise can make Virgos difficult to live with... Occasionally they tend to mistake scientific culture for heavenly wisdom...

Libra

Libra is the seventh sign of the zodiac. It is ruled by Vesta.
Its key phrase is "I balance".

Venus gives Libra charm and beauty of expression. Libra's energy is expressed in the present and in spontaneous action. It is a "group-working" sign, but independence is always retained in any form of association and partnership.

Marriage and friendship are particularly important to people born under this sign. They are often art oriented and can communicate intelligently to give form to their original ideas. Libra is the sign of justice, fair play, and loyalty in constant need of understanding and trust. Being an "air sign", Libra is an intellectual sign, constantly seeking mental stimulation.

Scorpio

Scorpio is the eighth sign of the zodiac. It is ruled by Pluto. Its key phrase is "I desire".

Scorpio is probably the strongest sign of the zodiac, showing great power of regeneration together with the ability to sustain effort and a strong drive. Scorpio's lives are often constant struggles and battles to reach out at impossible stars. Dislike of weaknesses together with deep generosity and compassion go with this sign. Scorpios are usually deep thinkers and have an excellent memory. They are interested in mystery and occultism.

They tend to prefer solitude and a secretive way of life to contacts with the "maddening crowds". Scorpios are not afraid of death because they understand the principle of cyclic earthly manifestations.

Sagittarius

Sagittarius is the ninth sign of the zodiac. It is ruled by Jupiter. Its key phrase is "I see".

Sagittarius is the sign of justice and freedom, energy, and activity. Jupiter protects Sagittarians so that it always gives them an ultimate chance in front of the worst disasters... It is a philosophical and religious sign always seeking approbation and harmony.

Impulsive, Sagittarians tend to jump to conclusions and to make important mistakes in their judgments. Sagittarians like to travel to faraway places. They are attracted to foreign cultures and countries and are prone to take long journeys abroad.

Capricorn

Capricorn is the tenth sign of the zodiac. It is ruled by Saturn. Its key phrase is "I use".

Capricorn is a down-to-earth sign, not merely satisfied with the minimum comfort and peace of mind that a "normal job" can allow. Capricorns have far-reaching goals with long-lasting ideas and desires, usually taking the long and fastidious way around, preferring gradual ascension to sudden changes. Their symbol is a mountain goat climbing slowly to the top, slowly but surely... Great working ability and determination are the keys to their success, giving to Capricorns the material security they need and the power of a high social position. They usually honestly believe that, because of their constant efforts, the world "owes them" success and recognition. Capricorns can appear to be "born old" and rather cold in their general behaviour. They are, nevertheless, sensitive and need to be appreciated for everything they do.

Aquarius

Aquarius is the eleventh sign of the zodiac. It is ruled by Uranus. Its key phrase is "I know".

Friendship and good company are particularly important to people born under this sign. They are sometimes eccentric in their attitude but also determined and tenacious. They may occasionally display a "know-it-all" attitude, and they are impatient with people they consider unworthy of their "superior qualities"...

Aquarians can be everything or nothing, but they will never remain alone for long. Their personal security depends almost entirely upon the quality of their relationships with other people. They are attracted to the electricity and electronics professional fields, often displaying enormous ability in research as well as in communication (radio, television, computers, the media, etc.).

Pisces

Pisces is the twelfth sign of the zodiac. It is ruled by Neptune. Its key phrase is "I believe".

People born under this sign are extremely sensitive to the thoughts and feelings of others. They are easily influenced because they unconsciously absorb other people's ideas and points of view. They desperately want to do the right thing but, as a rule, they lack sufficient willpower to attain, reach their goals. They often seem unable to decide and may give the impression of being constantly tired. Pisceans are not combative people but, when aroused, their anger is difficult to calm down... Jupiter gives them wisdom and trust while Neptune tends to lead them to a world of dreams. They may devote their lives to religion or become missionaries or artists such as musicians, painters, sculptors, or dancers.

Learn these quick descriptions to get a summary of each sign of the zodiac. It will help you memorise and visualise the possibilities of blending signs as it can be done with the SOLAR SIGN and the ASCENDANT.

As we progress, each month, you will learn more about the SIGNS, PLANETS, HOUSES and ASPECTS potential. Blending these "colours" will eventually make the whole picture.

Lesson 3

TRIPLICITY AND QUADRUPLICITY

Have you ever heard or read about

FIRE, EARTH, AIR, and WATER SIGNS?

Did you know that

ARIES, LEO, and SAGITTARIUS are FIRE SIGNS?

TAURUS, VIRGO, and CAPRICORN are EARTH SIGNS?

GEMINI, LIBRA, and AQUARIUS are AIR SIGNS?

CANCER, SCORPIO, and PISCES are WATER SIGNS?

FIRE

On Earth, all living creatures depend on these four basic elements. Fire seems to be the primary cause, the "big bang" of the astronomer's theory of the beginning of the universe. Fire serves us in many ways, but it can also destroy. It can warm things up, heat them or burn them, depending on the amount of heat generated. When fire was discovered in prehistoric times, it became a god, was worshipped, just like the Sun, mainly because it created heat and light, and was a substitute to the Sun, in winter and during the night.

In astrology, some signs have more "FIRE" than others. It simply means that they have more primary drive and spontaneous reactivity.

FIRE **signs** are "glowing signs". They express the need to shine and "burn".

ARIES is the first sign of the zodiac. It corresponds to the beginning of spring in the Northern hemisphere of the world. ARIES has the primary fire influence when the sun is bursting out giving life after the long winter. Trees blossom, nature awakens, and a new life cycle begins.

NOTE: The above description is only meant to give you an idea of the sign's tendency and quality both in the southern hemisphere of the earth.

ARIES is the first of the three FIRE signs, when heat is being activated, directly from the spark. "Action" is the key word to Aries" means of achievement. Its behaviour pattern is said to be impulsive, spontaneous or "CARDINAL".

In astrology ARIES is a FIRE - CARDINAL Sign

A few months later, in the Northern hemisphere of the Earth, summer brings about the best and worst qualities of the sun. It rises early in the morning and sets late in the evening. In some places, near the North Pole, there is not even what could be called a "night" during summer. The sun may disappear west, behind the horizon, but it reappears east less than one or two hours later...

We can say that in summer, the heat of the sun is constant or **"FIXED"**, except for occasional weather changes. From the 23rd of July till the 23rd of August, LEO rules and the sun is high in the Northern Hemisphere's sky. LEO is the second FIRE SIGN when heat is constant and burning. "Success and power" are the key words to Leos. They like to glow and shine, even in the simplest situations.

In astrology we say that LEO is a FIRE - FIXED sign

The third and last FIRE SIGN, SAGITTARIUS, begins late in November, when the last warm influence of the sun shines over the autumn colours of the Northern Hemisphere of the Earth, until the first days of winter, which begins on the 21st of December. During that time, the sun is flickering, not reliable enough to allow proper planning of outdoor activities because of unpredictable weather changes. Still, late in autumn, one can enjoy some beautiful and warm afternoons, taking a walk in the odorous woods, under the leafless trees. Such moments are most appreciated because of that "winter feeling" lying closely ahead in time...

The heat of the sun, late in autumn, is said to be changeable, or **"MUTABLE"**. SAGITTARIUS, then, is an active sign, subject to many changes according to situations and environments. It is the most adaptable of all fire signs.

In astrology SAGITTARIUS is a FIRE - MUTABLE sign

EARTH

From the big bang of the astronomers came the universe, the sun, and the planets and all the other suns and planets in the trillions of galaxies. We, on Earth, believe that life is meant to keep our feet firmly on the ground. We need to accumulate material possessions to render worthwhile the long hours we spend working to earn our money. We have what is called an "earthly nature". In the beginning there was the Earth and nothing else. Since then, things have changed, but the Earth has remained virtually the same. It has a "fixed" quality, one that is uneasily moved or changed.

TAURUS is the first EARTH SIGN of the zodiac. It also begins in spring (Northern hemisphere) like Aries, but one month later, when the earth is standing still, awaiting the rebirth of nature. TAURUS has a "**FIXED**" quality about it. It is attached and drawn to earthly possessions as well as to all the good things of life.

In astrology TAURUS is an EARTH - FIXED Sign

The second EARTH sign is VIRGO. It begins late in August, when summer, in the Northern Hemisphere of the Earth, is about to end. Nature is at the door of its "yearly death", still active and eager to put aside what has been harvested and acquired since the beginning of spring. All that activity must be well organised. Autumn and winter lay ahead. Nothing must be overlooked. The change in season brings about many weather changes. Virgo has this changeable or "mutable" quality. It is what we may call a "moody" down-to-earth sign.

In astrology VIRGO is an EARTH - MUTABLE Sign

The third and last EARTH sign is CAPRICORN. We are now in winter (Northern Hemisphere of the earth). Nature seems extinct. However, under the thick coat of snow, activity can still be observed. Life is resting, lasting on its reserve, and waiting for better days, when spring brings back the warmth that is needed. Nature is still, but active in an "underground" way.

In astrology CAPRICORN is an EARTH-CARDINAL sign

AIR

AIR is what we need to breathe and to live. Without air, fire would not be able to burn and the creation of water would be impossible. Without air the Earth would be a deserted place, lonely and silent, turning around and around aimlessly, much like the other planets of the solar system, where no life is apparent or at least, not as we know it on Earth.

Venus is like our planet. It is almost as big, and it takes almost the same time to travel around the Sun. One year on Venus is approximately two third of a year on Earth. But one day is equal to one year on Venus, because the planet needs as much time to turn around itself as it does to turn around the Sun... The temperature on the ground reaches 400 degrees centigrade, while it freezes on the other side. Venus is surrounded by a thick atmosphere mainly composed of carbonic gas. The air on Venus would be impossible for us to breathe, not mentioning the heat...

About **Mars**, quite a small planet, there have been a lot of talking and wrong beliefs. The "Martians" do not exist, at least not as you may have read their descriptions in science-fiction literature. There is not enough air on Mars to allow human, animal nor insect life. There is no evidence of any life form on any of the other planets of the solar system. Then, who knows what scientists may discover, thanks to their perpetual research and studies?

The prime quality of air is to be forever in motion, adaptable to any form and to any environment and impossible to grasp is one's hand. **Air** is the wind that we hear but cannot see. It blows and flows freely around us and around everything. **Air** is everywhere. AIR **signs** have many of these qualities.

GEMINI is the first one of them. It has the prime quality of forever changing, seeking movement and novelty. Air signs are linked to the intellect, the brain's function and its influence on communication skills and mobility.

In astrology GEMINI is an AIR-MUTABLE Sign

The second AIR SIGN, LIBRA, has a more determined kind of "wind blowing action". It usually blows in one direction at a time, diving more attention and certainty to its endeavours.

In astrology LIBRA is an AIR-CARDINAL Sign

AQUARIUS is also a versatile and changing sign. Compared to Gemini or Libra, however, it seems to have more "staying power". Aquarians tend to hold on their principles forever. They believe in standing still and doing absolutely nothing if it means defending such principles.

In astrology AQUARIUS is an AIR-FIXED sign

WATER

The fourth element is WATER. Except for some rare places, water seems to be present everywhere upon our planet. Let us not forget that only one fifth of the surface of the Earth is NOT occupied by water... Water is the basic need for life to commence and then grow. Without it, we would most certainly die. Life began in water, millions of years ago.

CANCER **is the first** WATER **sign**. It has the quality of the surface of the ocean, always in movement and strong, so useful to carry enormous vessels across the continents. Cancer is an active and determined, yet sensible and sensitive sign, just like the surface of the ocean is.

In astrology CANCER is a WATER-CARDINAL Sign

SCORPIO, on the other hand, belongs to the depth of the ocean. Down there, no light can penetrate. It is the kingdom of darkness and mystery, the night of nights... Down there, movement is only a dream, and life resembles death... Scorpios are attracted to the depth of the waters of life. They have strong and fixed feelings and beliefs. Their staying power makes them prone to a "live or die" attitude when they are confronted to hardship and obstacles.

In astrology SCORPIO is a WATER-FIXED Sign

The third and last WATER SIGN is PISCES. It has the "mid waters" quality, where forever changing currents bring cold and warm waters together, able to drag a good swimmer to the deep of the river or sea. Pisces has the changeable nature of the water between the surface and the bottom. It does not seem to know exactly what direction it should take in life...

In astrology PISCES is a WATER-MUTABLE Sign

The 4 elements: FIRE, EARTH, AIR and WATER form the basic screen for life to spread out and grow. The 3 elements: CARDINAL, FIXED, and MUTABLE complement each one of the four primary elements. There are 3 possibilities in each one of the 4 elements making the 12 signs of the zodiac.

* * * * * * * * * *

TRIPLICITY and QUADRUPLICITY are the names given to describe these two inter blending categories. See the corresponding chart supplied with this lesson and you will easily understand.

Between the 12 zodiac signs, there are:

3 FIRE signs: Aries, Leo, Sagittarius

3 EARTH signs: Taurus, Virgo, Capricorn

3 AIR signs: Gemini, Libra, Aquarius

3 WATER signs: Cancer, Scorpio, Pisces

(Triplicity)

Of which:

4 are CARDINAL signs: Aries, Cancer, Libra, Capricorn

4 are FIXED signs: Taurus, Leo, Scorpio, Aquarius

4 are MUTABLE signs: Gemini, Virgo, Sagittarius, Pisces

(Quadruplicity)

Reading the zodiac counterclockwise:

From ARIES, every fourth other sign is a FIRE SIGN and every third other sign is a CARDINAL SIGN.

From TAURUS, every fourth other sign is an EARTH SIGN and every third other sign is a FIXED SIGN.

From GEMINI, every fourth other sign is an AIR SIGN and every third other sign is a MUTABLE SIGN.

From CANCER, every fourth other sign is a WATER SIGN and every third other sign is a CARDINAL SIGN again, because CANCER is the third sign after ARIES, therefore the second CARDINAL SIGN.

In the primary analysis of a BIRTH CHART, **TRIPLICITIES and QUADRUPLICITIES** are used to get a general idea of an individual's character tendency. The principle is easy:

Figure out the TRIPLICITY and QUADRUPLICITY of each SIGN where you find a planet in the chart, then add up such TRIPLICITIES and QUADRUPLICITIES.

As part of this lesson, try now to work out your own chart's triplicity and Quadruplicity tendency. See how many planets are in Fire, EARTH, Air and Water Signs and which of the Cardinal, Fixed and Mutable qualities dominate.

To do this exercise, take the chart titled **FOR YOUR BIRTH CHART'S GENERAL TENDENCY** and do as follows....

1) In the first column you will find the symbol of each planet,

including two asteroids, Vesta and Chiron. We will explain their role later. *I have also included your rising sign. If you have a double rising sign, note both in the appropriate area of the chart.*

2) In the second column draw the symbol of the sign in which you find each one of the above in your personal birth chart and listed in the first column.

3) In the third column write the **TRIPLICITY** quality of the signs marked in the second column. (**Fire, Earth, Air or Water**)

4) In the fourth column write the **QUADRUPLICITY** quality of each of the signs marked in the second column (**Cardinal, Fixed or Mutable**)

5) Then add up the **TRIPLICITIES** collected

6) Add up the **QUADRUPLICITIES** collected

7) The totals will tell you what quality dominates your birth chart as far as the "positions of the planets" are concerned.

8) Then mark, in front of **"GENERAL TENDENCY"** whatever your result is.

NOTE that you may find equal number of planets in different elements and qualities. Using "sign rulership" and the rising sign will help you determine which element and quality really dominate your chart. This work can be done using the texts on each zodiac sign where the "rulers" are mentioned. Add 1 point to each planet in sign of rulership. (Ex: Venus in Taurus = 2 Earth and 2 Fixed).

SIGN	DATES	RULER	SYMBOLISM
ARIES	21/03 – 20/04	MARS	Initiative Activity Command
TAURUS	21/04 – 21/05	VENUS	Practicality Affectivity Possessions
GEMINI	21/05 – 21/06	MERCURY	Intellect Versatility Adaptability
CANCER	22/06 – 22/07	MOON	Sensibility Tenacit Family
LEO	23/07 – 23/08	SUN	Vitality Authority Power
VIRGO	24/08 – 22/09	CHIRON	Discrimination Method Sense of duty
LIBRA	23/09 – 22/10	VESTA	Harmony Friendship Balance
SCORPIO	23/10 – 21/11	PLUTO	Regeneration Secrets Energy
SAGITTARIUS	22/11 – 20/12	JUPITER	Freedom Exploration Elevation
CAPRICORN	21/12 – 19/01	SATURN	Ambition Conservatism Organisation
AQUARIUS	20/01 – 18/02	URANUS	Humanity - Originality - Independence
PISCES	19/02 – 20/03	NEPTUNE	Compassion - Universality - Renunciation

Signs by dates

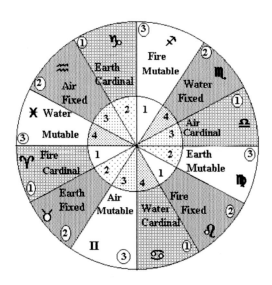

	FIRE	EARTH	AIR	WATER	Triplicity Quadruplicity
①	♈ Aries ①	♑ Capricorn ②	♎ Libra ③	♋ Cancer ④	CARDINAL
②	♌ Lio	♉ Taurus	♒ Aquarius	♏ Scorpion	FIXED
③	♐ Sagittarius	♍ Virgo	♊ Gemini	♓ Pisces	MUTABLE

Elements and qualities

Example chart to determine a general tendency

PLANET	SIGN	TRIPLICITY	QUADRUPLICITY
SUN	Leo	**Fire x 2**	**Fixed x 2**
MOON	Capricorn	Earth	Cardinal
MERCURY	Virgo	Earth	Mutable
VENUS	Cancer	Water	Cardinal
MARS	Aries	**Fire x 2**	**Cardinal x 2**
VESTA	Gemini	Air	Mutable
JUPITER	Cancer	Water	Cardinal
SATURN	Libra	Air	Cardinal
CHIRON	Sagittarius	Fire	Mutable
URANUS	Leo	Fire	Fixed
NEPTUNE	Scorpio	Water	Fixed
PLUTO	Virgo	Earth	Mutable
ASC (sign 1)	Pisces	Water	Mutable
ASC (sign 2)*	No second sign	Nil	Nil

Number of elements in: FIRE SIGNS: **6** EARTH SIGNS: **3** AIR SIGNS: **2** WATER SIGNS: **4**

Number of elements in: CARDINAL SIGNS: **6** FIXED SIGNS: **4** MUTABLE SIGNS: **5**
MY BIRTH CHART'S GENERAL TENDENCY IS: FIRE CARDINAL

For your Birth Chart's General Tendency

PLANET	SIGN	TRIPLICITY	QUADRUPLICITY
SUN			
MOON			
MERCURY			
VENUS			
MARS			
VESTA			
JUPITER			
SATURN			
CHIRON			
URANUS			
NEPTUNE			
PLUTO			
ASC (sign 1)			
ASC (sign 2) If needed			

Number of elements in: Fire: _____ Earth: ___ Air: ___ Water: ___

Number of elements in: Cardinal: ___ Fixed: ___ Mutable: ___

My birth chart's general tendency Is : _____

The result links me to (sign): _____

Lesson 4

THE PLANETS

ASTRONOMICAL AND ASTROLOGICAL POINTS OF VIEW

In this third lesson, we are going to learn about the planets from an **astronomical** point of view as well as from an **astrological** point of view.

The influence of each planet is important, but it must also be analysed in relation to the sign in which it stands.

In astrology we consider that the SUN and the MOON are planets. It is more convenient when we relate to them during a birth chart's general analysis. We see ourselves, then, as the "centre of the universe" because we seem to be standing still, surrounded by ever-changing skies...

Therefore, from our point of view on Earth, the Sun, the Moon, and the planets "seem" to turn around us. That is why we are the **apparent centre** of the solar system.

The planets are usually considered in order of their speed of rotation around the Sun. **The closest planet to the Sun is Mercury. It is also the fastest. The farthest planet to the Sun is Pluto, it's also the slowest.**

MERCURY rotates at an average distance of 57.9 million km from the Sun in just 88 days.

VENUS comes after at an average distance from the Sun of 108.2 million km, completing one revolution in just under 225 days.

The EARTH rotates around the Sun in 365.4 days at an average distance of 150 million km from the Sun. In a chart, the Earth the centre of the zodiac.

MARS, twice as big as MERCURY and yet much smaller than the EARTH, rotates at approximately 227.9 million km from the SUN, in 1 year and 322 days (almost 2 years).

VESTA is a small asteroid in the asteroid band between Mars and Jupiter. It measures between 456 and 562 km across. It revolves at an average 350 million km from the Sun in 3.63 years (more than three and a half years).

JUPITER, the giant planet, around 1,300 times bigger than the EARTH and more than 300 times its mass, rotates at 778 million km from the SUN in 11 years and 315 days (almost 12 years).

SATURN, further still and "only" 95.11 times the mass of the EARTH, rotates at 1,427 million km from the SUN in 29 years and 167 days.

CHIRON is also an asteroid, or rather a "comet residue". It measures around 160 km in "diameter". It orbits between Saturn and Uranus in 50.37 years. Its orbit is very eccentric with a distance to the Sun that varies between 1.3 and 2.8 billion km.

URANUS is 14.55 times the mass of the EARTH and rotates at 2870 million km from the SUN in 84 years and 7 days.

NEPTUNE, far, far away; 17.23 times the mass of the EARTH rotates at 4,496 million km from the SUN in 164 years and 280 days.

PLUTO, the last planet known today, was discovered in 1930. It is 100 times smaller than the EARTH and rotates at 5946 million km from the SUN in 248 years and 157 days. From

PLUTO the SUN seems no bigger than a bright star shining among millions of others in a clear summer night sky...

The SUN, considered as a planet in astrology because of its obvious influence upon every living thing, is said to rotate in 365 days and 6 hours, which is the time the Earth takes to travel around it. We call it "a year".

The Sun is a star, just like any other star in the universe, the ones we look at in wonder in a clear night sky. The Sun is fixed, and the planets turn around it.

The symbolism attached to the Sun, Moon, and planets, give the astrologer an insight into a person's motivations, home environment, education, personal impulses, emotiveness, and a lot more.

THE PRINCIPLES OF LIFE

I have regrouped the symbolism of these elements into "life principles". They are useful to gain instant information on behaviour and character traits.

THE SUN is the *MASCULINE PRINCIPLE OF LIFE.*

Its position in the chart tells about external life, vitality, authority, pride, impulsiveness, willpower, and energy. It also represents the father and any other form of authority to deal with during the entire lifetime.

THE MOON is the *FEMININE PRINCIPLE OF LIFE.*

Its position in the chart tells about the soul, the emotions, personal feelings, and inner life. It also relates to imagination, fecundity, memory, and artistic tendencies. It represents the mother or mother figure, motherhood, and the relationship with women in personal life

MERCURY is the *INTELLECTUAL PRINCIPLE OF LIFE*

Its position in the cart tells about intelligence, mental expression, communication ability, the potential to learn, the need to travel, curiosity, adaptability, the tendency to lie and the taste for the written or spoken words. Speech, and the quality of intelligent expression, brothers and brotherhood are also represented by Mercury.

VENUS is the *LOVE PRINCIPLE OF LIFE*

Its position in the chart tells about sensuality, charm, charisma, affectivity, love, artistic ability, taste for good food, beautiful things, decoration, music and singing. Venus also represents sisters, as well as female relatives and friends.

MARS is the *COMBATIVE PRINCIPLE OF LIFE*

Its position in the chart tells about active energy and the way it is expressed. It also tells about passions, sex drive, combativeness, aggressiveness, and martial or authoritarian tendencies.

VESTA in the *HARMONY PRINCIPLE OF LIFE*

Its position in the chart tells about the need for balance, harmony, and wellbeing. It represents the ability to preserve inner peace, moral wellbeing, and spiritual equilibrium.

JUPITER is the *EXPANSION PRINCIPLE OF LIFE*

Its position in the chart tells about the philosophical approach to life, the potential to succeed, material and spiritual evolution, the need for justice and fair play, respect of laws and regulations, financial satisfactions, good sense and equity.

SATURN is the *RESTRICTION PRINCIPLE OF LIFE*

Its position in the chart tells about the approach to work, obstacles, efforts, inhibitions, the past, personal worries and dilemmas, social difficulties and hardship, life's lessons, and karma. Time and patience are required to reach the most distant goals. They are represented by Saturn.

CHIRON is the *OBSERVING PRINCIPLE OF LIFE*

Its position in the chart tells about the potential to analyse and observe the realities of life. It also shows the ability to preserve good health, and how to deal with illness. Chiron is known as the "inner doctor". It represents our self-healing potential.

URANUS is the *TRANSFORMATION PRINCIPLE OF LIFE*

Its position in the chart tells about the ability to adapt to sudden and drastic changes, about revolutionary tendencies, inventiveness, ingenuity, the superior nervous system, inner contradictions, eccentricity, radicalness, and the need for freedom and independence.

NEPTUNE is the *SPIRITUAL PRINCIPLE OF LIFE*

Its position in the chart tells about personal aspirations and dreams, the unconscious mind, mysticism, artistic inspiration, attraction to the supernatural, to drugs, alcohol, tobacco, and medicine. It is the connection with the spiritual dimension of life.

PLUTO is the *REGENERATION PRINCIPLE OF LIFE*

Its position in the chart tells about the attraction to the mysteries of life, death, and sexuality. It represents the inner strength, self-questioning, self-destruction, destruction in view of reconstruction, and physical and spiritual regeneration.

The synthesis of the twelve principles is a crucial part of the astrological reading. From the meanings of the positions of each planet in the signs, we derive important information. Blending the principles of the planets with the symbolism of the signs is the key to a proper astrological reading.

The influence of the Sun is obvious throughout the year. It is the provider of life on Earth. Without the Sun, the solar system would not exist.

The dispositions of the celestial bodies around the Sun create a harmonious partnership that allows the Earth to be just at the right place to ensure proper development of life as we know it.

The Sun represents the day, therefore ACTIVITY, and symbolically, the POSITIVE POLE OF LIFE.

In the next lesson, we will discuss the influence of the Moon.

Lesson 5

The Moon

The Moon is the second most important celestial body because of its brightness derived from the sun. It closely and directly influences the surface of the Earth. The Moon rotates in about 27 days and 6 hours around the Earth, at an average distance of 350 thousand km from our planet.

The Moon represents night, therefore PASSIVITY and, symbolically, the NEGATIVE POLE OF LIFE.

In astrology the SUN is fire and daylight

The MOON is water and night.

In a chart, the Sun represents the *active* external energy, while the Moon represents the *passive* and internal energy. According to the positions of the Sun and Moon around the Zodiac, we can tell about the means of action in relation to environmental conditions, psychological tendencies as well as deeper feelings, family background, education, and long past motivations.

The Sun, the Moon, the eight planets and two asteroids used in this course have each what is called a **SIGN OF RULERSHIP.**

The observation of human behaviour has revealed that in a certain area of the zodiac, the individual energy of a planet becomes stronger and its influence is more remarkable.

In a "neutral sign", the planet is said to be PEREGRINE, or just "passing by". In another sign yet, that same planet is said to be EXALTED, because its influence is almost as strong as in its sign of RULERSHIP. In another sign again, it is said to be in

"FALL", because its influence seems reduced. It is said in DETRIMENT, in the sign opposite its sign of rulership.

The sign of DETRIMENT is the opposite sign to the sign of RULERSHIP.
The sign of FALL is the opposite sign to the sign of EXALTATION.

Here is the list of the planets with the signs of their rulership, exaltation, detriment, and fall. Refer to it to analyse your future charts.

THE PLANETS AND THE SIGNS

Planet	Ruler	Exalted	Detriment	Fall
SUN	LEO	ARIES	AQUARIUS	LIBRA
MOON	CANCER	TAURUS	CAPRICORN	SCORPIO
MERCURY	GEMINI	VIRGO	SAGITTARIUS	PISCES
VENUS	TAURUS	PISCES	SCORPIO	VIRGO
MARS	ARIES	CAPRICORN	LIBRA	CANCER
VESTA	LIBRA	AQUARIUS	ARIES	LEO
JUPITER	SAGITTARIUS	CANCER	GEMINI	CAPRICORN
SATURN	CAPRICORN	LIBRA	CANCER	ARIES
CHIRON	VIRGO	CAPRICORN	PISCES	CANCER
URANUS	AQUARIUS	SCORPIO	LEO	TAURUS
NEPTUNE	PISCES	SAGITTARIUS	VIRGO	GEMINI
PLUTO	SCORPIO	LEO	TAURUS	AQUARIUS

In all other signs, the planet is said to be *"peregrine"*.

NOTE: Apart from the rulership of each planet, I do not use the other notions in my practice of astrology. The above chart is my own perception of the strength and weaknesses of the various celestial bodies' positions. You do not have to apply these rules in your personal approach to astrological readings. The rulership of a planet is the only essential concept to memorise.

BLENDING

Blending the Sun's and the Moon's influences is a simple approach to a character analysis. The Sun represents the essential influence on human nature. The "Sun-sign potentials" are described in lesson 2.

It is easy enough to describe the basic meaning of a zodiac sign (or sun sign), but what happens when the Moon, Mercury and the other planets are found in various other signs around the chart?

We know, for example, that the Moon represents the "feminine principle of life", the emotions and feelings, the subconscious mind. The emotions and subconscious are influenced by the sign in which the Moon stands because it literally "absorbs" the influence of that sign to, in turn, influence the emotional development and expression of the person concerned.

The same method applies to determine the influence of Mercury, Venus, Mars, Vesta, Jupiter, Saturn, Chiron, Uranus, Neptune, and Pluto.

Read the list of aphorisms below to get accustomed the influence of the Moon according to its position in each zodiac sign. Do not take them for granted. **You will soon learn that the basic influence of a planet in a sign can be drastically modified by other elements in the chart.**

THE MOON IN THE SIGNS
(Basic interpretation)

MOON in ARIES

The emotions are expressed impulsively. The feminine principle becomes almost masculine here because Aries is a Fire sign ruled by Mars. It deals more with action than emotion. The emotional response to stimuli is spontaneous and intense.

MOON in TAURUS

The Moon here is in a strong position. It enhances the emotional tie with matter, nature, art, and the good and beautiful things of life. Wellbeing is expressed in a sensual rather than intellectual or spiritual manner.

MOON in GEMINI

The emotions are subject to various fluctuations and changes. Communication is an asset, but a tendency to fantasise or even to lie is present, especially during childhood. Brotherhood and friendship are important sources of motivation.

MOON in CANCER

Family ties and emotional security through harmonious relationships are most important for wellbeing. Emotions can be overwhelming and a source of excessive sensitivity. The Moon here also indicates a more emotional than rational approach to human relationships.

MOON in LEO

This position of the Moon confers pride and a sense for leadership. The desire to be admired or appreciated is strong. It can lead to an unconscious need to be the centre of attraction. The feminine tendency of the Moon is masculinised in this Sun-ruled sign. Pride may interfere with natural emotiveness.

MOON in VIRGO

The analytic characteristic of this sign may reduce the spontaneity of the emotions. Sensitivity is voluntarily limited to avoid over exposition to discords and disappointments. Artistic tastes and creativity centre on elaborate and intricately detailed works of art.

MOON in LIBRA.

The emotions are subject to variations due to a tendency to strive for balance and harmony in human relationships to the detriment of emotional stability. The spontaneous link between mind and feelings enhances spontaneous appreciation of intellectual and artistic creativity.

MOON in SCORPIO

The emotions are triggered by a natural attraction to the mysteries of life, sex, and death. Strong independent tendencies and inner energy enhance natural charisma and magnetism. At times, socialising is awkward because of blunt and somehow distasteful manners.

MOON in SAGITTARIUS

Gives the emotional pattern a philosophical and spiritual sense. It also confers a natural interest in foreign languages and cultures, philosophy, religion, and higher education. A good sense of humour, loyalty and self-confidence are also indicated.

MOON in CAPRICORN

This position bolsters patience and the ability to sustain long-lasting efforts. It indicates a preference for earthly targets, materialistic pursuits, and realistic endeavours. Shyness, introversion, and emotional self-control are also present.

MOON in AQUARIUS

The emotions are subject to sudden and unexpected changes. Laughter and tears, joy and sadness, sociability, and withdrawal, cohabit closely with this intriguing position of the Moon. Originality, humour, and spontaneous attraction to others favour social success and reputation.

MOON in PISCES

Intuition and sensitivity to human and geographical environments confer a natural ability to connect with the invisible and metaphysical side of life. Emotions become a source of inspiration that can border on daydreaming, with a lack of common sense and realism.

Remember that the above descriptions are just a glimpse of a much more complex influence of the MOON according to its positions in the twelve zodiac signs.

There are many other factors that can alter the basic influence of a planet in a sign. We have just seen what the Moon in Pisces means. Its effect would be more remarkable if the Sun were also in Pisces, because the two major principles of life would then be working in the same direction. But the Sun in Leo, for example, would slightly alter the influence of the Moon in Pisces, because of its rulership position in Leo.

Jupiter, Saturn, Chiron, Uranus, Neptune, and Pluto are known as SLOW PLANETS. It takes almost 12 years for Jupiter to go around the zodiac, 29.5 years for Saturn, and many more for Uranus, Neptune, and Pluto.

Those planets influence many more people than Mercury, Venus, Mars, and Vesta during their transit through a sign. Uranus remains up to seven years in a sign. Imagine how many births occur worldwide in such a long time! The influence of the slow planets (beginning with Saturn) can be referred to as "generational influence". Their position in the chart tells us about the individual's way to handle the tasks of life. Saturn relates to difficulties and hardship. It gives information on the possible results obtained from the efforts and determination we put into reaching goals and realising projects.

In future lessons, you will learn about the **"HOUSES"** and the

"ASPECTS", the crucial elements to perfect the analysis of a birth chart.

Back to the MOON...

The movements of the Moon are important because it takes only 27 days and 6 hours for our natural satellite to complete one full circle around the Earth, therefore around the zodiac.

Compared to Pluto with 248.5 years, you understand that the two "planets"[2] cannot have the same influence on human nature. The Moon changes sign every two and a half days, while Pluto may remain over thirty years in a sign.

The Moon influences everything on Earth by reflecting the energy of the Sun. The Sun remains the primary element. It is the god of light and the provider of life. The Moon is the goddess of night, the mother of life, giving light to the darkness, fascinating and mysterious.

The Moon influences the movements of the oceans (the tides) as well as the actual birth of children. Statistics would certainly show that more babies are born after a full Moon than before. It is a fact that the Moon and the feminine cycles are almost identical in time.

The Moon influences plants, animals, and human beings, especially children and immature or over-sensitive individuals. More crimes are committed when the Moon is full. If rain is expected, it will have more chance to fall within the first few days after a full or new Moon. Every drop of water in the oceans, rivers, seas, and lakes is subject to the attraction of the Moon. Scientists have even been able to measure the influence of the Moon in a cup of tea![3] Thus, the smallest quantity of water

---

[2] The Moon is not a planet. It is Earth's natural satellite.
[3] Read "Supernature" by Lyall Watson mentioned in lesson 1

is subject to low and high tides produced by the movements of the Moon. Since 70 to 80% of the human body is made up of water, how could we not be influenced by the powerful energy of our natural satellite?

The variations to the Moon's influence on individuals are linked to its position in the signs, as seen earlier in this lesson, but the overall "tendency" of a birth chart is also an important criterion. If the general tendency is EARTH FIXED, the Moon has a different influence than in a FIRE-CARDINAL chart. Its influence, however, is always stronger when it is found in a water sign such as Cancer, Scorpio, or Pisces, no matter what the general tendency of the chart may be.

After the Sun, the Moon is the most influential factor in anyone's horoscope because of the short time it takes to move away from any given position.

There is a method of forecasting known to astrologers as *LUNAR RETURNS*. It is based on the return of the Moon at the exact position in the birth chart. Lunar returns occur every 27.4 days. This technique is described in the second section of the ABLAS astrology course.[4]

Conclusion

The Sun and the Moon are the major factors to analyse in a birth chart. They serve to understand Arians, Taureans, Geminis, Cancers, Leos, Virgos, Libras, Scorpios, Sagittarians, Capricorns, Aquarians, and Pisceans much more accurately and subtly.

One hundred and forty-four possibilities emerge (12 Sun signs

[4] https://www.ablas-astrology.com/course.htm

x 12 Moon signs) leading us much further than "solar-sign astrology" based only on the 12 zodiac signs.

In this course we take into consideration the 8 planets and 2 asteroids, bringing the number of possibilities to an incredible figure of 144 000 000 000 000 and even more when including the Ascendant, Lilith, and the Lunar Nodes, the Part of Fortune and the Aspects!

Looked at in this manner, astrology becomes a very serious study indeed. The interpretation of a birth chart is a source of valuable information that allows to behave efficiently in accordance with life's circumstances triggered by astrological configurations.

Whether this knowledge is used for good or evil is up to the individual to decide. It is said, for example, that Hitler hired astrologer-advisers before and after he became Germany's Fuhrer. It is also mentioned in the Bible that astrologers (the Three Wise Men) had announced the birth of Christ and followed the "star of Bethlehem" to find the newborn. This is an evident symbol of astrology. "*To follow the stars*" should therefore mean "*to know someone's own astrological chart and act wisely to obtain the best possible results*".

Later in this book you will learn that one planet (or more than one) has the strongest influence. It is shown by its position in a certain area of the chart. That planet is called the "DOMINANT". You remember that ARIES is a sign ruled by Mars. If this planet is strong in the chart, its influence may have a greater effect than the Sun or the Moon. Later in this course, I will show you how to determine your own "dominant" using a simple system called "*planetary chains dominant search*", PCDS.

For now, and they will be the subjects of the following lessons, we will discuss the influences of Mercury, Venus, Mars, and Vesta in each one of the twelve signs. With that additional knowledge, you will broaden the analysis of your own birth chart.

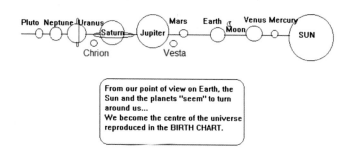

From our point of view on Earth, the Sun and the planets "seem" to turn around us...
We become the centre of the universe reproduced in the BIRTH CHART.

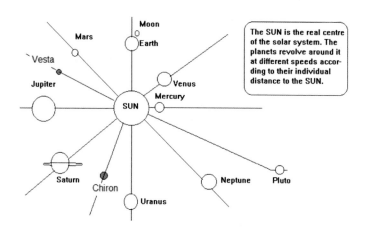

The SUN is the real centre of the solar system. The planets revolve around it at different speeds according to their individual distance to the SUN.

ABERRATION AND REALITY

(Geocentric and heliocentric systems)

This drawing illustrates the difference between the heliocentric and geocentric theories. The Sun is the centre of the solar system (heliocentrism). The Earth is the apparent centre of the Solar system (geocentrism). In astrology, the Earth is the centre of the chart.

THE PLANETS (Astronomical point of view)

Symbol	Name	Average distance to the Sun[5]	Revolution time[6]
☿	MERCURY	57.9	88 days
♀	VENUS	108.2	225 days
♂	MARS	227.9	1 year 322 days
⚶	VESTA	345	3 years 230 days
♃	JUPITER	778	11 years 315 days
♄	SATURN	1,427	29 years 167 days
⚷	CHIRON	2,025	50 years 153 days
♅	URANUS	2,870	84 years 7 days
♆	NEPTUNE	4,496	164 years 280 days
♇	PLUTO	5,946	248 years 157 days

The principle of each planet must always be analysed in relation to the sign in which the planet is found. In its sign of rulership, the influence is always stronger, but not necessarily dominant.

---

[5] In million kilometres
[6] Around the Sun in Earthly time, not around the zodiac (due to occasional retrogradation periods)

THE PLANETS (Astrological point of view)

Planet	Rulership	Keywords
SUN	LEO	**Masculine principle** - Vitality - Authority - Willpower Energy - The father - Social image.
MOON	CANCER	**Feminine principle** - Emotions - Feelings - Passivity - Moodiness - Fantasy - The mother.
MERCURY	GEMINI	**Intellectual principle** - Communication - Movement - Intellectual expression - Brother.
VENUS	TAURUS	**Love principle** - Sensuality - Charm - Affection - Creativity - Femininity - Cravings.
MARS	ARIES	**Combative principle** - Expression of physical energy - Passion - Sexuality – Masculinity.
VESTA	LIBRA	**Harmony principle** – Kindness – Compassion – Diplomacy - Justice - Equity - Moral values.
JUPITER	SAGITTARIUS	**Expansion principle** – Philosophy - Success - Opportunism - Generosity - Open-mindedness.
SATURN	CAPRICORN	**Restriction principle** – Constraint – Education Work - Obstacles - Difficulties - Pain - Wisdom.
CHIRON	VIRGO	**Observing principle** – Focus - Concentration - Attention to detail - Specialisation - Health.
URANUS	AQUARIUS	**Transformation principle** – Reformism - Originality Inventiveness - Eccentricity - Nervousness.
NEPTUNE	PISCES	**Spiritual principle** - Aspirations, dreams and hopes - Mysticism - Spirituality - Inspiration.
PLUTO	SCORPIO	**Regeneration principle** - Death - Mystery - Sexual Drive - Inner energy - Self-questioning.

Lesson 6

Mercury, Venus, Mars, Vesta in the signs

The lists of aphorisms included in this lesson, should be considered as reference material, together with the list relating to the Moon in each sign proposed in lesson 5. Throughout this course you will need to go back to those texts to support your first personal astrological readings.

It is important for beginners to refer to ready-made descriptions until they can memorise them, understanding the basic meanings of all planetary influences in a chart. After a while of daily practice, you will become accustomed to what they mean, and you will be able to use your own words to describe the planets' roles in anyone's birth chart.

In the present lesson, we will discuss the potential influences of Mercury, Venus, Mars, and Vesta in each one of the twelve signs. Let us begin with Mercury.

MERCURY

Mercury is the closest planet to the Sun. Place your own birth chart near you as you read on. As we progress in this lesson, you will begin the self-portrait to be completed by the end of this course. On your notebook, draw the symbol of Mercury, Venus, Mars, and Vesta, as well as the signs in which you find them in your birth chart.

As explained earlier, depending on the date of birth (and time of birth as far as the Moon is concerned) each planet may be placed in any one of the twelve zodiac signs. The sign in which a planet is found is a source of valuable information. Although only basic to begin with, the portrait you draw will become more and more precise and profound as you progress through each lesson. Remember that what the planet represents takes on the "colour" of the sign.

Mercury, first of the eight planets in order of distance to the Sun and revolution time, represents the intellect and the neuronal activity of the brain.

Mercury rules Gemini. That is the sign where Mercury is "at home". However, it does not mean that with Mercury in Gemini a person has a better or higher intellectual capacity than someone with Mercury in another sign.

It simply means that Mercury represents that sign and that any element (planet, House, etc.) in that sign depends on Mercury to perform in the person's chart and life.

It therefore means that **Gemini is a Mercurial sign**. But it does not mean that people born under this sign have Mercury in Gemini. In fact, Mercury can be found in other signs. **The same principle applies to every other planet in a birth chart.** Refer to the following list of aphorisms to understand the basic influence of Mercury in your chart.

MERCURY in ARIES

The intellect is overactive and at times rather aggressive and impulsive, with abrupt and sudden flows of unrestrained energy. The intellectual interests appear and disappear quickly. Communication is tensed and arguments are commonplace. Although it depends on the rest of the chart, this position of Mercury is less remarkable a male's chart. That is perhaps because Aries is a masculine sign. Short distance travels are decided in an instant. Headaches are also frequent with this position.

MERCURY in TAURUS

Mercury here confers a rather practical mind and an interest in material comfort manifesting in relationships often motivated by the pleasure derived from sharing the same food, the same ideas, and the same tastes. Music, painting, cooking, and the many good and beautiful things of life are a source of intellectual satisfaction. The manner of speech is usually rather pleasant. The learning process is slow, but the memory is usually good.

MERCURY in GEMINI

Mercury here is the impersonation of its mythological role of *messenger of the gods*. Quick-witted and intelligent, a person with Mercury in Gemini is always "on the go", but not quite persistent enough to reach the finish line. The Mercurian person easily adapts to new currents of thoughts and ideas, and to changing social patterns. Communication comes easy especially when the subject is light or superficial. Short distance travels are preferred. The nervous system and neuronal activity may become a source of concern.

MERCURY in CANCER

The intellect and communication process are subject to variations due to the emotional connotation of this sign. Family life is important and personal interests often include history or the family tree. Mental activity is enhanced by a correlation between sensitivity and objectivity. Mercury being under the rulership of the Moon, moodiness is likely to hinder one's natural ability to deal with important subjects objectively and rationally. Variations of the state of mind may have a disruptive influence on the primary digestive function (the stomach).

MERCURY in LEO

This position indicates an intellectual interest in arts, together with a creative mind. Pride and a tendency to have a strong image of oneself may interfere with the wellbeing of close human relationships. However, generosity, enthusiasm, honesty and stability of thoughts and ideas are usually conferred by this position of Mercury in the Sun-ruled sign of the lion. There is a tendency to be either excessively humble and shy, yet quite domineering and paternalistic.

MERCURY in VIRGO

This position confers a pragmatic and down-to-earth intellectual approach of life. A practical analysing mind favours success in business or retail work. However, a tendency to focus on details may temper the broader picture. This position is excellent for commercial, scientific, medical or office work, because it bestows a methodical approach and a good sense of order and classification. Mercury in Virgo is also found in the charts of hypochondriacs.

MERCURY in LIBRA

Mercury here confers diplomacy, good taste, and a genuine interest in balance and harmony. This position is found in the charts of musicians, writers, and poets. It is also favourable to mathematicians and people involved in justice, architecture, and politics. Intellectual behaviour is rather pleasant and positive, honest, and sensitive. It usually goes with a sympathetic approach to human relationship, which tends to increase popularity and the potential to succeed.

MERCURY in SCORPIO

The intellect and manner of speech are direct and insightful, but often sharp or caustic. An independent mind makes it complicated to keep relationships harmonious. There is a strong intellectual attraction to the unknown, an interest in scientific or human research, and a fascination for life's mysteries. In some cases, moral values need to be occasionally reasserted to avoid various clashes, misunderstandings, and a tendency to use charisma and authority to influence others incorrectly.

MERCURY in SAGITTARIUS

The intellect is attracted to religion and philosophy as well as to foreign countries and cultures. However, it may remain on a mental level rather than involving deeper feelings. Mercury here also indicates a spontaneous interest in long-distance travels, and foreign languages favoured by an ability to learn and acquire a high level of knowledge in many areas. A respectful approach of the notions of heavenly justice and wisdom is also indicated.

MERCURY in CAPRICORN

Mercury confers a down-to-earth intellect with long-term and long-lasting interests. The preference goes to conservative learning patterns and efforts to climb the social and professional ladder. Patience, reflection, and seriousness favour success and far-fetched objectives and ambitions. In some cases, lack of optimism and shyness come from a tendency to intellectual underestimation. Nevertheless, Mercury in Capricorn goes with a persistent and determined mindset.

MERCURY in AQUARIUS

Intellectual originality and virtuosity are indicated. The mind is connected to the universe around, interested in human nature and in the modern tools of communication. The downside of this position of Mercury is mental eccentricity that can lead to marginality. There is a degree of difficulty to focus on any one subject, and impatience. However, sociability with a charitable approach to human relationships enhances the potential to succeed.

MERCURY in PISCES

Logic and understanding processes rely on intuition and sensibility rather than rational reasoning to obtain better results. Imagination and inspiration are valuable assets to the art-oriented person. The mind is easily influenced by environmental ambience and vibrations. Connection to the invisible confers clairvoyant tendencies. An interest in religions and mystical subjects is also indicated.

Bear in mind that these quick descriptions are only meant to guide your first analyses. Later you will learn how much the basic influence of a planet in a sign can be modified by various other elements in the chart.

VENUS

VENUS is the LOVE PRINCIPLE of life. The sign in which it is found indicates how this principle is applied. Venus also plays an important role in the development and expression of our interest in the good and beautiful things of life. Food, clothing, the arts, and creativity are subject to the effect of Venus. Dipped into the energy of a sign, it expresses itself in accordance with the nature of that sign. Use the list of aphorisms below to understand the basic role of this planet in your chart.

VENUS in ARIES

Venus here confers ardent and fiery feelings in personal and intimate relationships. It also indicates sudden changes in the expression of love and friendship, and a degree of aggressiveness and competitiveness in seeking affection. Venus is not at ease in this sign because Aries is ruled by Mars, the god of war, turning the goddess of love into a warrior lover. A tendency to demand too much attention and to dominate loved ones may have spoiling effects on relationships because of such intense needs and desires.

VENUS in TAURUS

In its sign of rulership, Venus confers fixed and constant feelings and affections. Emotional security and stability are important to ensure and preserve wellbeing. Sensuality is well developed, and physical contacts are essential in personal intimate relationships. Artistic tastes centre on the beautiful in all earthly manifestations. Decoration, clothing, food, and music are some typical interests conferred by Venus in Taurus. This position also tends to preserve good health, thanks to one's spontaneous interest in the positive role of earthly matter.

VENUS in GEMINI

The love principle is certainly adaptable and versatile, but sometimes superficial. The need for variety, movement, and excitement can make it difficult to keep a steady relationship for long. A mentalised expression of love creates an attraction to more intellectual than carnal partners. This position favours social success, thanks to an innate ability to use words and imagination in a pleasant and charming manner. Like a butterfly going from flower to flower, this lover likes to discover and experiment before settling down durably.

VENUS in CANCER

Venus here shows how the love of family and home can make life agreeable for close ones. There is a tendency to be oversensitive and romantic, moody, and fluctuating in one's demonstration of love and affection. Emotional attachment to the home and family environment makes for a usually pleasant atmosphere and agreeable personal relationships. This position indicates a strong mother instinct and a keen interest in cooking, decorating, and creative activities. A compassionate and usually gentle nature favour popularity.

VENUS in LEO

This position confers ardent, passionate, and stable feelings in sentimental relationships. Personal pride, however, can interfere with emotions in romantic situations. Artistic taste and creativity are enhanced, together with an outgoing, sunny, and affectionate nature. Venus in Leo goes with a loyal and sincere approach to love and romance. It also indicates a tendency to take things too much at heart and to be easily hurt. Venus in Leo also seems to favour physical beauty. Charisma and positive personal magnetism are also present.

VENUS in VIRGO

Venus here confers an over-analysing approach to love and affection. The intellect interferes with direct and spontaneous reactions triggered by personal feelings and can inhibit and restrict the evolution of the intimate life. This position of Venus in Virgo is frequently found in the charts of unmarried people. Virgo confers highly critical standards of appreciation of the other person and of the self, together with a tendency to worry too much about loved ones. Artistic tendencies are present and can contribute to social and professional success.

VENUS in LIBRA

Venus here makes marriage, associations, and social relationships true affairs of the heart. They are a major factor of wellbeing. Hence, the "love potential" of Venus is spontaneously and often "theatrically" expressed. Venus here confers physical beauty, personal charm, and charisma. This position is especially favourable to artists, comedians, musicians, and writers. A constant search for harmony makes discord and arguments upsetting and unpleasant. Diplomacy and concessions are therefore usually preferred to painful arguments.

VENUS in SCORPIO

Love is mixed with strong sexual desires together with a deep and passionate approach to romance. Feelings are expressed with pride and possessiveness. Jealous and secretive, the person is moved by a sense of self-sacrifice to sublimate love. Profound resentment becomes a source of inner grudge when romantically deceived. This position often goes with love/hate types of intimate relationships. Artistic tastes lean toward strong, dramatic styles, with a touch of mystery, erotism and occult fantasy.

VENUS in SAGITTARIUS

In Jupiter's sign, Venus gives idealistic and spiritually oriented feelings and emotions. Friendliness and sociability go with this position. Close human relationships are based on ethics, morals, philosophy, religion, and other socially recognised values. Traditions are encouraged to preserve emotional wellbeing. Artistic tastes are rather flamboyant and expensive. Love is coloured with religious or philosophic convictions. Extreme generosity is a source of disappointment in a world where personal profit is a primary motivation.

VENUS in CAPRICORN

The love principle is "cooled down" by Venus in this sign. It may even confer a rather cold approach to intimate relationships. Introversion of personal feelings produces melancholy rather than "joie de vivre". Saying "I love you" does not come easy. There is a tendency to self-denial. Believing not to be nice or handsome enough does not favour spontaneous romantic and sentimental accomplishment. Celibacy or late marriage is frequent. Nevertheless, quiet as they may be, affections are profound and extremely durable.

VENUS in AQUARIUS

Venus here gives a suave, light, gracious and pleasant attitude to express love and affections. High moral standards are usually present in the search for meaningful sentimental relationships. A tendency to love-friendship relations may be a source of ambiguity and misunderstandings in private life. Free love and independence in marriage are common. The need for variety and excitement may favour celibacy rather than long-lasting partnerships. Original and unusual artistic talents can lead to social or professional success and recognition.

VENUS in PISCES

Venus here indicates an over-sensitive nature, prone to ambiguous romantic adventures and relationships. Mystery colours one's love life with an inclination for mystically oriented partners. Universal love on a spiritual level is often preferred to individual relationships. Religion may deeply influence the expression of love and creativity. Compassion and altruism toward mankind are also present. Music and dance may become a source of creative expression and satisfaction.

MARS

As we have seen earlier in this book, Mars represents the combative principle of life. The sign in which it is found in a chart indicates how this principle is expressed. Here is a list of aphorisms to help you analyse and understand Mars's basic influence in your chart and in your life.

MARS in ARIES

Mars here is in its sign of rulership where it confers a "primal" and spontaneous expression of combativeness. Action is the keyword to success with this position of Mars in Aries. Authoritarian tendencies, however, can alienate friendship and harmonious relationships with co-workers, friends, or family members. A tendency to feel threatened produces a need to develop self-defence skills. Dedicated martial artists or sports competitors are favoured from Mars in Aries in their chart.

MARS in TAURUS

Mars here confers a combative behaviour wherever material possessions are concerned. Financial success is favoured, together with a tendency to spoil loved ones and to be over generous in romance or friendship. However, selfishness and greediness may also be present, bestowing an ambiguous approach to earthly matters. Food, beauty, and the arts may favour professional and social realisation. The eagerness to satisfy personal desires may, however, become a source of chronic tension with the entourage.

MARS in GEMINI

Mars here confers an assertive and sharp manner of expression. Social life may be a source of chronic tension, due to impatience and a tendency to fervently impose personal opinions. Relationships with siblings are often tensed. Neuronal activity favours quick comprehension and quick learning skills. However, lack of endurance impairs long-term realisations. Self-discipline is needed to ensure concrete actions rather than theories.

MARS in CANCER

Mars here centres the combative principle on home affairs and family life. Its influence in this water sign confers a kind of "passive aggressiveness". Tenacity and determination depend essentially on the emotional state. To defend and protect one's family and home environment is a must that may develop far beyond the immediate human and geographical limits. Hence, chauvinistic, or nationalist character traits are often conferred by Mars in Cancer. A keen interest in the cause of the environment is also present.

MARS in LEO

This position is strong. Mars here confers creativity and good fighting ability. Pride motivates spontaneous commitment to deal with life's realities. Competitiveness, together with vibrant energy and inner strength help realise and achieve important goals. Fits of anger and bad temper are also present, with their disrupting incidence in social, professional, and personal relationships. The desire to fight for grand causes, sometimes at the cost of one's own life, is another characteristic of the influence of Mars in Leo.

MARS in VIRGO

Mars here gives energy and skill wherever work and duties are concerned. Minute precision and patience make it possible to undertake extremely intricate tasks. This position would certainly favour watchmakers or surgeons. Fussiness and perfectionism, however, may discourage from achieving any major project. Focusing on small details increases the tendency to excessive worry with their disruptive repercussions on physical and psychological health. The digestive system is vulnerable and can become a source of chronic discomfort.

MARS in LIBRA

This position shows that the combative principle is triggered by other people's requests rather than one's own needs. Always to be ready to help or defend close ones, Mars here favours family and social popularity. Mars in this Air sign tends to confer a jack-of-all-trades ability but not the means to concrete realisations. Diplomacy, counselling, and coaching are potential sources of professional success. The ability to control or dominate and direct others increases leadership abilities.

MARS in SCORPIO

Mars in Scorpio confers strength and a more effective approach to life's realities and responsibilities. Courage and a cold-blooded attitude to deal with hardship and difficulties are useful to do well in challenging situations. However, Mars here can also create offensive qualities, such as aggressiveness, excessive authority, forcefulness, and stubbornness. Sexual appetite is usually strong and may motivate prejudicial tendencies, health-wise or socially.

MARS in SAGITTARIUS

Mars here brings the combative principle to a more spiritual or philosophical level. Personal beliefs and moral ethics are a source of strong motivation. The ability to succeed is favoured by applying the social and legal rules. Excesses produced by Mars in this sign range from acts of heroism to radical religious tendencies that can alienate from pleasant social interaction. This position also increases the interest in sports and adventure.

MARS in CAPRICORN

Tenacity and determination are enhanced and favourable to the realisation of far-fetched goals. Ambition is a source of motivation. Time is a positive factor to fulfill personal ambitions. Leadership ability allows for more responsible professional positions. The Saturnian influence of Capricorn transferred to the energy of Mars increases spontaneous determination and endurance. But rigid authority prejudices social wellbeing.

MARS in AQUARIUS

This position confers a tendency to act in an original and unconventional way. Battling to impose reforms and social changes is a source of renewed stimulation. Inventiveness and spontaneous search for solutions to the most trivial problems of life does not deter from attending to much more important situations. However, excessive rebellion against the status quo may marginalise and deter the ability to remain in good terms with society. Relationships are tensed and unpleasant.

MARS in PISCES

In a water sign, Mars is not as virulent than in other elements. It does not make its influence weaker; it gives it a more subtle manner of expressing the combative principle of life. It confers a more intuitive reactivity based on higher principles, both philosophical and spiritual. Religious beliefs may stimulate the need to act to the point of losing touch with reality. Mars here enhances the ability to defend personal convictions derived from education or social trends, regardless of practicality.

VESTA

Vesta orbits in the *asteroid belt*[7] between Mars and Jupiter. I have given it the rulership of Libra. It represents our ability to preserve or restore inner balance and harmony. Our wellbeing depends on our ability to deal with life's realities and difficulties in a sensible and responsible manner. Diplomacy and compassion are also represented by Vesta. Its sign position clearly colours its primary influence to render it variously effective and useful. Here is a list of aphorisms to help you understand the role of Vesta in your chart and in your life.

VESTA in ARIES

Balance and harmony depend on the ability to act and decide. The energy put to the service of various life's goals is a source of inner tension. Impulsiveness causes multiple setbacks and various mistakes. To control personal impulses and other contradictory reactions is essential in maintaining a positive and constructive approach to life's events. When stability and efficiency become the main source of motivation, they prevent chronic destabilisation and promote success and wellbeing durably.

VESTA in TAURUS

Harmony and balance depend on the access to the good and beautiful things of life. Creativity favours wellbeing and success. Money is a means to please oneself and to benefit from what life has to offer to the astute buyer. Artistic talent can also play a role to promote social and professional

---

[7] The asteroid belt is a region in the solar system located between the orbits of Mars and Jupiter. It is occupied by a large number of solid objects of many sizes much smaller than planets. They are called **asteroids** or **minor planets**.

achievements. Love and material security are essential to maintain harmony and wellbeing in various areas of life. However, the quest for pleasure may tend to go beyond reasonable limits and produce pernicious yearnings.

VESTA in GEMINI

Intellectual complicity and spontaneous communication are essential to preserve balance and harmony in personal and social relationships. Reading, writing, travelling, teaching, and communicating in many ways are sources of wellbeing and accomplishment. They can motivate a career and favour professional success. However, lack of perseverance is also present. A shallow approach to the realities of life produces disappointments and errors with damaging consequences. Self-discipline is a must to benefit from Vesta in Gemini.

VESTA in CANCER

Family relationships and home environment heighten the necessary motivation and effort to maintain balance and harmony at home. Venus in Cancer confers a fluctuating approach to the realities of life. Personal wellbeing depends largely on the emotional quality of the immediate surroundings. However, excessive sensitivity may become a source of chronic physiological and psychological disorder. Motherhood often has a remarkable influence on the emergence of the need to search for inner peace and contentment.

VESTA in LEO

Creativity, personal charisma, and the need for love and recognition are viewed as essential sources of intimate wellbeing. Natural attraction to the brighter side of life favours higher levels of social and personal realisations. Vesta confers a compassionate approach to the needs and conditions of the underprivileged that may motivate spontaneous involvement in humanitarian or charitable activities. However, if talent and empathy are driven by pride and self-centredness, authenticity and sincerity are impaired.

VESTA in VIRGO

Harmony and wellbeing depend on the quality of human relationships in the social or professional environment. The ability to restore or preserve balance confers diplomatic tendencies that can influence the choice of a career. Health care is viewed as essential in pursuing and attaining personal objectives. However, excessive worry may contribute to the aggravation of various physiological disorders. It is necessary to avoid focusing on petty details to the detriment of the broader approach needed to solve most problems.

VESTA in LIBRA

This is Vesta's strongest position. Inner balance and harmony are essential values to preserve and feed. They motivate and encourage creativity, kindness, open-mindedness, and wellbeing, both personally and socially. Diplomacy favours pleasant and productive social, professional, and personal relationships. However, the desire to be good to others, and appreciated as a person, may overcome one's own needs and necessities. Alas, generosity and compassion do not ensure durable inner peace and comfort.

VESTA in SCORPIO

This position shows that sexuality is a major factor to preserve or restore inner harmony, balance, and wellbeing. A profound approach to personal relationships enhancoc thcir significance and positive potential. A tendency to feed on hardship to find the strength to overcome difficulties helps maintain a cold-blooded approach to the most troubling circumstances. However, the need to get too deeply involved in hazardous situations may prove detrimental to peace of mind and existential and satisfaction.

VESTA in SAGITTARIUS

Personal enjoyment and inner harmony are derived from philosophical, moral, and ethical values. Long-distance travels and a spontaneous interest in foreign cultures and languages are recurring sources of positive motivation and wellbeing. The respect of rules, laws, and traditions favour social balance and success. However, over-optimistic tendencies may prove detrimental and deceiving. Vesta here can also confer excessive opportunism together with a more cunning than genuine interest in human relationships.

VESTA in CAPRICORN

Inner harmony and balance depend on the rigour with which responsibilities are tackled. To comply with the realities of life and to accept their role and importance are necessary for personal wellbeing and achievement. The top of the mountain is a source of motivation to the climber eager to reach it rather than remain in the valley. Patience and determination are the keywords to personal realisation. Rigidity and lack of enthusiasm, however, may temper one's self-image and delay reaching the finish line in a reasonable time.

VESTA in AQUARIUS

Imagination and adaptability help maintain balance and harmony despite the ups and downs and sudden and unexpected changes of circumstances. Inner wellbeing is maintained by the diversity of human contacts that stimulate the ability to communicate in an original and creative manner. Quick reactivity is conferred to preserve or restore inner balance. Effective solutions and answers to most questionable situations come easy with Vesta in this sign. Let loose, however, originality can border on marginality with detrimental consequences.

VESTA in PISCES

Enhanced intuition and spontaneous connection to the invisible favour inner harmony and wellbeing. Creativity is a source of excitement and positive motivation. Artistic tendencies are often remarkable with this position of Vesta. The ability to progress in the most dubious situations is derived from spontaneous intuition. Music, dance, and various natural talents contribute to preserving or restoring inner balance and peace. However, lack of concrete direction backed by rational action may interfere with the positive use of innate potential.

* * * * * * * * * *

Once again, I insist on the fact that the influence of a planet in a sign is subject to the energy of such sign as much as to other elements. They will be discussed later in this course. If you do not recognise yourself in some of these short aphorisms, you will soon discover why.

What I want you to do is to **_rephrase_** what you have read about your Sun sign potential, about the positions of the Moon, Mercury, Venus, Mars and Vesta in according to their positions in signs in your own birth chart. You will then have to blend and synthesised to obtain a more accurate self-portrait. Although incomplete, it is a necessary step to the next level.

Another recommendation is to **use your own words** rather than copy/paste mine. Doing so from the very beginning of the course will make it much easier for you when the time comes to personally conduct astrological reading.

In the next lesson, we will discuss the influences of Jupiter, Saturn, Chiron, Uranus, Neptune, and Pluto in the signs. You will discover that the slower planets have a much broader influence on earthly life than the faster ones, from the Sun to Vesta.

Lesson 7

Planets in signs

From Jupiter to Chiron

In this lesson we will continue the study of the influence of the planets in the zodiac signs with **Jupiter, Saturn, and Chiron**. Uranus, Neptune, and Pluto are described in lesson 8.

These are the "SLOW" planets of the solar system. Their individual influence simultaneously concerns a much greater number of people in the same sign compared to any of the faster planets.

Jupiter remains an average of one year in a sign. Saturn need two and a half years to do the same voyage through a sign. Chiron stays from two to eight years in a sign, due to its eccentric orbit around the Sun.

* * * * * * * * * *

JUPITER

Jupiter is the first one of the slow planets. It takes almost twelve years to travel through the twelve zodiac signs, remaining an average of one year in each one. Jupiter is what I call the "*expansion principle*" of life. It represents our need and desire to progress and acquire. Be it for academic knowledge or material possessions, Jupiter represents our motivation to succeed socially and personally.

Jupiter is the largest planet in the solar system. It is almost 1,300 times the size of the Earth, revolving around its axis in just under ten hours. The energy produced by Jupiter is massive. The Earth rotates at an average distance of 150 million kilometres from the Sun, an ideal situation for life to develop as we know it on our planet. In comparison, at that same distance from Jupiter, all living creatures on Earth would be destroyed instantly by the radiation of the giant planet...

In astrology, the Sun is the giver of life, while Jupiter is growth and expansion. Perhaps this means that without the presence of Jupiter in the solar system, nothing on Earth would expand and progress... The sign where Jupiter stands in a chart, tells how the expansion principle is applied. Each sign influences the primary role of a planet. Let us discover in this lesson what it means for Jupiter.

Use the short aphorisms below to complement the self-portrait you began to draw in the previous lessons. **Remember that the primary influence of a planet is subject to other elements, some of which may drastically modify, alter, or sublimate its basic meaning in a chart.**

JUPITER in ARIES

In this sign, Jupiter confers instinctive leadership abilities and an interest in the philosophy of action, with a spiritual, or educational purpose. Spontaneous generosity and idealism are a strong source of motivation to succeed. However, excessive optimism may become a source of mistakes. The fiery nature of the sign confers a natural attraction to adventure and adrenaline-producing situations. Learning to channel active energy is necessary to lower the risks of incidents or accidents, and their costly consequences.

JUPITER in TAURUS

Success is inspired and motivated by the acquisition of the good and beautiful things of life. Money being the essential means to satisfy personal material desires, great energy is put to the service of social, professional, and financial realisation. There is a strong affective connotation to the idea of material security and stability. Artistic creativity is enhanced. Music, singing, cooking, sculpting, or painting are some of the natural talents to be exploited. Generosity often hides an intimate need for approbation and love. Friendships are usually profound and durable.

JUPITER in GEMINI

The idea of success depends on the ability to learn, to communicate, and to the potential to achieve positive human relationships. Moving places, meeting people, teaching, or writing are sources of renewed enthusiasm and involvement in numerous projects. The natural interest and attraction to the younger generations enhance intellectual activity and adaptability to social innovations and progress. However, excessive mental activity may induce a loss of rationality and difficulties to materialise ideas into concrete deeds.

JUPITER in CANCER

The philosophical approach to life is deeply marked by the nature of the family environment. The influence of the mother and the concept of motherhood are a source of renewed motivation and spiritual development. The relationship with the home and the homeland is strong. Evolution and social success depend on the ability to manage the emotional charge linked to one's origins. An excess of emotional vulnerability produces a need for personal protection by displaying an enthusiastic and optimistic face to conceal deeper affective distress.

JUPITER in LEO

There is an innate desire to become "someone", a hero, or an enviable member of the community. A positive attitude helps climb the social ladder and prosper in various ways. A mindful approach to the notion of success is linked to an innate need to become a leader, pleading the cause of the weaker and less fortunate, to help and protect them with genuine generosity. However, excessive attraction to high social status enhances opportunistic tendencies to the point of overpassing the moral or ethical limit in human relationships and interactions.

JUPITER in VIRGO

Traditional astrology considers it in "exile", but in my opinion, based on four decades of daily practice, I believe that is not an unfavourable position at all. Indeed, it confers a sense of the fair value of work and service to the community. It can also indicate a genuine interest in health and medicine, strong enough to motivate a choice of career. However, the critical tendency of Virgo can interfere with the natural generosity and enthusiasm represented by Jupiter. Conflicts of interest may have unfortunate repercussions in personal or social life.

JUPITER in LIBRA

This position confers a genuine interest in fairness and equitable moral values in marriage, close relationships, and partnerships. Generosity and a compassionate approach to human affairs favour wellbeing and positive motivations that boost popularity, both in private and social life. The ability to convince others of the merits of ideas and projects is another trait of personality derived from Jupiter in this sign. Success greatly depends on the quality of partnerships, rather than solely on personal effort. Choosing the right associates is essential to avoid errors and disappointment.

JUPITER in SCORPIO

This position confers an innate interest in occult sciences, mysticism, religion, and the mysteries of life and death. A spontaneous ability to communicate with the invisible world is often remarked. The attraction to the unknown motivates the search for secret information about people and events. Police investigators would certainly benefit from Jupiter in this sign. An attraction to unusual relationships and sexual partners may become a source of difficulties. This position of Jupiter also indicates a tendency to fluctuate between enthusiasm and morbidity that may lead to a nihilistic perception life.

JUPITER in SAGITTARIUS

This is Jupiter's rulership position, a sign where its influence is stronger than in any other. It confers more enthusiasm and a more spontaneously positive and optimistic approach to life. It enhances the interest in foreign countries and cultures. It extends the desire to learn to a wider variety of subjects and disciplines. Higher education and social rules and traditions are sources of strong motivation. However, the desire to progress and to succeed increases opportunism and the tendency to aim too high with accrued risk of social, moral and ethical setbacks and disappointment.

JUPITER in CAPRICORN

A realistic approach to life allows for more concrete and long-lasting results. The desire to succeed is strong, but the process of realisation is slow. A down-to-earth philosophy of life enhances the potential to build and prosper. Taking time to attain the desired objectives has a beneficial effect on the quality of the outcomes. A genuine respect of hierarchy and social order provides access to higher social or professional status. Rigour and rigidity may, however, cohabit with difficulty with detrimental effect on the ability to embark spontaneously in important schemes and projects. "Better safe than sorry" is the motto with Jupiter in Capricorn…

JUPITER in AQUARIUS

This position confers a broader understanding of human and social needs. No class, religion and racial distinctions are made in human dealings. There is a genuine appreciation of people for what they are, not for what they have. A philosophical inclination to share experiences with individuals from all walks of life is noticed. A progressist and anti-conformist approach to the realities of life motivates implications in charitable activities. There may also be bohemian tendencies triggering sudden changes of status due to a chronic need for fresh and unusual experiences.

JUPITER in PISCES

This is the most spiritual position of Jupiter. It confers understanding, compassion, and a spontaneous connection with the spiritual meaning of life. Empathy may be taken advantage of, but personal satisfaction stemming from a strong sense of duty, allows a more holistic than worldly approach to the most unpleasant earthly events and situations. Artistic creativity is enhanced and contributes to wellbeing as well as to social or professional realisation. However, excessive trust in others may lead to profound disappointment and disillusion.

SATURN

Saturn takes 29.5 years to complete its journey around the zodiac. Its influence has always been associated with hardship, passing time, and old age. Wherever it is found in a chart Saturn provides information on the way a person takes on the burdens of life. However, many births occur while Saturn transits a sign. Its position in the "Houses" and the "aspects" involving it in a chart provide valuable information to understand how this planet influences the mental, physical, spiritual, inner, and social development.

Saturn is wisdom, and wisdom takes time to acquire. It is the "karmic" planet par excellence. It shows the type of earthly mission we must take on, and the effort needed to deal with the reality of the task. Its position in a sign tells about the energy Saturn absorbs and transfers into our personal approach of the facts of life.

Here is a list of aphorisms to briefly explain how Saturn reacts in each zodiac sign.

SATURN in ARIES

The fire-cardinal energy of Aries makes Saturn uncomfortable in this sign. It confers a tendency to hesitate rather than to act or react spontaneously. However, taking time to attend to daily routines contributes to more constructive results. Saturn in Aries produces surges of energy that are sometimes difficult to control. It creates counter-reactions when time has come for major decisions. The positive side of this position is the ability to ponder and reflect instead of rushing to conclusions. Authority, impulsiveness, and aggressiveness have a karmic connotation that needs to be dealt with without compromise.

SATURN in TAURUS

The karmic value of this position is closely related to the materialistic earthly side of life. Food, money, and possessions may be considered as primary sources of concern and difficulty. Saturn here increases a tendency to dread the consequences of wrong decisions or inappropriate behaviour. Self-restriction stems from an innate need for self-protection. Financial reluctance and apprehension undermine creativity and the spontaneous expression of love and affection. Peace of mind and economic coherence depend on patience, endurance, and determination.

SATURN in GEMINI

Saturn here absorbs some of the lighter aspect of the sign of the twins: eternal youth. In appearance, at least... Intellectual development and communication are the main missions to accomplish in this life. A tendency to self-underestimation reveals that knowledge requires learning and that learning takes time. The quality of human relationships depends on the ability to express and share personal and communal thoughts and ideas. Feeling uncomfortable in the presence of others undermines the potential to build meaningful relations.

SATURN in CANCER

This karmic position of Saturn opposite its sign of rulership is often considered negatively in astrology. If it often indicates a life path or "mission" in relation with the home, family affairs and the ethnic or social background, it also confers a more rational approach to realities, difficulties, and emotional challenges. The mother or mother figure deeply influences the choices made to deal with personal and family hardship. However, once emotional ties to past events are overcome, determination, patience, and endurance favour a more enjoyable second part of life.

SATURN in LEO

The nature of Leo is linked to the need to accomplish, to impress and to become the centre of attention. Saturn here imposes more time to reach the desired level of performance and realisation. Although it may take longer to prosper, once achieved, the outcome is often exceptionally long-lasting. The creative quality of Leo enhances Saturn's influence on personal ambition and determination to obtain the best possible results. It is a matter of ego. However, the time factor may be a source of discouragement and alter the necessary drive to achieve life's mission.

SATURN in VIRGO

Despite obstacles and restrictions, Saturn's influence on the ability to succeed exclusively depends on work and duty. Virgo instils its fastidious and rational approach of life to Saturn's seriousness and determination. There is an innate need to undertake commitments, no matter how long it takes and how difficult they are. Progress is viewed on more personal than social angles. To remain at the bottom of the ladder or reach the highest level makes little difference to the way work, and responsibilities are perceived and accepted. Health and medicine may be part of the motivation to realise life's mission.

SATURN in LIBRA

Human relationships often have a profound karmic connotation. Saturn here emphasises the need for long-lasting personal involvement, privately, socially, and professionally. Such alliances may be sources of hardship, frustrations, and limitations. They are nonetheless a must to progress and to achieve long-lasting concrete results. Personal ambition depends on the quality of the other person or people involved in a joint venture. Unable to do it solo, it appears necessary to share and split the overall tasks and efforts to assume the time factor with more determination and avoid solitude.

SATURN in SCORPIO

Sexuality, death, and the unknown have a deep karmic connotation. Self-limitations and personal dissatisfaction make it difficult to accept fate to lessen the emotional weight and build on the ashes of past errors and misfortunes. Sexual Drive nourishes determination and the purpose to deal with and overcome life's unpleasant circumstances. A constant shadow seems to limit existential brightness and happiness. More fatalistic than adventurous, Saturn enhances resignation to undergo a later life path marked by solitude and a degree of austerity.

SATURN in SAGITTARIUS

Philosophy, religion, and karma are closely linked to become a source of reflection and acceptation of the limitations and burdens that earthly life imposes to foster moral progress. Time is viewed as a necessary process to understand and accept its lofty meaning. Restrictions may be self-imposed to assess one's determination and endurance. Travelling and connecting with foreign places and people have a common spiritual purpose. The energy used to deal with hardship helps face up to reality with a smile and a positive approach that favours the realisation of long-term projects.

SATURN in CAPRICORN

In its sign of rulership, Saturn enhances the natural connection with time. It is a strong position that improves patience and determination. Hardship is viewed as one of the unavoidable realities of earthly life. Long-term projects are sources of inspiration, although not joyfully expressed or anticipated. Social and professional realisation is a goal that may take many years to reach. A fatalistic rather than opportunistic thought pattern may alter the excitement and motivation to succeed. However, Saturn in Capricorn is often found in the charts of high-level executives and successful individuals.

SATURN in AQUARIUS

A karmic tie with humanity has a profound influence on the development of social life. People are considered as much a source of motivation and satisfaction than disillusion. Major efforts are needed to build solid and meaningful relationships. The diversity of human beings makes it exciting to participate in collective long-term projects with a common goal. Patience is required to deal with those who may be so different that it becomes a problem to connect with them. Unexpected changes are not appreciated; the nature of Saturn being more sedentary than mobile. However, major changes being considered fateful and part of one's destiny, they are usually dealt with successfully.

SATURN in PISCES

The natural connection between body and soul depends on life's difficulties and the necessary effort and time required to deal with them. A lofty approach allows for better results. Effort is considered from a spiritual rather than purely terrestrial point of view. Earthly life is made easier by accepting its many challenges. Saturn here confers more inspiration and intuition to concretely realise earthly projects. Saturn's realism impregnated by the heavenly influence of Pisces confers the ability to give time a chance to show the way to concrete and long-lasting success.

CHIRON

The asteroid Chiron was discovered in 1977. It orbits around the Sun between Saturn and Uranus and takes about 51 years to circle the zodiac. Astronomers believe it is a comet residue trapped between the combined fields of attraction of the two giant planets.

In mythology Chiron is one of the *centaurs*, half man, half horse, aggressive monsters devoid of intelligence. However, two of them, Chiron and Phobos, are good and charitable. Chiron is the son of Cronos (Saturn). He is thoroughly familiar with the art of hunting, warfare, medicine, and music. Unfortunately, during a battle against evil entities, Heracles accidentally wounds Chiron. Despite the diligent care the centaur receives, the wound does not heal. Unable to sustain more pain, Chiron decides to die. He exchanges his immortality with mortal Prometheus.

In astrology, Chiron is correlated with health and medicine. It represents our ability to diagnose, to observe, and to analyse. To me, Chiron also represents a karmic charge expressed by a degree of difficulty to manage the sectors of life represented by the House where it is found in a birth chart. Its position in a sign informs on physiological vulnerability of certain functions and organs. It also shows the potential to understand and to deal with health issues and other ordeals in a reasonable and practical manner. Read the aphorisms below to discover the influence of Chiron according to its position in your birth chart.

CHIRON in ARIES

The earthly karmic mission represented by Chiron in this sign is linked to the challenge of dealing with and controlling impatience, impulsiveness, and precipitation. Analysing the possible consequences of hasty decisions and reactions allows for fewer mistakes to be made and fewer incidents to deplore. Excessive authority often hides a latent inferiority complex resulting from painful incidents or accidents dating from the first year of life. Health issues tend to centre around the head: the skull, the hair, the ears, the teeth, the skin of the face or the orbits of the eyes.

CHIRON in TAURUS

Hat the Earth provides in food and other good and beautiful things, are part of the karmic mission. Money and personal possessions become a source of concerns and ruminations. The pleasures of life attract and repulse at the same time. The challenge is to accept the concept of the physical confronted to the metaphysical. It also seems important to decide if the present is more important than the future to which it is tightly attached. Health issues are likely to affect the neck area, the throat, the lips, the mouth, as well as the breasts and the thyroid glands.

CHIRON in GEMINI

Communication is one of the main challenges to take on as a karmic mission. There is an obvious need to master the art of talking, writing, and sharing thoughts and ideas. The intellect allows us to reflect and ponder on facets of the self to tackle a natural tendency to loftiness or arrogance. A shallow approach to human relationships can lead to moral errors that affect popularity negatively. Knowledge is a quest issued from an intellectual inferiority complex resulting from early-life limitations. The brains and the lungs are the main areas for health concerns. The nervous system and the upper limbs may also be

CHIRON in CANCER

Family, home environment and motherhood are essential parts of the karmic mission. Deep personal feelings are marked by unpleasant situations resulting from difficult relationships with loved ones. There is a need to better control emotions to avoid an inner sensation of vulnerability with its unfortunate consequences in personal life. Analysing irrational emotive reactions allows better understanding of their origin. Childhood holds the answers to irrational fears and anxieties. The stomach, the lymph, the body fluids, and the left eye may become health concerns.

CHIRON in LEO

Ego is a question of survival; it is essential to being alive and aware of the self. The need to be the centre of attention initiates various behaviour patterns that may produce contrary effects to what is anticipated. Analysing the reasons behind a tendency to "show off" is useful to understand a suppressed inferiority complex caused by unpleasant childhood situations and events. Artistic creativity helps exteriorise the awkward and distasteful. The cardiovascular system, vision in the right eye, and the spine may become causes for health concerns.

CHIRON in VIRGO

Work and duty are essential parts of the karmic mission. An innate interest in health and medicine may motivate a career or profession. Serving, guiding, and helping others are a source of constant inspiration. The ability to observe, analyse and diagnose contributes to success. It can also enhance a predisposition to excessive worry about health, hygiene, and physiological wellbeing. Focusing on details tends to conceal the broader picture on which they depend. The digestive function, the intestines and the nervous system are causes for health concerns.

CHIRON in LIBRA

Partnerships and personal relationships are essential to life on Earth. Karmic ties have a profound influence on behaviour patterns. Wanting to preserve harmony may result in hurtful disappointment. Looking after a partner's or relative's health requires strength and self-abnegation to the benefit of the person's wellbeing. The earthly mission is to preserve, protect or restore close relationships and to serve as a mediator to get people to connect genuinely. Unstable urinary and kidney functions, and lower back pain may become sources of health concerns.

CHIRON in SCORPIO

Death, sex, the obscure and the mysteries of life are a source of philosophical interest and motivation to shed light on the unknown. There is a tendency to sink deep into sombre phases, perhaps due to an innate need to discover what it is "on the other side". Unfortunate events may leave deep scars in the heart and the soul. There is an attraction to morbid phenomena and an innate interest in strange and unusual experiences. The physical body can spontaneously reject what it does not like and what it does not want. This process favours physical regeneration.

CHIRON in SAGITTARIUS

To study, to teach, to travel, to learn, and to share thoughts and ideas are essential to the achievement of life's karmic mission. Struggles with formalities and conventions are due to philosophical differences that cannot be resolved. There is a need to heal and to lead others to a better life. Being profoundly attached to moral and intellectual principles may attract adverse outside reactions. Feeling misunderstood enhances the desire to convince by becoming an example to others. The liver, blood circulation, and blood pressure may cause health concerns.

CHIRON in CAPRICORN

Social status is important. There is a karmic need to prove that getting to the top is possible and accessible to the brave at heart and the hard worker. Education plays a major role to enhance or annihilate self-esteem and innate gifts and natural potential. Climbing the social ladder may take longer than most but determination and patience help to get to the top. Time should be considered an ally, not an enemy, even though difficulties, setbacks, obstacles, and delays require more energy to get the job done. The bones, the joints, the knees, and the skin may become health concerns.

CHIRON in AQUARIUS

Socialising and social work are parts of the karmic mission. There is a need to help others in various ways. Involvement in humanitarian activities may be a means of achieving the ultimate goal of life. Rational observation helps find better solutions to the most difficult problems and situations. A natural tendency to criticise is derived from an innate ability to pinpoint defects and focus on how to repair them. Restoring, mending, and curing complement the various potentialities derived from Chiron in this sign. Blood circulation, the lower limbs, and the nervous system may become sources of health concerns.

CHIRON in PISCES

Beliefs are an essential part of the human's mind. Connecting with the soul or with the spiritual dimension of life to which we all belong, allows for a deeper understanding the reasons behind life on this planet. The ability to link the physical body with the higher spirit promotes efficient rational holistic treatments to many ailments. To embrace universality rather than individuality enhances natural talent and potential. Intuition is a guide, a source of inspiration. There is great sensitivity to music and to subtle vibrations. The hormonal system, the feet and the lungs may become sources of health concerns.

Lesson 8

Planets in signs

From Uranus to Pluto

In this lesson we deal with the last planets of the solar system. They are also the slowest. Uranus takes 84 years to revolve around the Sun. Neptune needs 165 years and Pluto 248 years. Their individual influence impacts a greater number of births in the same sign than any of the other planets. They are especially interesting to analyse on a global (world) point of view. Their positions in Houses in a birth chart are more appropriate to understand how the slower planets affect individual life.

This lesson includes three lists of aphorisms to guide your analyses of the positions of Uranus, Neptune, and Pluto in your birth chart. Let us begin with Uranus.

URANUS

Uranus is the planet of sudden release of energy that can trigger unexpected and revolutionary changes. It takes Uranus 84 years to complete its journey around the zodiac. Uranus can remain up to seven years in a sign influencing many more birth charts than Jupiter or Saturn. Its position in sign indicates how we cope with modern intellectual and scientific innovations and progress. Uranus is said to have an "electrical" influence particularly reaching the superior nervous system.

The sign in which it is found tells about a generation of people and their ability to cope with drastic changes, to adapt, to invent, and to move forward promptly in the areas represented by the sign where Uranus is found. To individualise its influence, the "*House*" position and the "*aspects*" hold the answers. They will be explained in future lessons.

URANUS in ARIES

Drastic changes in social organisation have a strong influence on the ability to act and react. The first sign symbolises a new beginning, a new start. Initialising new projects is part of the behaviour of people born with Uranus in this sign. They are inventive and quick to respond. They always seem ready to rebel against the status quo. They fight to impose new concepts and ideas, but they also fight to combat reforms. Above all, they need to learn to slow down to avoid mistakes, accidents, conflicts, and painful breakups. Their vital energy may be subject to extreme highs and lows.

URANUS in TAURUS

There is a profound need to change the way nature and what it provides is considered. Food and feeding habits are subject to major innovations. The relationship between work and money is organised in an original manner. Using modernised or revolutionary tools of communication improves the ability to realise unprecedented social and material changes. There is a tendency to marginalisation due to a difficulty to accept laws and regulations. Instability may result and create a tortuous financial life path. Erratic eating inclinations may become a source of health concerns.

URANUS in GEMINI

Verbal and written interactions are essential to human life. Uranus here enhances originality, intellectual enthusiasm, adaptability, and the capacity to reach others and exchange thoughts and ideas spontaneously. Inventiveness and originality feed a strong need to reform communication by means of new concepts and the use of modern tools. Drastic changes in education and teaching methods are encouraged. They are a source of motivation to move forward with the times rather than stick to traditions. The nervous system and the lungs may become sources of health concerns.

URANUS in CANCER

The concepts of family, motherhood and patriotism motivate a strong need for major changes. Considered marginal by some and progressist by others, novelty is, however, essential to adapt to future necessities rather than keep on nurturing conventional models from the past. Bohemian tendencies are noticeable, although dependent on social, moral, and family situations. Single parenting is more attractive than the traditional home-life model. Frequent changes of residence are preferred to sedentary living. The stomach and the lymph may become sources of health concerns.

URANUS in LEO

Creativity is inherent to human nature, although it varies in intensity and value from one person to another. Originality calls for novelty and reforms of the meaning of creation. The expression of love is a source of sudden changes of direction. Instability may be considered a means to remain free and individualistically responsible. Unconventional forms of art are preferred to classic standards of the past. There is a need to change egotistic values to more universally useful forms of expression. The cardiovascular function may become a source of health concerns.

URANUS in VIRGO

Work and health are primary concerns that require constant re-evaluation to preserve social stability and progress. Uranus here expresses the need to change, to reform, and to transform conventional standards to innovate and allow more freedom in employment and innovations in health-related areas. There is a need to move away from routine work that generates boredom and a loss of interest in the daily tasks. Original ideas about hygiene and duty may create unusual behaviour at home and socially. Digestion affects the nervous system and may become a source of health concerns.

URANUS in LIBRA

Humans are not solitary creatures. They need each other to share, to progress and to develop. Uranus here indicates a strong need to reform the basics of personal relationships. Freedom and independence in marriage are more important than the legal contract. Marginal or unusual partnerships may result. Unconventional means to communicate profoundly modify couples' connections. Laws and regulations in marriage and other forms of association or partnerships are revolutionised to accommodate new trends. The lower back, kidneys and urinary functions may become health concerns.

URANUS in SCORPIO

Sex is the most basic but essential way to procreate. It is the natural means that nature provides to transcend death by giving life. Uranus here indicates a need to reform sexuality to modernise it and express it more freely. Unusual practices are meant to provoke senses and satisfy profound needs to abide by the idea that whatever begins must invariably end. Attraction to the unknown and to the darker side of human nature, may create self-destructive tendencies viewed as essential to favour inner regeneration. The reproductive system and bowel function may become sources of health concerns.

URANUS in SAGITTARIUS

Some believe that God was "invented" to create a monotheist religion intended to better control populations. Uranus here produces a strong need for freedom regarding philosophical thoughts and ideas. There is a tendency to reform and transform spiritual and ethical standards. Independence and originality characterise the revolutionaries who seek to renovate the moral and ethical landscape of society. Attraction to foreign cultures allows important gathering of information to serve the motto: "Learning is growing." Erratic hepatic function and blood pressure may become sources of health concerns.

URANUS in CAPRICORN

Tradition and hierarchy are essential to maintain social order. Uranus here creates a need to reform old-fashioned laws and change the way to deal with authority. Unusual projects and objectives develop from an attraction to new and unconventional tools and equipment. Climbing to the top requires determination and adaptability to the environment. Uranus here produces frequent modifications of direction that may lead to marginalisation. Inventiveness is a valuable asset to make the best out of the most unexpected and apparently unfavourable situations. Bones and joints may become sources of health concerns.

URANUS in AQUARIUS

The age of Aquarius is also the age of reality TV, mediatization of privacy and proliferation of the most complex and innovative devices to communicate with millions of people instantly. Dependence on electronic gadgets favours social predators who format youngsters to satisfy their mercantile purpose. Uranus here enhances the ability to quickly understand and show great ingenuity. There is also a tendency to voluntary marginal behaviour intended to drastically change and reform society. The nervous system, the peripheral blood circulation and the lower limbs may become sources of health concerns.

URANUS in PISCES

The need to believe is deeply rooted in societal archetypes. Religion plays a major role for thousands of years to control populations to ensure social order and stability. Uranus in this sign indicates a strong need to reform, transform and innovate. Philosophically inclined to new ideas and concepts, the adventurous spirit proposes nonconformist and marginal methods to tackle blind faith and irrational beliefs. An innate interest in holistic medicine is a vector for profound changes in social opinion and tradition. The respiratory system and hormonal function may become sources of health concerns.

NEPTUNE

More than any other of the slow planets, Neptune and Pluto in a sign have a profound influence on a whole generation of people. Moreover, their respective energy has a considerable impact on the course of history. That is why we use what these planets reveal in *world or political astrology*.

For the moment, read this lesson, try to understand the influences of Neptune and Pluto to supplement and end the chapter of this course about the planets in the signs.

Neptune is a very distant and extremely slow planet. To give you an example; in January 1890 Neptune was beginning its long transit in Gemini and at the end of December 1999, it was beginning its long transit in Aquarius. Neptune had travelled through only eight signs in 110 years! In fact, Neptune remains approximately fourteen years in each sign. That is why so many people born during such a long period have Neptune in the same sign in their birth chart.

Neptune is the first of the two slowest planets to have what can be called a definite *generational influence.* Hence, it plays an important role on the development of societies. Neptune is the *dream principle* of life. It represents faith, intuition, inspiration, and the natural connection between body and soul. The following set of aphorisms is meant to guide your analyses. Do not take them for granted, though. Other elements come into play to enhance or temper the natural influence of any celestial body in a chart.

NEPTUNE in ARIES

Neptune was in Aries, between 1861 and 1875, influencing a new generation of researchers and astronomers who tuned their head (Aries) to the sky. Many discoveries were made; some of which came out of the minds of enlightened, intuitive scientists. Occultists like Helena Blavatsky emerged and changed the spiritual concepts of the Western world. Neptune will return to transit in Aries from 2026 until 2040. Space manned missions to Mars (ruler of Aries) will become a reality and initiate a new era of discoveries for humanity. The less positive aspect of Neptune in fiery Aries influences some to act and react strongly and aggressively on presumptions rather than on fact and reality. Religious fundamentalism will also become more aggressive and irrationally determined.

NEPTUNE in TAURUS

It indicates a period from 1875 until 1889 during which a kind of idealism developed regarding the use of money and material resources. It marked the beginning of both Capitalism and Communism.

NEPTUNE in GEMINI

Between 1889 and 1902, Neptune marked a generation of people who did a lot to develop the intuitive and creative faculties of the mind that gave birth to the cinema at the end of the 19th century. There were major advances in communication since the invention of the telephone by Graham Bell in 1876.

NEPTUNE in CANCER

The transit lasted between 1902 and 1916, inspiring stronger psychic ties with the concepts of home and family. Religion had an emotional rather than intellectual significance. This position created excessive patriotism and ideological attachment to the home and country.

NEPTUNE in LEO

Neptune here conferred certain artistic talents to many people born between 1916 and 1929. This position enhances romantic tendencies and idealism in love, friendship, and other close relationships. Neptune in Leo illustrates the roaring twenties when unwise speculation and extravagant spending in pursuit of pleasure and lust led to financial ruin and to the great world depression of the thirties.

NEPTUNE in VIRGO

From 1928 until 1943 Neptune influenced a generation whose creative and imaginative faculties were thwarted by adverse material circumstances. The transit lasted through the period of the Great Depression and a part of World War II. Neptune here indicates a tendency to develop psychosomatic illnesses because of an over-sensitive approach to health and hygiene. Surges of anxiety derived from the influence of Virgo can lead to impractical methods and projects. Calculations based on unrealistic data produced incorrect results. This generation of people was deeply marked by uncertainty and disillusion when rebuilding the world from its own ashes was not a dream come true, but a painful reality.

NEPTUNE in LIBRA

From 1943 until 1957 Neptune here represents the post-war generation, people who brought about new concepts in the areas of marriage and partnership in general. The relationship itself became more important than the legal paperwork or contract. This led to an increasing divorce rate. The resulting broken homes produced uncertainty in the younger generation. The real value of relationship obligations became a source of error and disappointment. Inspired and sensitive, the artistic tendencies of this generation are enhanced by Neptune in Libra. It favours comedians, actors, musicians, and writers. These people found inspiration by connecting with the spiritual, some of them taking drugs or other substances to produce altered states of perception.

NEPTUNE in SCORPIO

Between 1957 and 1970, Neptune in Scorpio touched a generation led by basic natural desires. Sex, drugs, and alcohol became a formidable commercial exploitation with a harmful influence on morality and ethics. Drug addiction and alcoholism became an easy means to escape the "sad reality of life". A few people found true spiritual regeneration, but the greater number was marked by the negative effect of such destructive behaviour. However, clairvoyant abilities are also conferred by Neptune in Scorpio, together with profound sensitivity. The birth of the hippie movement in the sixties brought about a more sensible approach to nature's richness which led to the development of modern holistic medicine.

NEPTUNE in SAGITTARIUS

This position concerns people born between 1970 and 1984. They have a yearning for higher ethical and spiritual values in human customs. They dream of "spiritualising" society. Their inspired perception is found in music and art. Interactions with foreign lands for cultural exchanges is also important to their moral and intellectual growth. They have a mystical and metaphysical approach to the meaning of life. Spiritual healers, brilliant lecturers and philosophers are other products of the positive influence of Neptune in this sign. However, they are descendants of the hippie generation, of fake prophets and gurus who preached a better world for their own personal gain.

With Neptune in Sagittarius in their chart, some may be tempted to replicate a similar behaviour.

NEPTUNE in CAPRICORN

People born between 1984 and 1998 have Neptune in Capricorn. They display an innate sense of authority. Their intuition is down-to-earth. They want to keep their feet firmly on the ground, but their head is in the clouds. They want to succeed, and they have a good intuition when it comes to choosing the best way to get to the top of the mountain they want to climb. Some are too irrational, making grandiose plans that cannot be realised. Some understand that time is an unavoidable factor to include in their schemes. They are the most successful ones. To them, the soul is more a concept than a reality. Until they are proven wrong, they keep firm on their positions and beliefs.

NEPTUNE in AQUARIUS

This position concerns people born between 1998 and 2012. They have a genuine humanitarian philosophy and a spiritual approach to the meaning of life. They need to interact with others using modern tools of communication. They are intuitive and genuinely interested in the wellbeing of their entourage. They may get involved in charitable organisations to help the underprivileged. They are spontaneously connected, reaching out to the world in the hope of changing the essence of life threatened by the selfish behaviour of the older generations. The downside of Neptune's influence is a lack of objectivity and bohemian behaviour due to a certain confusion to adapt and accept laws and regulations.

NEPTUNE in PISCES

This position concerns people born between 2012 and 2026. Mystical, sensitive, and insightful, they are spontaneously connected to the spiritual dimension, where they may seek refuge when the realities of earthly life become too harsh. They tend to absorb the environmental energy like water in a sponge. Their extreme sensibility makes them vulnerable to negative and positive influences alike. Some are unable to distinguish between good and evil, between right or wrong. Some, with a higher IQ may become charismatic spiritual leaders. They will be teachers to those lost souls who will benefit from such lofty education. The downside of this position of Neptune is a tendency to lustfulness and an attraction to narcotics or alcohol, as well as fundamentalist religious practices.

PLUTO

As far as we know today, Pluto is the farthest planet in the Solar System. It revolves on an eccentric orbit at an average distance of 5,946 million km from the Sun and can remain up to 32 years in a sign. It takes over 248 years to complete one full circle around the zodiac. Imagine how many births the same position of Pluto can affect during its transit through a sign!

According to Greek mythology, Pluto is the god of death and the guardian of hell. He is the son of Saturn and brother of Jupiter and Neptune. When the planet was discovered in 1930 by US self-made astronomer Clyde Tombaugh[8], astrologers wanted to assess Pluto's possible influence on earthly life. They analysed many thousands charts of famous and more common people and, despite obtaining different results, they gradually agreed on one common theory.

Pluto's position in a sign shows how a generation of people profoundly and radically questions the status quo to regenerate the areas of life represented by the sign transited by Pluto. The process is like destroying an obsolete building to build a new one in its place. However, Pluto does not guarantee reconstruction. On the contrary, it may only motivate destruction.

The regeneration principle operates according to the influence it receives from the sign in which it stands. Therefore, wherever Pluto is found in a chart indicates how this principle operates at various levels. Read the list of aphorisms next to get accustomed to the energy of Pluto. Do not stop at your own sign's, read them all.

---

[8] Clyde William Tombaugh was born on February 4, 1906, in Streator, Illinois, US.

PLUTO in ARIES

Pluto is quite fierce and can be very destructive in Aries, the combative and competitive sign. Pluto here generates a large amount of energy to launch new projects. The need to destroy old traditions to impose new concepts was obvious during the period between 1823 and 1852. It was a time of extensive colonisation when force seemed the only way to defeat and conquer territories and countries alike. The next transit of Pluto in Aries will begin in 2066…

PLUTO in TAURUS

In Taurus, Pluto indicates a tendency to question and revolutionise the economy and its materialistically profitable connotation. Pluto transited here between 1852 and 1882. Because Taurus represents food, agriculture and the good and beautiful things of life, there was an overwhelming need to radically transform and modernise. The Industrial Revolution that led to the establishment of numerous factories throughout the world and to the first problems of unemployment and desolation. The era of the "Machine" had begun.

PLUTO in GEMINI

Pluto was in Gemini between 1882 and 1913. It coincided with a period of complete regeneration in communication at all levels and in all areas of life. A new way of thinking emerged, and the transport industry was revolutionised by the invention of the automobile and the aeroplane. Edison, Tesla, Bell, and others discovered the uses of electricity for modem technology and communications. Individually, Pluto encouraged a tendency to question and destroy the old ways of thinking to comply with the exigence of the extraordinary progress that took over the world in the twentieth century. Healthwise, this position may trigger various brains and neurologic disorders.

PLUTO in CANCER

Pluto began its long transit in Cancer in July 1913. World War I began in July 1914. World War II followed in 1939 when Pluto was nearing the end of its transit in this sign. In Cancer, Pluto marked an era of great patriotic concerns. The death of millions of people and children of all ages brought fear and destruction to many parts of the earth. The individual influence of this position is seen in a tendency to question and transform family ties and values. To rebuild on the ashes of the old world became an upmost necessity, but the task had to be led in a totally different manner, with the idea that deadly conflicts and global destruction would never again be a menace. Healthwise, Pluton in Cancer seems to trigger various pathologies affecting the digestive system and the lymph.

PLUTO in LEO

This position marked a generation of people whose education and growth were deeply influenced and strongly motivated by the events of World War II. Pluto transited in Leo between 1939 and 1957. Its effect is seen in the direct suffering caused by family losses, and in the psychological and affective impact of such disastrous times in world history. Pluto generates a need to question and transform with great courage and a sense of responsibility to help the weak and vulnerable. It confers a definite ability to express deeper feelings and emotions in new forms of art and in human relationships. Healthwise, when involved in discordant configurations in the chart, Pluto in Leo may produce cardiovascular pathologies, as well as eye and spine ailments.

PLUTO in VIRGO

Pluto was in Virgo between 1957 and 1972. People born then tend to question, reform, and transform their work environment. They need to destroy the "old school" to build a totally new concept. The role of the syndicates and other leadership-contesting movements emerged and eventually led to situations such as riots and demonstrations in various parts of the world. They are good examples of the influence of Pluto in this sign. Excessive worry about working conditions and health issues produce various pathologies affecting the digestive system. A constant effort is needed to avoid over-concern and its distressing effects on wellbeing.

PLUTO in LIBRA

People born between 1972 and 1984 with this position tend to question and seek reforms and regeneration in the areas of personal, social, and professional partnerships. There is a profound need for fairness and equity that may lead to revolts and other revendication movements. Artists challenge the old school to rejuvenate the status quo and impose a different approach of their work in literature, theatre, cinema, and music. Pluto in Libra also indicates a strong desire to reform the justice system to restore its neutrality and clarity. The kidneys, bladder, and the lumbar region may become sources of health concerns.

PLUTO in SCORPIO

This is Pluto's sign of rulership where its influence is strong and profound. The transit lasted between 1984 and 1996. It indicates an attraction and an interest in the occult, the mysteries of life and death. People born with Pluto in Scorpio are usually determined and cold-blooded. They are not afraid to die. Some may even show masochist leanings due to their unusual resistance to pain. Plutonian types of professions are preferred to more conventional careers. The army, the police force, the funeral industry, perilous or hazardous activities, and any profession that can satisfy their physical need for adrenaline. The reproductive system and the colonic function may become sources of health concerns.

PLUTO in SAGITTARIUS

Pluto in Sagittarius affects people born between 1996 and 2009. They belong to a generation seeking to regenerate the administration and justice system of their country with worldwide consequences. Some may develop a rather nihilist philosophical approach to life and lack positive drive to more constructive achievements. Regeneration seems necessary to obtain a more insightful meaning and purpose to higher studies, academic knowledge, and communication. Relations with foreign countries and cultures may deeply change due to fateful events, such as pollution, pandemics, and other calamities. These people grow up in difficult times. They need to be strong and remain optimistic, however negative the events may be. Blood pressure and liver function may become sources of health concerns.

PLUTO in CAPRICORN

This position concerns people born between 2009 and 2024. They will be motivated by a much-needed reorganisation of the world's banking system. They will strive to get rid of the common perception of money and profit. They will find it necessary to avoid increasingly frequent frauds, and dysfunctions at the highest levels of society. They will create a more equitable evaluation of people's incomes. They will strive to eliminate all kinds of dictatorship and other authoritarian behaviour. To avoid a global war or revolution, it will seem urgent to these people to revise and transform the notions of power and social status. Bones, skin, and joints may become sources of health concerns.

PLUTO in AQUARIUS

From 2024 onwards, we can expect a global phenomenon of total social regeneration. Aquarius represents social and geographical environments, peoples, and populations. Those born between 2024 and 2043 will live to destroy society in view of building a new world. The previous transit of Pluto in this sign began in 1779, when monarchy in France and America was nearing the end of its reign. Chaos ensued, but revolution eventually led to Republic and democracy. In 2024, the Internet may crash and be replaced by a more suitable system of communication. Control of the population will become so tight that it will create remarkably fierce reactions. The victims of these dark times will become sources of inspiration for the strongest and most determined ones to fight for a better world even at the cost of their life. The central nervous system and the peripheral blood circulation may become sources of health concerns.

PLUTO in PISCES

Pluto will transit this spiritual, mystical, and religious sign between 2043 and 2068. It may produce a total regeneration in these areas and the destruction of the old churches to the benefit of new laws and new mystical and religious approaches. At the same time, our planet will be almost completely drained from its natural fossil resources. Other consumable forms of energy will have already appeared. Wars for oil will not be possible anymore. Energy will be derived from the Sun and other natural sources. Disasters related to gas, water pollution, seismic activity, and floods will be common during this transit. People born with this position of Pluto may deplore a weakness of the respiratory system and of the lower limbs, especially the ankles and feet. Psychosomatic illnesses will also be more frequent.

Once again, use the descriptions in this lesson and the previous ones to analyse your own chart.

See if you recognise yourself in the aphorisms relating to Jupiter, Saturn, Chiron, Uranus, Neptune, and Pluto in the signs.

Keep in mind that such short interpretations need to be considered lightly. They only serve the first-step analysis progression in your study of astrology. Many other elements will be progressively added to make this self-portrait as faithful as possible.

Note:

Do you know why a planet may enter a sign twice, a few months to one year apart? It is because of the **RETROGRADATION** *phenomenon. All planets, except the Sun and the Moon, retrograde at different times during their revolution around the zodiac. But of course, none of them change their sense of rotation around the Sun. They do not slow down, stop and reverse. The "Retrogradation" is an "optical aberration".*

The various speeds and distances from the Sun imply that all planets take different times to revolve around the Sun. Here on Earth, we neither feel the speed of rotation on its axis (1,674 km/h) nor the speed of its revolution around the Sun (29.78 km/s). Therefore, when the Earth "overtakes" another planet on its orbit, it looks like that planet is moving back. A similar sensation appears when you are sitting in a moving vehicle that overtakes another one on its way.

This is the retrogradation phenomena. Although only a visual illusion, it has a physical effect. The influence of the retrograding planet decreases. Around a chart, a retrograding planet is marked with the capital letter R.

Lesson 9

The dominant one

There are several methods out there to work out the dominant planet/s in a birth chart. Years of practice have eventually led me to contribute to another way of determining the most important planets in a chart. Using the rulers of signs and Houses daily to analyse the many charts requested from my numerous clienteles, it became evident to rely on rulership to elaborate this simple, but I believe efficient, approach to the dominant one. I called it *"the technique of the planetary chains"*.

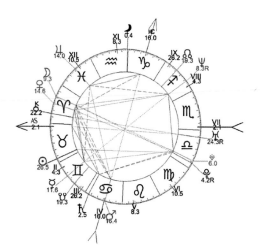

I will use the chart on the left to demonstrate how it works. First you need to make a list of the elements taken into consideration, from the Sun to Pluto. Then apply the principle of rulership to draw the planetary chains.

In this chart, the Sun is in Taurus, a sign ruled by Venus. Venus is in Aries, a sign ruled by **Mars**. Mars is in Cancer, a sign ruled by the Moon. The Moon is in Aries, a sign ruled by **Mars**. We stop here because Mars has already been mentioned once in the chain. There Mars is the leader of this first chain.

The second element to consider is the Moon. It is found in Aries, a sign rules by **Mars**. Mars is in Cancer, a sign ruled by the Moon. *We do not stop at the Moon because it is the reference element, not an element in the chain.* The Moon is in Aries, a sign ruled by **Mars**. Once again, Mars is the leader of the second chain.

Next comes Mercury. It is in Gemini, in its own sign. The chain stops here.
Then comes Venus. It is found in Aries, a sign ruled by **Mars**. Mars is in Cancer, a sign ruled by the Moon. The Moon is in Aries, a sign ruled by **Mars**. Once again, Mars is the leader of the chain.

Next, we turn to Mars. It is in Cancer, a sign ruled by the **Moon**. The Moon is in Aries, a sign ruled by Mars. Once more, we do not stop at Mars, because it is the reference element, not an element in the chain. Mars is in Cancer, a sign ruled by the **Moon**. Hence, the Moon wins the leadership of Mars's chain.

Vesta is the next element to consider. It is in its own sign, Libra. The chain ends with **Vesta**.

Jupiter follows. It is in Pisces, a sign ruled by **Neptune**. Neptune is in Sagittarius, a sign ruled by Jupiter (same remark as above about being the reference element). Jupiter is in Pisces, a sign ruled by **Neptune**. The chain ends with the leadership of Neptune.

Saturn is the next element to consider. It is in Cancer, a sign ruled by the **Moon**. The Moon is in Aries, a sign ruled by Mars. Mars is in Cancer, a sign ruled by the **Moon**. Once again, the Moon wins a chain leadership.
Chiron is the next one to consider. It is in Aries, a sign ruled

by **Mars**. Mars is in Cancer, a sign ruled by the Moon. The Moon is in Aries, a sign ruled by **Mars**. This is another leadership win for the god of war 😊

Uranus now. It is in Libra, a sign ruled by **Vesta**. Vesta is in Libra. The chain ends here. **Vesta** is the leader.

Neptune is second to last. It is in Sagittarius, a sign ruled by **Jupiter**. Jupiter is in Pisces, a sign ruled by Neptune. Neptune is in Sagittarius, a sign ruled by **Jupiter**. Jupiter wins leadership of this chain.

Pluto is the last element to look at. It is in Libra, a sign ruled by **Vesta**. Vesta is in Libra. The chain stops with the leadership of Vesta positioned in its own sign.

All we need to do now is counting the number of leadership wins for the element found at the end of each chain. **Mars obtains 4 wins. Vesta: 3. Moon: 2. Mercury: 1. Neptune: 1. Jupiter: 1**

Mars is the dominant one, followed closely by Vesta. The energy of the person concerned is therefore quite strong. This lady is a double Taurus (sign and Ascendant) with Venus in Aries next to the Moon. That says a lot…

The technique of the chains is an ideal exercise to get used to juggling with the rulers of the signs. The quicker the better. Just like learning to name the signs quickly in the right order, then in the reverse order, is an excellent exercise to memorise the logic of their placements around the zodiac the chain technique helps to recognise their rulers instantly.

Now we want to compare our result with the general tendency of this chart. Here it is.

Sun	Taurus	Earth	Fixed
Moon	Aries	Fire	Cardinal
Mercury	Gemini	Air x 2	Mutable x 2
Venus	Aries	Fire	Cardinal
Mars	Cancer	Water	Cardinal
Vesta	Libra	Air x 2	Cardinal x 2
Jupiter	Pisces	Water	Mutable
Saturn	Cancer	Water	Cardinal
Chiron	Aries	Fire	Cardinal
Uranus	Libra	Air	Cardinal
Neptune	Sagittarius	Fire	Mutable
Pluto	Libra	Air	Cardinal
Ascendant	Taurus	Earth	Fixed

The result is:

4 Fire, 6 Air, 3 Water, 2 Earth
2 Fixed, 4 Mutable, 9 Cardinal

The general tendency is AIR-CARDINAL

Air-Cardinal with dominant Mars… Air-Cardinal means a Libra tendency while the ruler of Aries, the opposite sign, is the dominant planet. It undoubtedly indicates a strong personality, pulled between the need to temporise (Libra) and an impetuous nature that may be quite a handful to control when aroused…

Now, check your own birth chart and work out your dominant planet. Then compare it with your general tendency. What useful information about your personality can you derive from this exercise?

Next, you will learn about the Houses. What they are, what they mean and how they are affected according to their positions around the zodiac.

Lesson 10

The Houses
(Part 1)

In this lesson you are going to learn about the *HOUSES,* what they are, what they mean and how they are placed and analysed in relation to planets and signs.

You must understand thoroughly this week's lesson to keep up with the pace of the course and comprehend the essence of astrology for the development of your skill.

Let us begin...

The *date of birth defines the Sun Sign* while the *time of birth determines the "rising sign" or Ascendant.*

The zodiac is divided into twelve sections allocated to the twelve signs. They are placed counterclockwise, beginning with Aries to end with Pisces.

There is always a moment when the sun rises on Earth, and a moment when it sets. Between these two moments, the sun "seems" to circle the Earth, from left to right, from east to west. But, in fact, everyone knows that it is the Earth that turns, in the opposite direction, from right to left or from west to east, not the Sun... This reverse vision of the zodiac explains why in astrology the signs and Houses evolve *counterclockwise* and that east becomes west, and west becomes east.

The Ascendant on the left of the chart represents the east. House VII or Descendant on the right of the chart, across from the Ascendant represents the west. In addition, The MC (House X) represents midday, and the NADIR (House IV) represents midnight.

In Astrology when we consider the Houses, we consider the rotation of the Earth, not the apparent movement of the Sun.

You know now that you belong to such or such sign simply because, when you were born, the Sun, in relation to the Earth, was transiting that sign. Of course, everyone knows that the Sun is fixed. It is the Earth that turns around it in one year...

Consequently, as far as the zodiac signs are concerned, the journey of the Earth around the Sun is the astronomical reality. The revolution takes 365 earthly days and 6 hours, or one year. That is why you need to know your date of birth to determine your Sun sign or zodiac sign.

The Earth also rotates around itself on an invisible axis in 24 hours 56 minutes and 4 seconds precisely. This rotation defines the day and the night. From dawn to dusk, from dusk to dawn.

For someone born at 11 p.m., the Sun is on the other side of the Earth. That does not change the "Sun Sign" or "Zodiac Sign" of that person, but it determines their "**Rising Sign**" or "**Ascendant**", also known as "**House 1**" written in Roman number: I.

HOW is it done?

See the drawing titled "**A YEAR IS A DAY**" on the following page and imagine that a person was born on the 21st of March at 6 a.m. The Sun is in Aries, no matter what time of the day it is. This is the zodiac sign of this person.

But what is the person's Rising Sign?

On the bottom drawing of the illustration on the following page, you see that at 6 a.m. the Sun is rising above the horizon. It stands on or near the cusp (beginning) of the first House (also called the **Rising Sign** or the Ascendant). In this case, the

Rising Sign is usually the same as the **Sun Sign**.

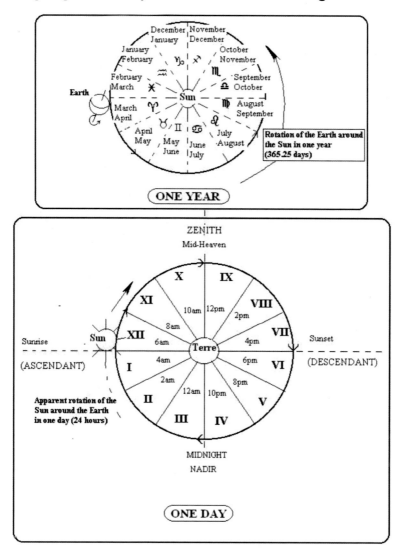

A YEAR IS A DAY

Remember:

For a birth at sunrise any day of the year, the Sun is on the eastern horizon, therefore on (or near) the cusp of the first astrological House, the *Ascendant*.

Another example…

For a birth on the 14th of July at 11:30 a.m., the Sun is in Cancer. This is the ***Sun sign*** or ***zodiac sign***.

Question: in what ***House*** is the Sun at 11:30 a.m.?

Use the chart provided on the next page of this lesson. Simply move up **clockwise** from 6:00 a.m. toward 11:30 a.m. You should stop in House X, between 10:00 a.m. and noon near the cusp of the **Mid-Heaven** or **MC** or **House X**.

Conclusion? The time of the day defines the position of the Sun. At 11:30 a.m. it stands in the tenth House. In the example above, whatever the time of birth, on the 14th of July, the Sun is in Cancer.

Question*:* "In what sign is the **Ascendant** or **House I?**"

With a pencil, ***mark the sign CANCER in HOUSE X.*** Going down, **counterclockwise**, mark the following zodiac sign, Leo then Virgo, then Libra, until you fall into the first House, the section of this hypothetical chart that begins at 6:00 a.m.

The answer is "EITHER" VIRGO or LIBRA.

Why?

On the 14th of July, the Sun is somewhere around 21 degrees in Cancer. At 11:30 a.m. it is not standing exactly on the "cusp" (beginning) of House X. Also, depending on the place of birth (latitude and longitude), **the Houses are not equal, whereas the zodiac signs always are.**

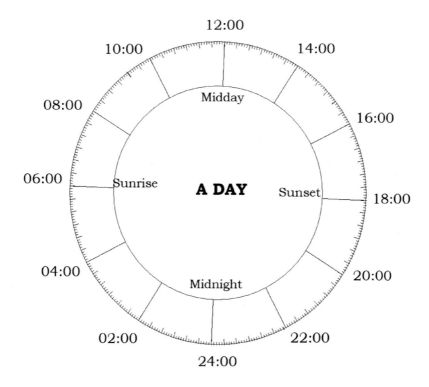

(There is a method of placement of the Houses called "equal house system". In the present course, we will use the Placidus House system, based on the inclination of the Earth's axis.)

If you find the above explanations difficult to understand, don't worry… We will clarify this matter in future lessons. 😊

Right now, all you need to remember is that the zodiac signs are determined according to the course of the Earth around the Sun in **ONE YEAR,** and that the Houses correspond to the **apparent course of the Sun** around the Earth in **ONE DAY.**

There are 12 SIGNS and 12 HOUSES. Each *SIGN* corresponds to a period of approximately *one month.* Each *HOUSE* corresponds to a period of approximately *two hours.*

The *FIRST HOUSE is called ASCENDANT or RISING SIGN because* it begins at **sunrise**.

Opposite the First House is the *SEVENTH HOUSE also called "DESCENDANT".* It corresponds to the moment when the Sun sets on the western horizon. **It begins at the same degree in the opposite sign to the Ascendant.**

At midday, the Sun is at the highest position above the Earth. In astrology we call this point in space: *MID-HEAVEN or MC* (in French: MILIEU DU CIEL or in Latin: MEDIUM COELI - MIDDLE OF THE SKY). It is the position of the *TENTH HOUSE.*

Opposite House X begins *HOUSE IV* or NADIR or **IC** (from the Latin: IMUM COELI) corresponding to the middle of the night (Midnight).

These *four HOUSES* are the major and most important sectors of a Birth Chart. They are called ANGULAR HOUSES.

The ANGULAR HOUSES are:

- House ONE (I) or ASCENDANT or RISING SIGN.

- House FOUR (IV) or NADIR or IC.

- House SEVEN (VII) or DESCENDANT.

- House TEN (X) or MID-HEAVEN or MC.

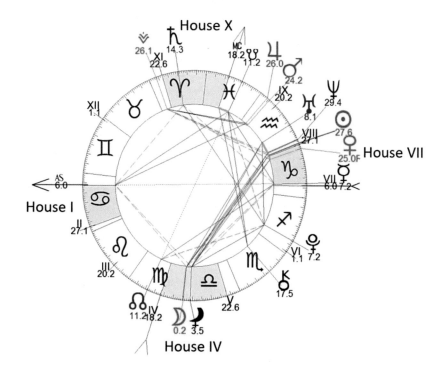

The four angular Houses

The eight other Houses are known as **CADENT** and **SUCCEDENT** Houses.

A Cadent House is the last one in each quadrant of the zodiac. A quadrant begins with an Angular House. Then comes a Succedent House, followed by a Cadent House, preceding the next Angular House. There are four quadrants, each one begins with an Angular House and ends with a Cadent House. See the chart below for more details.

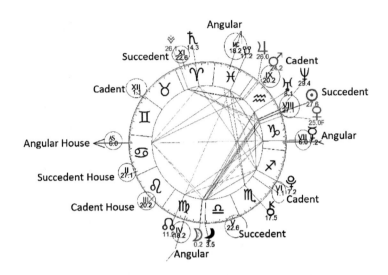

Each one of the twelve Houses corresponds to one or more area/s of life which can be related, in their essence to the symbolism of the corresponding zodiac sign.

You remember the key phrase of *ARIES: "I AM "*. Aries is the first sign of the zodiac.

The *First House,* or *Ascendant, or Rising Sign,* has the same key phrase, but it corresponds to the ***inner personality,*** whereas the Sun sign represents the external personality. There is often a big difference between the outer self and the inner self. The Sun sign represents the way we need to be seen, while the Ascendant represents who we intimately are…

House II corresponds to ***TAURUS*** with the key phrase *"I HAVE "*. House II deals with material possessions and the ability to earn money to acquire such possessions. Food and the good things of life are also linked to this House, symbolically attached to Venus, ruler of Taurus.

House III corresponds to *GEMINI* with the key phrase "*I THINK*". House III deals with the mind, the intellect, communication, short distance travels as well as brothers and sisters because Gemini, ruled by Mercury, is the sign of communication, youth, and brotherhood.

House IV (NADIR or IC) corresponds to *CANCER.* We know that Cancer-born people are family-oriented. Therefore, House IV deals with family affairs, home environment, as well as with the second part of one's life, when a person has reached the age of having a home and family of his own, becoming a parent or grandparent. It also corresponds to the mother and mother instinct.

House V corresponds to the sign *LEO,* the artistic and romantic sign. The solar sign "par excellence" because it is ruled by the Sun. House V deals with the affairs of the heart (love and romance) and with creation (artistic) or procreation (children). It also gives good information on the amount of luck in the native's life.

House VI corresponds to the sixth sign, *VIRGO.* It deals with work, service, and health.

Now, take the drawing titled *"THE HOUSES",* and notice how the six sections **below the horizon** line correspond to nighttime, while the six sections **above the horizon** line correspond to daytime.

Nighttime is symbolically the self, the inner truth of a person. *Daytime* is symbolically the self, confronted to the outside world.

The "I" of the NIGHT HOUSES becomes "WE" in the DAY HOUSES.

Note that HOUSES I, II, III, IV, V and VI are diametrically opposed to HOUSES VII, VIII, IX, X, XI, and XII in a chart.

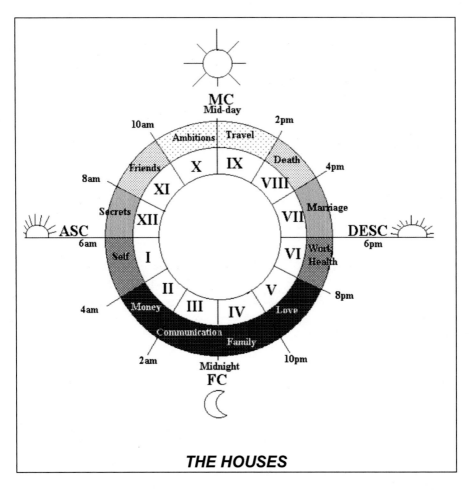

THE HOUSES

House VII or DESCENDANT corresponds to the sign LIBRA, which is a sign of partnership, and human relations. House VII deals with marriage and with all the important contracts and associations of someone's life. House VII is opposed to House I or Ascendant. The "**I am** " of House I becomes "**we are**" in House VII when we marry or associate with other people in any kind of business, sentimental or social venture.

House VIII is opposed to House II and corresponds to the sign Scorpio. It represents death as opposed to the "**I am**" and "**I have**" processes. It also corresponds to joint resources and corporate money such as shared property, inheritances, and all common action to deal with the material aspects of a relationship or partnership. Like the eighth sign, Scorpio, it also deals with sex in a transcended way such as Sigmund Freud's approach to his psychoanalysis research.

House IX is opposed to House III and corresponds to the use of the mind within the social structure. Philosophy, higher education, and other thought processes belong to this House. It also deals with travel, like House III, but in a more serious and profound way such as long journeys in foreign countries, migrations, and scholastic exploration. House IX corresponds to the ninth sign, Sagittarius.

House X or MID-HEAVEN or MC corresponds to the tenth sign, Capricorn. It deals with personal ambition within the social structure. It is opposed to House IV, projecting the family and home environment's influences outwardly to expand and progress socially. From the warmth and safety of the nest, one day the bird learns to fly to become an active member of the community with all the dangers and satisfaction it engenders. House X also represents the father, hierarchy, and authority.

House XI is opposed to House V and corresponds to the eleventh sign, Aquarius. It deals with social life, friends, and enemies. House V being the creative House, in House XI this potential is shared with the community and projected outwardly. House XI is concerned with group creativity rather than personal creativity as it is the case for House V.

House XII corresponds to the twelfth sign, Pisces and is opposed to House VI. House XII deals with secrets and long past and often forgotten motivations. It also has a karmic connotation in the sense mat it can give information on the general tendency of the previous incarnation. It is the prebirth House in which karmic memory is kept. As opposed to House VI dealing with personal work and health, House XII gives information on the inherited disorders or physical afflictions. House XII also deals with mystery and limitations at work and in the will and ability to serve the community. House XII also deals with the soul and the natural connection with the spiritual dimension to which we all belong.

* * * * * * * * * *

This first acquaintance with the House symbolism should allow you to derive further knowledge to improve the analysis of your own birth chart by **blending the Houses and the Signs**.

The process and calculations necessary to determine the Ascendant and positions of the Houses are part of the **ABLAS astrology course**.[9] They are not included in this book.

Observe your Birth Chart and see how, from the ASCENDANT down to House Seven or Descendant, the space of each House differs.

For example:

House I or ASCENDANT may be at 10° in   LIBRA
House II at 7° in SCORPIO
House III at 12° in SAGITTARIUS
House IV at 18° in CAPRICORN
House V at 2° in PISCES
House VI at 28° also in PISCES

The zodiac signs are equal and cover each a space of 30° (degrees) around the 360-degree circle.

---

[9] To enrol in the course, visit https://www.ablas-astrology.com/course.htm

Why are the signs equal and the houses unequal?

Observe the zodiac drawing below.

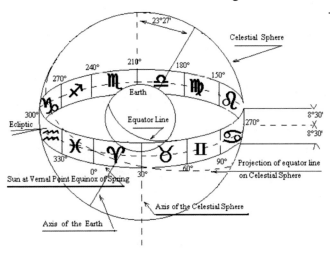

You see that the Earth stands and turns in the centre of what is called the *ecliptic*

The circle was divided into twelve equal sections corresponding to a period of about thirty days (one month). Regardless of any geographical position on Earth, our planet remains at the same degree in the same sign. The zodiac is a division of the year and each sign corresponds to a 30-degree section of the 360-degree circle. However, Aquarius lasts for 29 days and Pisces for 30 days, Aries for 31 days, etc.

From this, it may be deduced that the apparent course of the Sun around the Zodiac is variable. In summer days last longer than nights. Similarly, in certain signs the Sun needs more time to go through. In astrology, there are signs of "short" and "long" Ascensions. A term attributed to the variations explained above.

See the list titled **"SIGNS and DAYS"** included with this week's lesson.

Looking at the drawing of the zodiac again, you notice that the "axis of the Earth" is not perpendicular to the astral plan but slightly *on an angle.* This angle is exactly 23 degrees 27 minutes wide (23° 27').

Consequently, when the Sun shed light over our planet during a 24-hour period while the Earth turns around on its oblique axis, some parts of its surface get more sunrays than others over the same period. This is especially true of the seasonal differences between the northern and southern hemispheres.

Now, look at the drawing called **"HOUSES on EARTH"** on the following page.

The EARTH turns at a CONSTANT speed around its axis but the ANGLE on which it leans allows more exposure at some places than others.

At the EQUATOR line the exposure would be quite constant, but the farther above or under that line the wider the sunrays angle becomes.

This means that during the same period of time, 2 hours for example, because of the oblique position of the Earth compared to the sun, (A) receives more rays than (B) at certain moments of the day and less at others.

On the drawing, you will easily notice the differences.

For (A), House XI is wider than House XII which is smaller than House I. For (B), House XI is smaller than House XII, and much smaller than House I. For (C), House IV is smaller than House III, which is much smaller than House II.

On the other side of the Earth the same pattern applies symmetrically.

However, as much as the orange like quarters forming the Houses are identical, House X is different for (A), for (B), and for (C) and so are all the other Houses on the chart. This means that the House disposition changes according to the place of birth in latitude and in longitude.

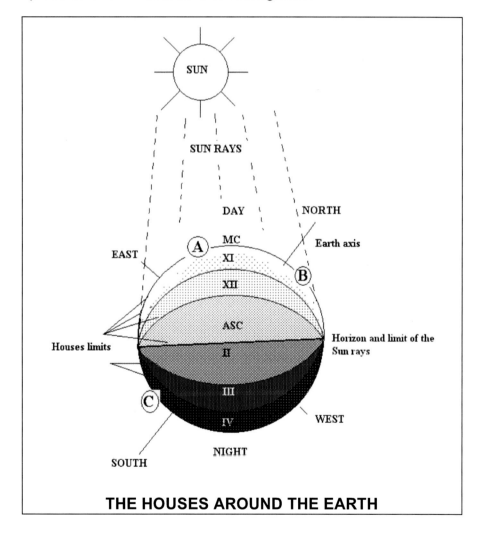

THE HOUSES AROUND THE EARTH

See the list below of what you must understand at this point.

1) There are twelve (12) astrological Houses of variable width (**in this course, we use the Placidus system of domification**).

2) Each House represents a two-hour period (twelve Houses correspond to twenty-four hours)

3) The "**night-Houses**" (I, II, III, IV, V and VI) *are symmetrically opposed to the **day-Houses** (VII, VIII, IX, X XI, and XII)*

4) Depending on the latitude of birth the House disposition changes in accordance with latitude and longitude.

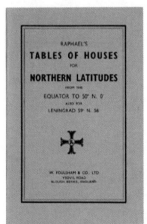

To locate the Houses positions manually, you need to refer to a book called "*TABLE OF HOUSES for northern latitudes*" such as the one pictured on the left.

The next point to investigate concerns the position of the Houses in certain signs rather than others.

Take the next drawing titled: "The zodiac and the Houses" on the following page.

On this drawing *you notice the celestial strip called "zodiac" and* in the centre of which runs the *ecliptic.*

As the Sun travels along the ecliptic in one year, it goes through each one of the twelve signs of the zodiac.

On the drawing, you see that the Sun is in Taurus. We can deduct that is late April or May. Taurus runs from 20th April until 21st May.

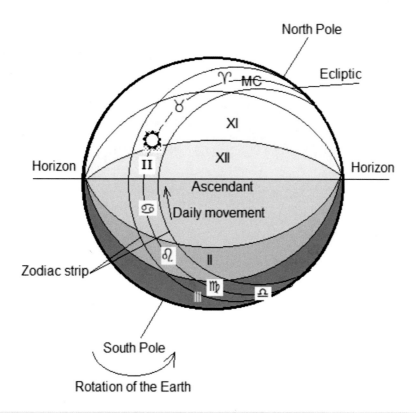

Rotation of the Earth

The zodiac and the Houses

At the time this drawing was done, the SUN was just rising above the Horizon. We know then that it is around 6 o'clock in the morning. The time of 6 a.m. should correspond to **House I** or **Ascendant** or **rising sign** as we have seen earlier.

Along the ecliptic, the Sun runs from left to right (see the arrow of the drawing). If House I begins in Taurus, House II may begin in the next sign, Gemini, House III in Cancer, House IV in Leo, and so on until the last House.

Whatever the time of birth is, the Sun is in Taurus in April and May. However, according to the time of birth, and place, it may stand in any one of the twelve Houses.

For a birth at midnight in April or May, it moves the whole zodiac down to **House IV** found **in Taurus** where the Sun is.

To end this lesson, answer the questions below. A little practice is often more efficient than a long discourse…

QUESTION 1

What is   the fundamental difference between a zodiac sign and a House?

QUESTION 2

Why are the signs and Houses disposed counterclockwise in a Birth Chart?

QUESTION 3

To what HOUSE are opposed:

a- HOUSE V ……………………………………………..

b- HOUSE XII ……………………………………………

c- HOUSE III …………………………………………….

QUESTION 4

To what SIGN corresponds:

a- HOUSE V…………………………………………….

b- HOUSE XII …………………………………………..

c- HOUSE III …………………………………………..

Lesson 11

The Houses
(Part 2)

THE "SOLAR HOUSES"

Is it possible to draw a chart without a Time of Birth? Yes, it is! Simply use the position of the Sun to draw the cusp of the first House, then place the cusps of the following Houses at the same degree in each other sign.

For example, if the Sun is 24° in Sagittarius, place House I there, House II at 24° in Capricorn, House III at 24° in Aquarius, and so on until you complete the circle.

This is called a SOLAR CHART for midday. Midday allows a median position of the Moon, the faster moving object around the chart.

Although I mostly prefer to have a precise time of birth to draw a chart, I have gradually recognised the value of the Solar Chart. This method was used by the ancients for the common people who seldom knew their time of birth, let alone their day of birth. I apply this technique to do a forecast for each zodiac signs in videos that I post on my YouTube channel[10]. So many people tell me how accurate these simple forecasts are that it motivated to look at many of the charts I analyse both ways, from the Solar point of view and from the time of birth point of view. Try it out to verify for yourself. The result is quite bluffing. It shows the person from a different angle, perhaps more externally than internally. Nevertheless, such a reading is quite revealing of many personality facets.

[10] My YouTube channel is at https://www.youtube.com/ASTRORORO

The present lesson is meant to teach you how to work with Houses in signs. This is what we are going to discuss now.

The Houses in the signs

A House in a sign describes how the areas represented are dealt with. The energy of the sign is transmitted into the House, just like the planet in a sign is coloured and influenced by the energy of such sign. It is simple to understand and rather simple to apply. Once you know the meaning of the signs, blend it with the meaning of a House and you will obtain a correct interpretation.

Some examples

In the chart below, the **Ascendant, or House I is in Taurus**.

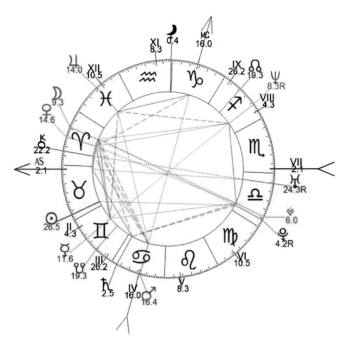

The Ascendant represents the inner personality, the "true self" compared to the "social mask" represented by the Sun-sign. In Taurus, it simply indicates a down-to-earth personality, attracted to the good things of life.

House II in Gemini indicates a nonconformist approach to money and what it buys, such as books, communication tools, travels, and mentally inspiring products. Earning money may also be derived from the above.

House III is also in Gemini, accentuating the natural ability to communicate and to learn, with a need to travel and to enjoy sharing thoughts and ideas with the entourage.

House IV in Cancer accentuates the importance of family values. The home environment, both human and geographical, is a source of strong emotional stimuli and motivation.

House V in Leo enhances creativity and the need for love and approbation. It also indicates a tendency to play a dominant role in romantic relationships.

House VI in Virgo and Libra (intercepted sign) indicates two distinct possibilities workwise. There is a rational and well-organized approach to professional duties, together with an ability to play a conciliating role at work. Health concerns may centre around the digestive system and urinary function.

House VII in Scorpio deals with private, social, and professional close relationships which are intense and profound, occasionally difficult, and hurtful.

House VIII in Sagittarius indicates a philosophical and rather positive approach to the mysteries of life and death. Money is appreciated for its role to strengthen family ties.

House IX also in Sagittarius shows a connection with foreign countries, long-distance travels, and a predisposition for higher education, politics, and social activities.

House X (MC) in Capricorn confers a rational and responsible approach to professional and social status. The ambition is to reach a summit, no matter how long it takes and how high it is.

House XI in Aquarius enhances the need to socialise by interacting actively in human and geographical surroundings.

House XII in Pisces and Aries (intercepted sign) deals with past events concealed in the subconscious, from where they motivate a paradoxical tendency to passively absorb and impulsively react to external stimuli.

The meanings of the Houses

Earlier in this book, I briefly described the Houses and the areas of life they represent. For a long time since I began to seriously study astrology in 1975, I wondered why the Houses were linked to the areas of life described in textbooks. Whatever I read on the subject did not appease my hunger for a satisfying explanation. For example, I read that House IV represents the mother in a male's chart and the father in a female's chart. To me, it made no sense. It seemed to be just another gratuitous theory emerged from the active minds of non-practising "self-proclaimed" astrologers. I also read that a "square aspect" (we will study "aspects" in future lessons) was positive because the square is the base of the pyramid…

I want to share with you my own theory to explain rationally the meaning of each House.

Birth is represented by the Ascendant because its exact position is essentially determined by the time of birth. Contrary to the zodiac sign largely defined by the moment of conception, the Ascendant depends on a voluntary action of the baby when the time is ripe to come out of the mother's womb and officially become a citizen of the world. That is why I believe the Ascendant represents the inner personality, the true self, the authenticity of a person. Arguing that birth from Caesarean is not the moment chosen by the baby is receivable. In that case, certain elements in the chart indicate such an event together with its consequences on the development of personality.

The Sun is light. It allows us to see and to be seen. It also plays a major role on the development of the physical body without which we could not be seen. Hence, the Sun sign represents who we are physically and the role we play socially. It is from the Sun that we derive the energy to interact with other Sun signs (people) all our life.

However, we have a "second personality", one that is often much deeper and more meaningful than the role we play to be recognised and considered as a person and a member of the community. That other side is represented by the Ascendant.

What happens when the Ascendant is in the same sign as the Sun? The person is said to be a "double Aries", "double Taurus" or double any one of the other signs. Usually, it indicates great intensity. But it is not an absolute rule at all. There are two major differences to consider. They relate to the position of the Sun. See the example charts on the following page and try to find the difference.

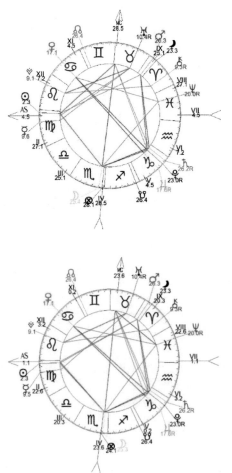

Have you found the difference? Easy... In the top chart on the left, the Sun is in House XII. In the chart below, it is in House I. House XII is the "locker House" where we keep safe what we do not want to share with the outside world. The Sun in House XII tends to shine within. People with the Sun in House XII usually find it difficult to play their part spontaneously. They feel better and safer in the shade rather than in direct sunlight. Whatever their sign, there is a "Pisces" tinge to their behaviour and general attitude. Pisces is the twelfth sign...

On the contrary, when the Sun is in House I or Ascendant, natural energy flows much stronger. It increases spontaneity and impulsiveness. People with the Sun in House 1 are impetuous and eager to be in the spotlight. There is an "Aries" tinge to their behaviour and general attitude, because Aries is the first sign of the zodiac, symbolically related to the first House, the "I am" House.

However, other elements in the chart may confirm or contradict such basic approach to both placements of the Sun. They will be discussed in future lessons.

House II follows, and we know that it deals with matter, money, and food. Why is it so? The moment of birth is a transition between one element (liquid) to another (air). This is the baby's first contact with matter. Matter is what counts… Food is one essential matter. Without it, we die. During gestation, the foetus is fed via the umbilical cord. Once born, the baby is fed by the mouth. Hence, House II shows how we deal with food and material possessions, and the money earned to acquire what we need to stay alive. If the first encounter with matter at birth is not right, this may disturb the development of financial and material performance for a lifetime.

House III is next. It represents the first cry, before which the baby is manipulated by the medical staff to ensure proper breathing and lung function, not forgetting the vocal cords! If there is a problem at this stage, it may impact the cerebral, intellectual, or mental performance, with a direct effect on the ability to communicate and to neurologically perform well.

House IV represents the baby's first encounter with the mother outside of the uterus. It is meant to be a great moment for the newborn. It usually is, but there are exceptions. The first contact with our mother links us to our roots, our origins, our family tree, and to our environment, from our family's place of residence to the country where we will live.

House V represents the newborn's first affective reaction to the first contact with the mother. Habitually very good and a source of instant satisfaction, the first encounter with our mum determines how we express our feelings and our creativity. A problem at this stage may impair our love life and the other areas represented by House V.

House VI is associated with the first feed and the first digestion process outside of the mother's womb. This is usually what the newborn does after the first affective reaction to the first encounter with the mother. Proper digestion is a must to stay in good health. The first vital lesson is learnt. From then on, it becomes a daily duty to work for food and eat properly to stay alive and well. Health depends largely on what we eat, and on our ability to preserve our environment from potential threat emanating from improper hygiene and feeding habits.

House VII represents the way we deal with personal relationships, such as marriage or other types of regular partnerships, both private and social. Our approach is linked to what happened on the day of birth after the six preceding sequences described above. It was our first encounter with our siblings, our father and other members of the family, friends of the family and other visitors. The quality of this event is important because it determines how we interact with other people for the rest of our life.

House VIII is opposed to House II. The first encounter with the matter of life is also determined by food. Once the newborn has had the first feed, there is only a little while before some of what was absorbed is rejected. This is the first poo! We must eat to keep alive. Eating is linked to House II. House VIII represents death. Later in life it represents what we do with the "food of life", such as money and material possession. Some spend it all, some save up. House VIII also represents the potential to save and make our capital grow.

House IX is opposed to House III linked to the first vocal expression of the "joy" to be alive 😊. House IX represents the earliest awareness of the "cry potential". Hungry? Cry and you will be served. Uncomfortable? Cry and Mummy will take you in her arms. Etc. Later in life, the development of the ability to learn what is best and more constructive greatly depends on how successful the cry potential has been during the first day and first year of life.

House X (Mid-Heaven) is opposed to House IV linked to the mother and the family. It represents the father or father figure, authority. The cry potential may or may not have the desired effect. If not, it needs to be reviewed to make it more efficient. A crying baby is often quietened down by the father's voice. Lower impedance has a calming and reassuring effect, except if the voice is too strong and transforms into a scream. Fear takes over and can deter the newborn's ability to progress adequately. Later in years it influences the potential to succeed socially and professionally. Dealing with authority and hierarchy is profoundly linked to the early relationship between father and child.

House XI is opposed to House V, related to the first affective reaction after birth. It represents the innate ability to derive attention, affection, and approbation from a simple smile or giggle. It is the first attempts to "make friends" with those around who came to visit and meet the newborn. Later in life, House XI shows what we can do to be appreciated by others, to have friends and to have our place in the community. It also represents the influence of others on the development of the ego and social behaviour.

House XII is opposed to House VI, linked to the first feed and first digestion process outside of the mother's womb. The process of birth and the following events have drained the baby's energy and alertness. Sleep and dreams are represented by House XII. It is also linked to the intrauterine period where babies tend to go back in dreams during their first year of life and more. Later, **House XII** deals with the perception of the past, with the connection we all have with the spiritual dimension, with the invisible and with the oneiric activity. We all need to dream. It is an essential part of our psychological and physiological balance. Dreams can help us understand, but they can also hold us back in fear of doubt about ourselves and our future. If the newborn's first sleep has been disturbed, it creates an uncomfortable passive conflict between dream and reality.

What next?

With the added knowledge about the meanings of the Houses, you can now improve the first-step analysis of your own birth chart done according to the positions of the planets in. Here is what to do *step by step*.

- Write your Sun sign potential according to the list included in lesson 2.

- Write your Ascendant potential using the Sun sign potential list once more.

- Find the position of your second House in the sign from your own Birth Chart

- Turn to the supplementary section included in this lesson.

- In your notebook write the description corresponding to the position of House II in your chart.

- Repeat the same process for the other Houses.

IMPORTANT RULE TO REMEMBER: "If a House includes two signs, take note of both in your analysis. In that case, two Houses include two signs (the opposite houses) and twice two others begin in the same signs."
See the example chart on the following page for more details.

- Once you have done this, read what you have compiled and honestly rearrange the text to fit your personality as close as possible. Using your own words is essential to your progress and understanding of astrology.

The result of your personal approach based on the information from this course will be part of your assignments to complete using the online form.

As the Course goes on, you will add up details over details

until you finally complete the whole picture.

Consult the supplementary sections for future reference as you progress with the course.

In the next lesson, you will learn about the positions of the "rulers" of each House in every one of the twelve signs and twelve Houses. You will begin to interblend signs, Houses, planets, and aspects. The meaning of a House in relation to the rest of the chart is the key to the analysis. It is equally useful to forecast future events based on the transits of the planets around the zodiac.

In this birth chart of a person born in Edinburgh, Scotland, almost 56° north of the equator line, you see that Houses XI, XII, V and VI and VII included one intercepted sign. At the same time, Houses I and II, III and IV, VII and VIII, and VIII and IX begin in the same sign. Houses I and II in Gemini. Houses III and IV in Cancer. Houses VII and VIII in Sagittarius. Houses IX and X in Capricorn.

The Houses dispositions around the chart depend on latitude. Except for those using the equal House system.

EXERCISE

Fill in the empty spaces according to your own birth chart.

1 - Write below in what sign you find each House in your birth chart.

House I		House VII	
House II		House VIII	
House III		House IX	
House IV		House X	
House V		House XI	
House VI		House XII	

2 – What are the ruler/s of each of the above Houses?

House I		House VII	
House II		House VIII	
House III		House IX	
House IV		House X	
House V		House XI	
House VI		House XII	

3 – In what sign/s you find the ruler/s of each House in your chart?

House I		House VII	
House II		House VIII	
House III		House IX	
House IV		House X	
House V		House XI	
House VI		House XII	

4 - Write in what House/s you find the ruler/s of each House

House I		House VII	
House II		House VIII	
House III		House IX	
House IV		House X	
House V		House XI	
House VI		House XII	

Supplementary section
THE HOUSES IN THE SIGNS

The Night-Houses

HOUSE I (ASCENDANT)

In Aries:

The intimate personality is intense, passionate, and sometimes aggressive or impulsive. This is revealed more in private life if the sun sign is different from the Ascendant. This position confers an active energy conducive to engagement and combat. Moderation is, however, advised to avoid slippages due to the Fire-Cardinal tendency of the first sign of the zodiac.

In Taurus:

Although more peaceful than Aries; when Taurus sees red, it is difficult to calm its anger. The epicurean nature of this sign encourages the taste for the pleasures of life, especially with family and close relationships. The culinary art, music, painting, and sculpture are bestowed by this Venusian rising sign.

In Gemini:

Intellectual activity and communication are essential parts of private life and intimate relationships with their repercussions in social life. A superficial or light approach of intimacy is sometimes noticeable. It confers a jack-of-all-trades nature, unwilling to take on long-term tasks or projects.

In Cancer:

Private life revolves primarily around the concepts of family, home, and residence. Emotions are strong and sometimes difficult to control. Patriotism and chauvinism are conferred by a certain taste for history. Genealogy can also be one of the areas of interest.

In Leo:

This fire sign strengthens the energy of the Self through the position of its ruler, the Sun. The ego is strong. It is expressed or imposed in private life. The attitude is chivalrous and protective of those around. Creativity is an asset conferred by this sign, together with a strong ambition to succeed.

In Virgo:

Anxiety, generated by a strong need for accomplished duty, together with a perfectionist, critical and self-critical tendencies are the main characteristics of the Virgo Ascendant. If they are more expressed privately, such predispositions also have an impact in social and professional life.

In Libra:

The search for harmony and balance in intimate life produce both the potential to find inner peace and the feeling of being perpetually at odds with oneself unable to achieve the desired unity. Libra also confers a somewhat theatrical approach to personal expression. Creativity and good taste are present.

In Scorpio:

Do not underestimate the determination conferred by this Ascendant. It is at the origin of the greatest achievements, as much as the worst disasters. Inner strength and determination are qualities that are not always welcomed nor appreciated by the entourage. Lack of flexibility and long-term resentment are also indicated together with a rather solitary and independent nature.

In Sagittarius:

This sign conveys enthusiasm and a lively nature that are more especially expressed intimately with possible repercussions in social life, depending on the general tendency of the chart. Positivity and generosity motivate spontaneous engagements in entertaining playful and cultural projects.

In Capricorn:

Stable and rather sedentary, private life is intended as a long-term project. Patience and determination allow the realisation of durable personal achievements. A pessimistic, fatalistic, or taciturn tendency is also observed. Personal ambitions can suppress the underlying need for peace and tranquillity.

In Aquarius:

Electric and erratic, the nature of the ego is multifaceted. Extreme originality can marginalise and create difficulties to manage a stable private life. However, the adaptability conferred by this sign allows for amazing acrobatic prowess to successfully manage difficult situations quickly and effectively.

In Pisces:

This sign confers great sensitivity and permeability in private environment that can interfere with the pragmatic and realistic approach of daily routines. Natural connection with the spiritual dimension of life preserves or restores balance and wellbeing. The self is subject to subtle fluctuations that can produce personality disturbances or give access to the highest levels of thoughts and feelings.

HOUSE II

In Aries:

With this position of House II, we often earn and spend money impulsively or unwisely. This sign confers a fighting and sometimes aggressive behaviour to defend one's financial interests. Eating habits are erratic or extremely strict and can be a source of various disorders, digestive or otherwise.

In Taurus:

With this position of House II, we can be conservative and calculating, but equally generous when possible. This is the natural position of House II. It indicates a strong attachment to material values and food for personal wellbeing. Money is mainly spent on practical or decorative objects.

In Gemini:

This position confers a nonconformist approach to finances. It is difficult to achieve serious savings or to plan a budget and stick to it for a long time. However, this sign increases the flexibility and the talent necessary to make ends meet. Money is often spent to travel or to satisfy intellectual needs.

In Cancer:

Money is preferably used to improve family life or the place of residence. Inheritances can play an important role in financial progress. The second part of life is often rewarded for the efforts made and the work done over time to acquire and enjoy the good and beautiful things of life.

In Leo:

Money is a source of positive and effective motivations to promote financial success. Some is spent on works of art or charity. Gambling can also be considered despite the risks of loss and bankruptcy. Most of the time, food is preferred hot, spicy, and more Mediterranean than Nordic.

In Virgo:

Practicality and method in the management of income and general finances are indicated. Commerce, pharmacy, or medicine can be considered to earn a living. Health concerns can become a source of excessive spending. Feeding habits can produce digestive embarrassment and discomfort.

In Libra:

Sharing money and material resources is considered to preserve or restore harmony in human relationships. Generosity with loved ones can become a cause for excessive spending. The need for justice and fairness motivates and confers a moderate approach to material realities.

In Scorpio:

Certain difficulties are to be expected about inheritances or financial investments. Money is used, either only for survival or to gain power and move up the social ladder. This is often the cause for serious financial problems, but the Scorpio confers determination and resilience.

In Sagittarius:

Money has more moral than material value. It is often used to help others, especially children, so that they can enjoy excellent education. Personal expenses are motivated by the need to share or to reach coveted objectives. Financial success is often favoured during the second part of life.

In Capricorn:

Money is earned from work, with long-term objectives in mind. Slow saving is preferred to making quick revenues from casual job positions. The ambition is to build up wealth slowly because it allows more time to prepare and realise. Frugal feeding habits are sometimes noted to cause health concerns.

In Aquarius:

Money is very often used for social causes or to help the community. Social relationships and friends are often the source of financial ambition. Money can be earned in professions related to the public, in electronics, IT, or in the media. Feeding habits are often irregular and casually coordinated.

In Pisces:

A lack of material practicality is frequently noticed. The influence of others motivates engagements in projects or activities that may cost more than they pay back. Intuition, however, is useful to avoid pitfalls and to succeed despite the risks involved. Food can be both a source of subtle pleasures and harmful excesses.

HOUSE III

In Aries:

There is a tendency to impulsive and aggressive reactivity. Heated discussions and debates are preferred to quiet diplomatic conversations. The mind is sharp, but the memory is rather short. Moves are hastily arranged but may lack correct preparation. Speed is an asset if subtly controlled and applied.

In Taurus:

The mental process is based on down-to-earth values conferring a practical mind and a spontaneous interest for the good and beautiful things of life. Communication is favoured by Venusian manners, charm, and charisma. A tendency to unexpected fits of anger is also conferred by House III in this sign.

In Gemini:

This is the natural position of House III. The mind is quick and adaptable. Often superficial, however, the learning process is good, but long-term memory is lacking. Travelling and communicating is a major facet of the personality. Gemini increases awareness, intellectual and mental adaptability.

In Cancer:

The mind is mainly occupied with family matters and the place of residence. The family tree and history are subjects that can motivate ardent research bringing much emotional stimulation and intellectual satisfaction. Interest in children can also lead to education or childcare careers.

In Leo:

The ego is expressed with intelligence and a certain grandeur.

Leadership and higher social level relationships stimulate this solar mind. Opportunism can produce a tendency to favour affability rather than authenticity in society. Intellectual leanings are usually flamboyant and colourful.

In Virgo:

The intellect is rather rigorous and pragmatic, moved by a need to classify and organise. Hygiene is considered of primary importance to preserve from illness. A tendency to focus on petty details may create excessive worrying that affect rational thinking, mental serenity, and contentment.

In Libra:

Some artistic qualities are evident, especially comedy. Partnerships are vital to preserve psychological balance. There is a profound need to be in touch with others, sharing ideas, opinions, and concepts, communicating freely and abundantly to the point of losing the initial subject of the conversation.

In Scorpio:

A spontaneous or innate intellectual interest in the mysteries of the invisible influences or forces operating behind any manifestation of life, leading to an innate interest in the occult sciences. The need to search for truth can produce uneasy situations in human relationships and communication.

In Sagittarius:

This position usually goes with a marked interest in higher education, philosophy, religion, and subjects in connection with the nature of the soul. Long-distance travels, foreign countries and cultures are also part of the intellectual interests. Good spirits and enthusiasm favour quality relationships.

In Capricorn:

This position often confers an excellent memory. Mental processes can be slowed down, but time is a beneficial factor of success. Intellectual endurance is an asset to carry out long-term projects. An interest in financial investments is present, although pessimism can limit positive realisations.

In Aquarius:

Intellectual pursuits are oriented toward social life and cultural exchanges. Human relationships are essential, as there is a strong need to be surrounded with friends or acquaintances to feel useful and appreciated. Electronics, physics, IT, and mathematics are areas of interest contributing to success.

In Pisces:

Extreme sensitivity to the opinions of others enhances permeability to the ideas and thoughts of the entourage. Spirituality and intuition favour success in areas where intelligence and subtility are essential values. Meditation and religion are other sources of personal or professional interest.

House IV (IC)

In Aries

Difficult family relationships may have affected childhood. Domestic tension and excessive authority are later in life often responsible for underlaying frustration and irritability at home. There is a strong need to impose strict rules and codes of conduct, while actively defending family interests

in Taurus

There is a taste for decoration and beautiful surroundings in the home environment. Money is spent to make it as comfortable and warm as can be. A rural atmosphere is often preferred to living in the city. The family background is usually jovial, light-hearted, and epicurean, close to nature and its goodness.

In Gemini

This position tends to indicate a rather intellectual family background. Brothers and sisters play an important part during childhood and education. Friends tend to become members of the family and the home is a place for cultural, intellectual, or more simply, enjoyable social activities.

In Cancer

This is the natural position of House IV in the fourth sign. Strong attachment to the home and family as well as to the mother is very frequently observed. Much is done during most of the lifetime to attend to and satisfy the needs of the family. Water proximity is important in choosing the place of residence.

In Leo

The home environment is preferred as luxurious as possible, whatever the means and the cost. Nothing but the best will do for children and all family members. A protective attitude allows for a more secure and comfortable family life. However, excessive ambition may become a source of financial drawbacks.

In Virgo

Practical, orderly, and methodical, the approach to the home environment is a source of constant dissertations to ensure proper hygiene and cleanliness. The home is often used for both living and work. A family business or a business ran from home is also frequent with House IV in Virgo.

In Libra

Harmonious relationships with family members are of prime importance to preserve wellbeing and serenity in personal life and partnerships. The family background may be artistic in some way. Arts and beauty are essential and spontaneously expressed in the home environment.

In Scorpio

Family difficulties in early childhood create underlying uneasiness later in life. The home environment is often surrounded by mysterious events and situations that can make it uncomfortable but quite intriguing and fascinating. Hereditary qualities are a source of spontaneous talents or motivations.

In Sagittarius

This position often indicates a family background with strong philosophical and moral beliefs. They confer a rather idealistic point of view when it comes to home environment and values. Seeking comfort and luxury is motivated by natural generosity in close relationships and with family members.

In Capricorn

Early childhood can be marked by excessive discipline and a difficult relationship with one of the parents. The ambition to achieve material success may be greater than the need for a conventional family life. The home may also be the place for work or to run a family business is an option.

In Aquarius

Friends are considered like members of the family. The home is unusual and the place for discoveries and social gatherings. Much coming and going is observed within family life. Parents are considered like friends or enemies, depending on the rest of the chart. Frequent changes of residence are likely.

In Pisces

The uncertainty of the sign makes it difficult to decide upon a precise way of life when it comes to family relationships and home environment. The idea of a "heavenly mission" can be present and a source of motivation to the overall attitude and actions. Spiritual family ties are also indicated.

House V

In Aries

One can fall impulsively in love with this position of House V. The luck factor is fluctuating and often poorly managed. Artistic creativity is focused on strong and intense subjects. Children tend to annoy and cause clashes at home, but the attitude is strongly protective of loved ones.

In Taurus

Sensuality dominates. The underlying value of a relationship seems more important than the person concerned. Fidelity in love is in favour of long-lasting partnerships. Beauty in art is a source of deep emotional reactions. Creativity is a way to bring wellbeing more than financial wealth.

In Gemini

Somewhat light-hearted, love life can be subject to frequent changes due to a constant search for novelty and excitement. The intellectual side of a love or friendship relationship is a must. Children are a source of spontaneous motivation and sympathy. There is an ability to be forever young at art.

In Cancer

Love and romance are somehow motivated by the need for a comfortable home. Heredity and family traditions may greatly influence the development of creativity. House V in Cancer confers a stronger maternal instinct, enhances fecundity and the desire to have children and a secure family life.

In Leo

This is the natural position of House V. Love is keenly needed and leads to passionate relationships. Luck is an important factor of success. Artistic creativity is encouraged. Painting and the visual arts are preferred. Beauty and charm are values that inspire shallow rather than profound human relationships.

In Virgo

Feelings tend to be over-analysed and dissected to the point of annihilation. Shyness is also noticed in the presence of the opposite sex. Romance and the workplace are often related. The luck factor is rather low because of a lack of belief in it despite a natural taste for the good and beautiful things of life.

In Libra

Romantic relationships are more a means of stimulating the intellectual or artistic appetite than purely motivated by love. A theatrical attitude is adopted in situations when emotions are directly affected. The need for companionship can overrun the search for the ideal partner and result in disappointment.

In Scorpio

The love principle becomes sexual in this sign. The artistic tastes include surrealism and the occult arts. Interests in black magic can also develop. Childhood is an important period during which death in some way may have played a troubling role. Romantic feelings are profound and expressed passionately.

In Sagittarius

Love and romantic relationships are often linked to a strong need for social promotion. Luck is a source of protection in many ways. To believe in it favours its spontaneous manifestations. Partners are a source of artistic inspiration or personal achievement. Generosity may be hiding opportunism.

In Capricorn

With this position, there is no plan to rely on luck to succeed in life. There could be a tendency to stay away from romance or to frequently change partners until the right one is met. This is often achieved when turning thirty, with long-term perspective. Sentimental engagement is taken very seriously.

In Aquarius

This position makes one more a friend than a lover. Romantic relationships must also be intellectual. Luck may strike suddenly and unexpectedly. Artistic talents are original, avant-garde and sometimes marginal. Curiosity leads the search for the perfect partner. A child-at-heart attitude is also observed.

In Pisces

Love, artistic creation, and the pleasures of life are often linked to religion or some form of spirituality. Music and dance are vectors of success and wellbeing. Universal love can be the basis of a missionary vocation. As a rule, there is shyness and reserve as well as uncertainty of feelings and desires.

House VI

In Aries

Arguments with co-workers, headaches and other health problems related to the position of Mars, ruler of this House, are frequent. Leadership abilities are evident and can motivate a military career and all professions in which action and physical effort are a must to succeed.

In Taurus

Work is often related to food, farming, decorating or music. Good relationship with co-workers depends on the aspects and position of Venus and Chiron in the Birth Chart. There seems to be a natural fondness for domestic animals, plants, and nature. The neck area may become a source of health concerns.

In Gemini

Journalists, writers of short novels as well as travelling representatives and communication mediators often have their sixth House in Gemini. It makes one prone to job changes as well as to unorthodox or nonconformist chose of the profession. Health concerns relate to locomotion and the respiratory system.

In Cancer

Work within the family scene, personal residence, or in a family business is common with this House position. Public relation, teaching young children, work related to the water, fishery, navigation, water treatment, biology or ecology are possible choices. Digestion may become a source of health concerns.

In Leo

The leadership quality of Leo favours the natural ability to control people and to achieve prominence due to a determined solar attitude at work. Creativity and craftsmanship are important and may become a major source of positive motivation. Health issues are mostly related to the heart and spine.

In Virgo

This is the natural position of House VI. Work and service are of utmost importance and carried out with all the skill and attention the task requires. Worrying too much and focusing on minor details may affect the quality of work. Intestinal function may become a source of health concerns.

In Libra

A harmonious and friendly working atmosphere is essential to produce the best results. The arts and work relating to human relationships may be preferred. Balance and harmony motivate the choice of professional path. Sore bones, rheumatism, or kidney function may become sources of health concerns.

In Scorpio

Work related to death or money, such as undertaker, lawyer, notary, or accountant are some of the areas of professional accomplishment. Determination and the ability to sustain effort favour executive positions. The reproductive system or colonic activity may become sources of health concerns.

In Sagittarius

Work and duty form a moral whole that motivates and promotes success. Respect for rules and hierarchy promotes evolution with good potential to reach to the highest professional level. Possible health concerns relate to the area of the hips, thighs, as well as blood circulation and the liver function.

In Capricorn

Ambition, determination, and skill favour a slow but more complete professional realisation. Hierarchy is highly respected. Conventional ways are preferred to the unorthodox approach to work and duty. Gradual progression improves work quality. The bones and the joints may cause health concerns.

In Aquarius

Work in such fields as mathematics, electronics, social welfare, and all forms of unconventional and sometimes marginal types of professions are chosen. Many changes may occur and affect stability. Health problems may relate to the superior nervous system, and vein circulation, especially in the legs.

In Pisces

Uncertainty may hinder from finding the most suited profession. Religious tendencies may motivate the need to be of service to the community. Work related to water, gas, medicine, and chemistry are possible choices. The hormonal system and the lower limbs may be sources of health concerns.

The Day-Houses

House VII

In Aries

There is a tendency to get married young. Aggressiveness or tension is felt with partners, both at work and privately. Diplomacy is a major asset to manage human relationships. The position and orientation of Mars in the chart are major elements to observe to better understand the role of this House.

In Taurus

Love is the essential motivation to marry. Sharing similar artistic tastes is an advantage. Loyalty and faithfulness are important values that favour long-lasting relations. The positions of Venus and Pluto need to be assessed to get a proper analysis of the pros and cons of this House situation.

In Gemini

Mental interactions and communication are essential in both personal and social relationships. There may be less romanticism, but more intellectual excitement. The roles of Jupiter and Mercury in the chart must be considered to better understand the influence of this House position.

In Cancer

Marriage is viewed as essential in creating a stable home and family life. The mother or mother image and family background may profoundly influence the choice of a partner. The positions of the Moon and Saturn in the chart need to be analysed to get an in-depth insight of this House position.

In Leo

Creativity is expressed in marriage, as much as in personal and social partnerships. Such relationships may be important to favour success and wealth in some way. The roles of the Sun and Uranus in the chart must be assessed to understand the quality and viability of all significant relations.

In Virgo

A tendency to over-criticise and overanalyse can affect marriage and other types of important relationships. Business associations are a source of success when rigour and a sense of order are applied to the partnership. Chiron and Neptune determine the underlying potential in this area of life.

In Libra

This is the natural position of House VII. Marriage and important relationships are a major source of motivation. The dispositions of Vesta and Mars inform on the eventual tendency to oscillate between harmony and tension to determine the underlying potential of success or failure in this key area of life.

In Scorpio

Difficulties or wellbeing in marriage and other important relationships depend on the influence of Pluto, ruler of Scorpio, in relation with Venus, ruler of the Ascendant. Sex and money may play a key role to motivate the commitment. Divorce or separation can be hurtful and a source of strong financial discord.

In Sagittarius

Marriage may be considered a way to spiritual achievement or social ascension. More than one marriage or similar relationship is likely. The dispositions of Jupiter and Mercury in the chart tell about the underlying sincerity or opportunistic personal approach of such important engagement.

In Capricorn

Marriage may be delayed until 28 to 30 years of age. Spontaneous sympathy and attraction to older partners are often observed. Long periods of solitude and celibacy are likely. The dispositions of Saturn and the Moon in the chart are key factors to determine the true potential in this important area of life.

In Aquarius

This position indicates a strong need to preserve independence after marriage. Friendship is a value on which relational harmony depends. There is a protectionist tendency that may overcome rational limits and affect the relationship. Uranus and the Sun are key factors to analyse the value of this major area.

In Pisces

Marriage can be motivated by dreams and idealistic hopes. Disillusions are often due to a passive approach to personal relationships. The dispositions of Neptune and Chiron indicate how private and other important partnerships are likely to evolve and produce in other areas of life.

House VIII

In Aries

The way to deal with material possessions is often impulsive and defensive. The mistakes made produce reactions that may increase tension in relationships because of financial discords. All investments must be planned and organised as well as possible to avoid setbacks due to precipitation.

In Taurus

This position seems to promote longevity, especially if Venus is well disposed in the chart. Money is important and used for the acquisition of earthly goods, with a view to bequeathing to descendants. Inheritance or a major financial opportunity favours a higher socio-economic level.

In Gemini

A childhood experience may be at the source of profound questioning and interest in the mysteries of life and death. Personal relationships have an important influence on finance management. Money saved is linked to a sense of freedom as much as security. The idea of investment motivates spending.

In Cancer

The death of a loved one during childhood can be the cause of great sensitivity about the subject. Money and material possessions are often accumulated to improve family life and communal property. Inheritances may substantially improve the state of finances, more often during the latter part of life.

In Leo

Heart can be the cause of death, especially if the Sun is involved in strong dissonances in the chart. The leadership qualities of the sign make it possible to take on important responsibilities and achieve great material and social success. Property management skill is also represented by this House position.

In Virgo

Worry about general health, for oneself and for others, can produce a troubling fear of death. The sense of duty prevails and allows success in commerce and health-related activities. There is an extremely responsible attitude to manage finances. Sexuality is often more intellectualised than spontaneous.

In Libra

Money is viewed to promote harmony and balance in personal and social relationships rather than for commercial or personal interests. The idea of death motivates actions to preserve wellbeing. Uneven financial balance can become a source of excessive worry and dependence on the banking system.

In Scorpio

The idea of death creates an innate interest in occult sciences. Sexuality is fuelled by the need to transcend death by giving life. There is a natural talent for money management and investments. However, a nihilist tendency may impair the potential to succeed financially.

In Sagittarius

A philosophical interest in the mysteries of life comes from the idea that death is only a physical ending opening to other life cycles. The theory of reincarnation may create a desire to gain wealth to contribute in some way to the next life. A lofty approach to money matters makes it easier to solve problems.

In Capricorn

Longevity is often defined by the presence of House VIII in Capricorn. Sexual needs are rather well controlled and persist until later years of life. Finance management is taken seriously. Resilience and determination favour a constructive approach to money matters despite adverse circumstances.

In Aquarius

The idea of death seems to intellectually stimulate early interest in occultism and other mystical or so-called occult subjects. Inventiveness and adaptability are applied in the areas of money and joint resources. The end of life is foreseen as original, unexpected, and sudden. But it is not always so...

In Pisces

The mystical meaning of death can be expressed in art or in strong religious beliefs. A holistic perception of earthly life is preferred. Therefore, intuition may contribute to financial success. However, lack of realism and too much reliance on fate or lucky star would be a source of errors and financial disillusions.

House IX

In Aries

Indicates a rather aggressive and dominating way of thinking wherever spiritual or philosophical values are concerned. Travels to foreign countries are likely to be decided suddenly and can become a source of problems or difficulties with local authorities. Enthusiasm and reactivity characterise this position.

In Taurus

A rather down-to-earth philosophical approach to life tends to confer a sedentary preference to long-distance peregrinations, except for holidays. A taste for the good things of life is a source of motivation that favours success in areas where moral and material values cohabit in good intelligence.

In Gemini

The philosophical principle of life is intellectualised to improve communication in social relationships and associations. Involvement in schools, universities, and other similar structures are some of the outlets for the ever-curious mind. Interest in foreign cultures and countries is also indicated.

In Cancer

Family and social origin interest and motivate a certain way of looking at life when relating to the system, rules, and laws. The mother can play or have played an important role in the choice of studies. Settling down far away from the place of birth is often remarked with this position of House IX.

In Leo

Pride and egotism can stand in the way of any real

philosophical achievement. However, the creative potential of the sign can lead to great spiritual realisation. Art, education, politics, involvement in associative activities, and long-distance travels are a source of moral and social enrichment.

In Virgo

Practicality and conservatism confer a down-to-earth philosophical approach to life. Over criticism and analysing of the world around can prevent social life and spiritual satisfactions. Long-distant travels are usually not favoured due to the amount of stress and worries they tend to produce.

In Libra

Philosophy is developed through marriage, partnerships, or social relations. There is a profound interest in foreign forms of expression, in art and other mediums. Travels are often envisaged as a source of intellectual fulfilment. The notions of justice and equity are foremost in the general approach of life.

In Scorpio

Mysticism, occultism and the supernatural are spontaneously abundant sources of intellectual stimulation. Life is seen as a regenerating cycle for the purpose of improving the soul. Spiritual convictions are often led by strong sexual impulses. Philosophical discord with others are likely.

In Sagittarius

This is the natural position of House IX. Spiritual achievement is highly respected and a strong incentive, through intellectual and moral discipline, to social or political leadership. Attraction to foreign countries and cultures comes from an innate need to learn and to experience higher levels of knowledge.

In Capricorn

Work and efforts are the philosophical foundation to a perfect life. A sedentary tendency is likely, although far-distant travel may be necessary at work or for reason beyond personal decisions. Spirituality is often perceived as a means for moral comfort rather than to obtain concrete results.

In Aquarius

There is a strong attraction to the mental and spiritual stimulation needed to progress and succeed. Unorthodox and sometimes marginal styles of religious or spiritual involvement can confer bohemian tendencies. They can also lead to genuine involvement in social welfare programs and organisations.

In Pisces

Philosophical beliefs are essentially motivated by emotions and feelings. Religious convictions can be strong and stemming from family background and education. Intuition and extreme sensitivity can produce visions, clairvoyance, or astral travel capacities. Outside influences create moral confusion.

House X (MC)

In Aries

This position of the MC is found in the chart of military people, business entrepreneurs, athletes, and competitors in various disciplines. However, it may also indicate a life path marked by clashes, conflicts, accidents, and tension. The father image is strong and often influences the choice of a career.

In Taurus

Career achievement depends on the affective cohesion between creativity and the ambition to succeed. Architecture, interior decorating, the arts, painting, music, and singing are some areas of potential achievement. Food, nature, agriculture, beauty, or cosmetics are other possible choices.

In Gemini

The ability to communicate is a prime asset to succeed in areas where sharing ideas, travelling, meeting people, and making good use of the power of the mind are essential. Curiosity and versatility may, however, induce a "jack of all trades" approach that may alter the potential to succeed durably.

In Cancer

This position is often found in the charts of people engaged in politics, and in careers related to the public. History, genealogy, family affairs, water, and emotional subjects are sources of inspiration and motivation. The influence of the mother or mother image may play an underlying role In choices made.

In Leo

The ambition motivates enthusiastic engagements in the

realisation of important projects. The desire to lead and dominate produces ambitious charismatic leaders. Creativity is fuelled by a strong ego that plays a major role in career achievement. The father or father image is a strong underlying influence.

In Virgo

Astrologers usually decide that Virgo is not a strong position for the MC. However, this sign confers excellent methodical, analytical abilities, and meticulousness that can lead to a successful career and realisation of ambitious goals. Sense of responsibility and service are useful in many professional areas.

In Libra

Success is often derived from judicious partnerships and collaboration. There is a natural artistic trait favouring a successful career. A strong need to share and be with others enhances personal motivation and potential. Periods of doubt and uncertainty may prevent direct access to concrete realisation.

In Scorpio

There is potential to succeed in occultism, astrology and other sciences dealing with the mysteries of life or the unconscious mind. Police investigation, medical or biological research, psychology, marine-life protection, or taking care of the deceased are possible areas for career success.

In Sagittarius

Teaching, religion, philosophy, long-distance travel, sports, and other open-air related careers are some of the better choices for a successful career. Enthusiasm and a positive approach to hierarchy and professional responsibilities make it easier to climb up the social ladder and realise personal ambitions.

In Capricorn

This is the natural position of the MC, in the tenth sign. Ambitions are a strong source of motivation, but success can be delayed by personal or social difficulties. Career objectives are usually down-to-earth and motivated by rational reasons that allow time to play in favour of long-lasting realisations.

In Aquarius

Electronics, IT, the media, or social interest are some of the keys to a successful career. Originality, adaptability, and inventiveness allow for a large range of possible choices. A tendency to change due to constant attraction to novelty may create a more bohemian than rational approach to social realisation.

In Pisces

Religion and spirituality, mysticism, and humanism are possible sources of inspiration to a successful career. There may be confusion and uncertainty on the right path to choose. Art, music, dancing, psychology or parapsychology, and parallel sciences are other areas of potential achievement.

House XI

In Aries

Friends and enemies tend to cohabit and produce an uneasy social atmosphere. There can be a tendency to dominate friends that can make relationships difficult. Many changes are observed in friendship and social settings, both human and geographical. Gossiping is another source of tension.

In Taurus

Friends are an important part of the active daily life. There is a tendency to befriend easily to create a pleasant atmosphere or to obtain some sort of approbation or recognition. Fidelity allows friendships to perdure, thanks to a sincere amount of affection emanating from the emotional nature of the ties.

In Gemini

Intellectual relationships are important and a source of attraction to social circles that can provide enough mental stimulation and variety to feed ever-changing needs and great curiosity. This position seems to favour youthful and dynamic communication skills. However, friendships tend to be ephemeral.

In Cancer

Friends are treated like family and dearly valued. The home can become a place for social gatherings and entertaining. Children have a friend-like relationship with their parents. However, emotionality can alienate from social contacts. Shyness is not unusual with this position of House XI in Cancer.

In Leo

There is a need to be the centre of attention in social meetings and among friends in general. The attraction to higher social standards can motivate altruistic tendencies that may be a source of success and recognition. Helping, counselling, and guiding others, bring popularity and personal satisfaction.

In Virgo

Co-workers are considered as friends. Social life is closely related to the profession. Excessive criticism can, however, create various tensions and conflicts at work. This position can also contribute a tendency to play an important role in union activity to defend or preserve workers' rights.

In Libra

There is a natural and innate need to make artistic friends with delicate manners and good taste. The Romantic partners are considered more as friends than lovers. There may be some difficulty to decide on a setting or environment to settle down and develop a coherent and stable social life.

In Scorpio

There is an innate attraction to unusual and mysterious people that can lead to perfect and profound enjoyment, as much as disturbing situations, and social difficulties. Treachery and karmic enemies may confer a tendency to develop a degree of paranoia that hinders the prospect of a satisfying social life.

In Sagittarius

There is a spontaneous attraction to wealthy and well-established social friends, or to spiritual or religious social movements. Intellectual relationships are a source of renewed enjoyment and motivation. Friendship may develop while travelling or with people from foreign countries.

In Capricorn

There is an innate attraction to older and more experienced friends. People of good standing in the community, who are serious and respected, are preferred to any other types of social relationship. A tendency to keep away from the madding crowd is usually due to some degree of timidity.

In Aquarius

This is the natural position for House XI in the eleventh sign. Friendship and social life are a must. A tendency to navigate from one friendship to another may last until the right person or group of people is met. Original, eccentric, or marginal individuals are a source of interest that may deter social stability.

In Pisces

The Neptunian quality of the sign confers a natural preference for spiritual and lofty friends and social environment. There is an attraction to religious as well as artistic and intelligent beings. However, relationships with unreliable or distressed individuals may hinder social stability and pleasure.

House XII

In Aries

Tends to create difficulties and deeply rooted motivations going back to the early days of life or passed incarnations. Life may then be felt as a constant struggle and search for inner truth. Peace of mind does not come easily. An effort to forget the past would restore and preserve peace of mind and wellbeing.

In Taurus

The material aspect of life is not considered vital enough compared to love, romance, and intellectual or artistic needs. Life may be a chronic source of ups and downs until the importance of social and moral stability to achieve personal goals and inner peace of mind is understood and applied.

In Gemini

There seems to be a karmic need to learn, to communicate, to meet people and to make use of the intellect in many other valuable ways. Superficiality may, however, be observed. It may stem from an inferiority complex. Neuronal tension is a source of mental fatigue and forgetfulness.

In Cancer

Family problems may cause strong reactions in relation to early life's difficult events or relationship with one of the parents or with both. There is an unconscious strong connection to the mother that may influence the entire life path. Peace of mind and serenity seem mostly favoured during the later years of life.

In Leo

Pride and egotism may alienate from accepting or realising

personal mistakes. Meticulousness and criticism about others confer a tendency to feel "too good for this world". Long passed motivations are probably linked to a working-class aristocratic background difficult to accept for such a "royal" sign.

In Virgo

Work and service is probably what is lacking in the individual's will to succeed. "Heavenly" talented he may always take what good comes to him for granted, not realising the true opportunities of his life. A working-class background may be one of the deep-rooted motivations to reject normal social conduct. For such reasons, success can be delayed until the meaning of duty is fully understood.

In Libra

Artistic gifts allow to act with people like a comedian on stage. This is only a shield to hide deeper feelings from a misunderstanding audience or entourage. Difficult relationships with co-workers tend to produce multiple job changes. A very personal sense of duty and service seems to stand in the way of success as a member of the community.

In Scorpio

Difficulties in early years of life or a "close encounter" with death may have conferred an innate sense of the afterlife and of good and evil. Religious or mystical beliefs about life's events as purposely imposed for karmic reasons. Peace of mind is derived from rational answers to irrational questions.

In Sagittarius

Spiritual achievement is considered with much interest to fulfil materialistic ambitions. Intellectual aspirations may be difficult to achieve despite the moral implication. A wealthy or religious background dating to a past incarnation may be responsible for a certain idleness regarding personal realisation.

In Capricorn

Ambition, conservatism, or materialism may be a source of passive rebellion against moral status quo. Rejection of parental behaviour can lead to bohemian tendencies. Moral accomplishment and inner peace depend on the amount of work done to deal with mixed feelings of guilt and victimisation.

In Aquarius

Nervousness and impressionability may be linked to early childhood disturbing situations. Unconventional surroundings and unusual family habits may have produced uncommon moral values. A superiority complex can lead to social prominence to the detriment of inner peace and wisdom.

In Pisces

This is the natural position of House XII in the twelfth sign. Clairvoyance, if present, is often derived from early childhood spiritual experiences. Karma canters on faith and trust in heavenly powers. A sense of sacrifice to serve the community is present, but inner peace relies on the ability to control impulses.

Supplementary Section

The Planets in the Houses

Interpreting the meaning of a planet in a House is important because it shows how such planet affects the area represented by the House in question. Such influence must be analysed in relation to the planet considered as the **ruler of a House in a sign and in a House**, as explained in the lesson and shown in the other supplementary sections provided with this astrology course. To understand how a planet works in such or such House, simply refer to the corresponding House general meaning. This will help you to quickly grasp how the analysis must be conducted.

Remember to **never base your analysis on one planetary influence alone.** On the contrary, take the good habit of blending them as you progress. This will avoid contradictory statements that may discredit your reading.

THE SUN

In House I

This position enhances the potential to express the inner self, especially if this House begins in the Sun sign. It confers an innate need to "shine" and be noticed in a varying pressing manner depending on the sign involved (Fire signs are more intense than Earth signs). Position comparable to the Sun in Aries.

In House II

This position enhances the desire for material possessions and money. There is an affective need for material possessions that may produce a defensive behaviour and a tendency to focus on personal acquisitions. Food and nature are other sources of interest. Position comparable to the Sun in Taurus.

In House III

This position enhances the desire to communicate and to be on the move. Interests are numerous and heteroclite. Mental energy is fuelled by intellectual projects, travels, and amusing human relationships. There may be a tendency to shallowness and gossiping. Position comparable to the Sun in Gemini.

In House IV

This position enhances the importance of family relations and the need to live in a comfortable home. Interest in history and patriotism are observed. The father or father image may be linked to the role of the mother for various reasons. Position comparable to the Sun in Cancer.

In House V

This House is "naturally ruled" by the Sun and enhances

creativity and romanticism. The need for love may be expressed artistically as well as in personal relationships. The ability to take advantage of opportunities is also conferred and enhanced by a strong ego. Position comparable to the Sun in Leo.

In House VI

This position enhances the need to work to be of service to others in various ways. There is a prevalent interest in health and medicine. It may lead to a career as much as to a tendency to excessive worry that to the point of developing a hypochondriac tendency. Position comparable to the Sun in Virgo.

In House VII

This position enhances the need to get actively involved in a meaningful relationship such as marriage. There is a natural ability to be useful and appreciated by others. It also confers a tendency to be more efficient in group rather than personal activities. Position comparable to the Sun in Libra.

In House VIII

There is a natural interest in the mysteries of life and death. An innate attraction to the hidden side of life can lead to lifelong involvement in research with sustained determination and passion. Sex drive, inner strength and regeneration potential are enhanced. Position comparable to the Sun in Scorpio.

In House IX

There is a spontaneous interest in long-distance travel, higher education, and philosophy. High moral principles help overcome many obstacles by being sincere and authentic. Life's circumstances are perceived as positive and useful to progress. This position is comparable to the Sun in Sagittarius.

In House X

This position enhances the desire to succeed and to reach a higher social status, no matter how long it takes. Ambition makes dealing with others at work and privately a source of tension. The father or father figure is a major influence in all important choices made. Position comparable to the Sun in Capricorn.

In House XI

This position indicates a friendly and sociable nature. There is a need to be a "lighthouse" for friends as much as for the community with a strong desire to help in any possible way. Dislike of solitude confers a tendency to depend on others for company. Position comparable to the Sun in Aquarius.

In House XII

There is a need to hide and keep personal energy and talents within rather than share them with others. The connection with the spiritual dimension of life is enhanced. The past is a source of answers to many existential questions. The idea of karma prevails. Position comparable to the Sun in Pisces.

THE MOON

In House I

This position enhances femininity and confers sensitivity and creativity. Emotions need to be controlled and channelled to harmonise private relationships and the energy of the inner self. The influence of the mother is strong and may be a source of emotional surges. Position comparable to the Moon in Aries.

In House II

This position renders emotionally attached to material possessions with various fluctuations due to dependence to the good things of life. Food has a strong influence on the ability to channel emotional outbreaks. Nature has a positive influence. Position comparable to the Moon in Taurus.

In House III

This position enhances the need for intellectual stimulation to create emotional reactions and make life more interesting or exciting. Movement is the keyword to being alive. There is strong emotional need and ability to communicate and express feelings effectively. Position similar to the Moon in Gemini.

In House IV

This House is symbolically ruled by the Moon. This position therefore enhances the emotional nature of the family sphere. It also indicates the importance of the mother or confers a strong mother instinct. Creativity is expressed through children and art. Position comparable to the Moon in Cancer.

In House V

This position enhances the ability to create and to express emotions through art and love. Children have a privileged position. They are a strong motivating factor. Emotional pride causes memorable fits of anger. The mother has an influence on the development of creativity. Position comparable to the Moon in Leo.

In House VI

This position enhances the emotional need to work and be of service to others, although this is subject to various fluctuations linked to the nature of our natural satellite. There is an interest in health and medicine. Hypochondriac tendencies are often observed. Position comparable to the Moon in Virgo.

In House VII

This position enhances the emotional need for harmony and wellbeing in all kinds of partnerships, both private and social or professional. There is a tendency to spontaneously help others. Excessive personal involvement may leave a feeling of ingratitude. Position comparable to the Moon in Libra.

In House VIII

This position indicates an emotional attraction to the mysteries of life and death. Anything to do with the occult generates interest. Sexual needs are enhanced. Financial investments may be responsible for the accumulated wealth but also for ruin or bankruptcy. Position comparable to the Moon in Scorpio.

In House IX

There is an emotional interest in philosophy, spirituality, religions, and academic knowledge. Intellectual human relationships are favoured. Interests in ancient history and foreign cultures are often observed. The home may be chosen far from the place of birth. Position comparable to the Moon in Sagittarius.

In House X

The mother or mother figure has a dominant position and may influence or motivate the choice of a career. Emotions are a source of motivation to accomplish personal or professional missions. Lack of emotional self-control is detrimental to social stability. Position comparable to The Moon in Capricorn.

In House XI

There is a motherly approach to human relationships, friendships, and socialising in general. The emotional interactions with others may motivate involvement in charity or charitable organisations. Impatience could deter long-term commitments. Position comparable to the Moon in Aquarius.

In House XII

There is a tendency to withdraw rather than openly express emotions. Emotional fluctuations are often derived from the intrauterine period or troubling family secrets. A strong karmic tie with the mother may be a source of spiritual motivation or moral depression. Position comparable to the Moon in Pisces.

MERCURY

In House I

This position enhances the ability to communicate and to express ideas and opinions in a spontaneous and sometimes impulsive manner. People born with Mercury here are intellectually interested in learning more about themselves to understand who they really are. Position comparable to Mercury in Aries.

In House II

Money is spent for intellectual purposes such as reading, travelling, and studying. There is an interest in food and nature, and a need for a privileged environment where thinking and reflecting are favoured. The intellect relies more on practice than theory. Position similar to Mercury in Taurus.

In House III

This is the natural rulership position of Mercury. Here its influence is greatly enhanced and favours intellectual activity. It also creates a natural ability to communicate and express one's own ideas, although they may remain trivial or superficial. Position comparable to Mercury in Gemini.

In House IV

This position enhances the natural ability and desire to communicate with and about family members. A keen interest in past events relating to the family tree and various family members is also present but depends on the sign position of Mercury in the chart. Position similar to Mercury in Cancer.

In House V

This position usually goes with an artistic mind. The intellect strongly influences romantic life and creativity. Communication with children, teaching, and interaction with loved ones are favoured in accordance with the sign position of Mercury in the chart. Position comparable to Mercury in Leo.

In House VI

The intellect and need to communicate strongly intervenes in the work environment and the overall accomplishment within the professional arena. Excessive health concerns may lead to a medical career or to psychosomatic illnesses. Position comparable to Mercury in Virgo.

In House VII

This position enhances the desire and ability to communicate with others, especially close ones such as partners, both in private and professional or social areas. Mercury can, however, tend to hinder the desire to communicate especially about oneself. Position comparable to Mercury in Libra.

In House VIII

This position enhances the intellectual interest in the mysteries of life and occult sciences. Money and the material side of life produce a taste for financial investments. Research, investigation, psychology, or psychiatry are some subjects that may motivate a career. Position similar to Mercury in Scorpio.

In House IX

This position enhances the desire to learn, to discover and to progress on the mental and intellectual plans. There is an attraction to foreign countries and cultures and a disposition for foreign languages. The need to learn is motivated by a desire to share. Position comparable to Mercury in Sagittarius.

In House X

This position enhances the potential to use the intellect and the ability to communicate to succeed socially and professionally. Careers in teaching, public speaking, politics, journalism, or in the media are some of the areas of possible success and achievement. Position comparable to Mercury in Capricorn.

In House XI

There is an innate need to communicate with others freely. Friends and social acquaintances are a source of renewed motivation for the expression of thoughts and ideas. A sincere interest in humanity may become the basis to a community-oriented career. Position comparable to Mercury in Aquarius.

In House XII

This position indicates a mystical or spiritual way of thinking, an intuitive mind, and a preference for the imaginary rather than in the real world. A tendency to withdraw may be derived from past events or traumas. The need to connect with the soul is prevalent. Position comparable to Mercury in Pisces.

VENUS

In House I

This position enhances the natural need for love and romance and dependence on affection. It often confers a certain vulnerability in private relationships due to a strong need to be appreciated at all cost. Creativity and artistic tendencies are present. Position comparable to Venus in Aries.

In House II

This position enhances the desire to possess, to earn money and to spend it for sentimental reasons. Sensibility to the beautiful surpasses the practical aspect. There is a strong need for approbation. Venus here is found in the charts of collectors, artists, or renown chefs. Position comparable to Venus in Taurus.

In House III

This position enhances the ability to communicate in a pleasant manner to convince in various ways. Sociability and friendliness are also conferred. The love principle is intellectualised producing talent in writing, public speaking and music making. Position comparable to Venus in Gemini.

In House IV

This position enhances family ties and interests in family affairs with a genuine appreciation for anything to do with the home and family environment. Venus here enhances procreation and the desire to have a family in a pleasant and natural environment. Position comparable to Venus in Cancer.

In House V

This position greatly enhances the natural ability and desire to love and be loved and appreciated. Pride and possessiveness in romantic relationship are observed. Having children and a loving family are a prime motivation. Artistic creativity is significantly increased. Position comparable to Venus in Leo.

In House VI

This position indicates a sense of responsibility in love and romance that may lead to a tendency to worry too much. There is dependence on wellbeing in the work arena. Professional choices are based on personal taste rather than exclusively financial conditions. Position comparable to Venus in Virgo.

In House VII

This strong position enhances the need to be loved and to love others, privately, socially, and professionally. Overdependence on affection is observed, with the possibility of moral disappointment and disillusion. The more you give, the more they take... Position comparable to Venus in Libra.

In House VIII

This position indicates a tendency to consider love on the physical and metaphysical plans. Sexual Drive is strong and may influence personal feelings to the point of getting deeply involved for physical rather than spiritual reasons. Difficulties in romance are likely. Position comparable to Venus in Scorpio.

In House IX

This position enhances the importance of love and affections in a philosophical or spiritual rather than emotional way. There is a need to express feelings in a profound and lofty way. Love is sometimes found in a far distant land. Spiritual creativity is enhanced. Position comparable to Venus in Sagittarius.

In House X

This position indicates that love is a top priority. It influences major choices and decisions in relation to the career and the realisation of important projects. Art may also be a source motivation and an avenue to a successful career. Feelings are expressed assertively. Position comparable to Venus in Capricorn.

In House XI

This position indicates a spontaneous empathy toward others issued from a need to be appreciated socially as much as privately. Creativity is motivated by an affectionate perception of humanity. Friendships are numerous and occasionally ambiguous. Position comparable to Venus in Aquarius.

In House XII

This position confers a spiritual approach to love and affection. It may also indicate a tendency to secret or imaginary love affairs. A predisposition to hide personal feelings to protect privacy is also observed. The past may be a source of ambiguous creativity. Position comparable to Venus in Pisces.

MARS

In House I

Mars is the natural ruler of House I where it enhances the ability to fight and to defend oneself in a rather aggressive way. Impulsiveness is responsible for various incidents and for extraordinary decisions that may save lives, thanks to heroic acts in perilous situations. Position comparable to Mars in Aries.

In House II

This position enhances the natural ability to fight to defend and protect material possessions. A tendency to spend impulsively may create various problems and financial shortcomings. There is a need to exercise patience to avoid conflicts for materialistic reasons. Position comparable to Mars in Taurus.

In House III

This position enhances the natural desire to express ideas and to impose them in an assertive manner. There is a need to slow down and to be more careful when talking, writing, or driving. Difficulties at school, or with brothers or sisters are also observed. Position comparable to Mars in Gemini.

In House IV

This position enhances the natural need to defend and protect one's family and home environment. It also indicates a tendency to argue and to generate conflicts within the family sphere. Excessive authority with loved ones may be responsible for domestic disorders. Position comparable to Mars in Cancer.

In House V

This position enhances the natural tendency to direct love

affairs and romantic relationships. This may lead to various disruptions and breakups. Excessive authority or reactivity with children, and overprotection of loved ones may also become a source of tension. Position comparable to Mars in Leo.

In House VI

This position indicates a strong desire to dominate and to show authority and leadership aspirations at work and in health or medically related matters. A natural liking of aggressive animals is also observed. This position may also motivate a career in surgery or the military. Position comparable to Mars in Virgo.

In House VII

This position indicates various tensions in private relationships to the point of becoming detrimental to wellbeing in marriage and other types of close partnerships, both private and social. The need to lead and to direct others is the cause for discord and breakups. Position comparable to Mars in Libra.

In House VIII

This position indicates an intense sexual drive linked to a tendency to dominate partners. This may lead to conflicts which could profoundly threaten inner wellbeing. Hygiene is to be considered seriously to avoid health issues. Self-control of inner tension is necessary. Position similar to Mars in Scorpio.

In House IX

This position enhances the desire to defend moral principles and to fight injustice in a determined, spontaneous, and sometimes aggressive way. Various problems with the law or the administration would be due to mistakes made from impulsive reactions. Position similar to Mars in Sagittarius.

In House X

This position enhances the desire to be first, to lead and to dominate one's own life, enforcing personal decisions to succeed. The father or father figure has a strong influence on the development of authority, ambitions, and choice of career. Action is the key to success. Position comparable to Mars in Capricorn.

In House XI

This position enhances the need to be of service to others in an active and spontaneous, but rather impulsive way. Overactive involvement in collective activities lead to fatigue and loss of vigilance. Excessive authority can have disturbing social consequences. Position comparable to Mars in Aquarius.

In House XII

This position tends to hinder natural combativeness, rendering it more spiritual than terrestrial. There is a need to act in secret due to a feeling of being a potential victim of betrayals. Karmic enemies are occasionally met. Paranoiac tendencies are seldom observed. Position comparable to Mars in Pisces.

VESTA

In House I

It favours inner peace and harmony. Wellbeing depends on how the self is perceived. Vesta confers a positive vibration rate that enhances charisma and charm. Its soothing energy softens any "hostile" presence in the immediate surroundings. Position comparable to Vesta in Aries.

In House II

Earthly foods, creativity, art, and the appreciation of the good and beautiful things of life are essential to inner wellbeing and harmony. A balanced budget means more enjoyment without the worry of being caught up by excessive spending. Position comparable to Vesta in Taurus.

In House III

The intellect functions on the notions of balance, harmony, and fairness. These essential values promote mental wellbeing, with happy repercussions in human relationships. Siblings and friends are essential to ensure inner joy and peace. Position comparable to Vesta in Gemini.

In House IV

This position promotes family harmony or reduces the intensity of any difficulties represented by adverse configurations in the chart. Diplomacy and fairness increase popularity and improve the quality of life in the home and close environment. Position comparable to Vesta in Cancer.

In House V

Vesta here promotes creativity and love in art and romantic relationships. There is a strong need for appreciation and approbation. Musical creativity is enhanced. Balance and harmony are prevalent values. Children are a source of inspiration. Position comparable to Vesta in Leo.

In House VI

Vesta here protects health and promotes harmony at work or dealing with daily routine and responsibilities. There is a need to restore or preserve balance that may motivate medically oriented careers. Success relies on subtlety and charm. Position comparable to Vesta in Virgo.

In House VII

Personal and social partnerships are fuelled by a positive approach meant to preserve harmony and balance in the relationship. Caring for others ensures inner satisfaction and wellbeing. A tendency to overdo it may trigger disappointment. Position comparable to Vesta in Libra.

In House VIII

Innate understanding of the cycles of life and death is a source of positive energy that helps maintain inner peace and harmony. Finances are protected by a positive and honest approach to material responsibilities. Inheritance is likely. Position comparable to Vesta in Scorpio.

In House IX

The notions of balance and harmony are a source of positive motivation to study, discover, travel, with a philosophical perception of life in all situations. The need to learn and to share favours teachers, writers, journalists, and politicians. Position comparable to Vesta in Sagittarius.

In House X

Ambitions are fuelled by a need to do well and to be appreciated and in harmonious relationship with the idea of success. The aspiration to reach the top while preserving inner peace and wellbeing is a major source of positive motivation. Position comparable to Vesta in Capricorn.

In House XI

Preserving balance and harmony in social relationships makes it easier to deal with others, even in the most delicate situations. Friends are a source of enjoyment and positive motivation that promotes inner peace and wellbeing. Position comparable to Vesta in Aquarius.

In House XII

Inner peace and harmony depend on the ability to get away from the madding crowd. In the quiet comfort of a special place, the soul can rest and allow body and mind to recharge in positive energy. True spirituality needs no words. Position comparable to Vesta in Pisces.

JUPITER

In House I

This position enhances generosity and the natural ability to be good to oneself and to others. It also indicates a tendency to put on too much weight, both physically and socially. Jupiter protects, but it can also create major problems. Enthusiasm needs to be controlled. Position comparable to Jupiter in Aries.

In House II

This position enhances the ability to make money together with great generosity. Jupiter here seems to protect material interests; it can also produce excesses that greatly affect finances. The love of good and beautiful things can be both a source of joy and trouble. Position similar to Jupiter in Taurus.

In House III

This position enhances the natural desire and ability to learn and to express oneself in an intelligent and entertaining way. There is a tendency to overdo it and to consider one's ideas as absolute truth. A genuine interest in foreign countries and cultures is observed. Position comparable to Jupiter in Gemini.

In House IV

This position enhances the need to be present on the family scene with kindness and open heartedness. There is a preference for larger-than-usual places of residence. The mother's positive influence often plays an important and generous role during the entire lifetime. Position comparable to Jupiter in Cancer.

In House V

This position enhances creativity and generosity with loved ones. Excesses are frequent, due to a need for approbation and admiration that exceeds the ability to reason and control kindness. Love of the beautiful and creativity favour success and social prominence. Position comparable to Jupiter in Leo.

In House VI

This position enhances the spontaneous desire to work with a generous approach to day-to-day tasks. Jupiter enhances the ability to climb up the social ladder, improving one's professional position by taking advantage of various opportunities and fruitful collaborations. Position comparable to Jupiter in Virgo.

In House VII

This position indicates the need to be generous with others, especially private, social, or professional partners. A tendency to be over-present for others may be taken advantage of. However, remaining positive ensures a philosophical approach to the worst situations. Acts a bit like Jupiter in Libra.

In House VIII

This position enhances natural interest in the mysteries of life, money, and sex. Inheritance and financial investments are favoured. Positive energy is used to improve material conditions with far-reaching goals and ideals. Losses are mostly due to excessive generosity. Position comparable to Jupiter in Scorpio.

In House IX

Jupiter is strong here and indicates a philosophical approach to life. Ambition and natural talent, together with an innate taste for studies, travels, and foreign cultures favour intellectual achievements. Politics, teaching, writing, and counselling are potential choices. Position comparable to Jupiter in Sagittarius.

In House X

This position enhances the potential to succeed professionally. Spontaneous generosity provides positive energy to reach the highest summits. Opportunistic tendencies are indicated and may play in favour of social accomplishment and self-realisation. Position comparable to Jupiter in Capricorn.

In House XI

This position enhances the desire to be of service to others in a spontaneously generous way. An interest in social and humanitarian causes motivates a need to help others with an open-hearted approach that may create both joy and disappointment. Position comparable to Jupiter in Aquarius.

In House XII

This position enhances the need for a more spiritual and divinely meaningful life, although it may be awkward to express one's own ideals and to act accordingly. Jupiter here may trigger a missionary career ambition. Religious beliefs motivate in a positive way. Position comparable to Jupiter in Pisces.

SATURN

In House I

This position indicates patience and determination, but a low consideration of oneself. Nevertheless, time allows for progress and concrete achievement. Self-realisation often occurs around thirty years of age when all is done to realise important life projects. Position comparable to Saturn in Aries.

In House II

This position indicates a conservative approach to the material aspect of life. Attention should be given to the food intake to avoid eventual physiological consequences of an inappropriate diet. A tendency to self-restriction may alter spontaneous enjoyment of the good things of life. Acts a bit like Saturn in Taurus.

In House III

This position indicates difficulties in studies due to adverse circumstances or lack of motivation that repress the desire to learn and communicate. The influence of the elderly on the development and evolution of the literary interests and capacity. Position comparable to Saturn in Gemini.

In House IV

This position indicates chronic home disturbance and a fatalistic approach to family responsibilities. It may also indicate a proletarian background that could temper the ability to climb up the social ladder. The influence of an older relative is often observed. Position comparable to Saturn in Cancer.

In House V

This position indicates sentimental frustration due to lack of companionship. It may also hinder procreation and creativity.

Time is a major factor in the development of personal life. Realisation is more likely around 30 years of age or much later, at about 60. Position comparable to Saturn in Leo.

In House VI

This position indicates that work and health may have karmic origins with a strong influence on the choice of a career. Periods of unemployment are possible, sometimes due to a difficulty-to-put-oneself-forward once the goals are set. Health may hinder employment. Position comparable to Saturn in Virgo.

In House VII

This position has a strong influence on the ability to share and cooperate with other people, especially in private life. This may lead to prolonged periods of celibacy and solitude with detrimental effect on personal wellbeing and moral or emotional health. Position comparable to Saturn in Libra.

In House VIII

This position indicates a life path marked by significant economic setbacks. Hence, a parsimonious approach of finances and joint resources. Libido is reduced. Unfortunate events may have produced an apprehension about death and the mysteries of life. Position comparable to Saturn in Scorpio.

In House IX

This position indicates a life path marked by problems to solve and obstacles to surmount within the social sphere on administrative and legal plans. A pessimistic philosophy of life does not motivate higher studies. There may be a karmic tie with a foreign land. Position comparable to Saturn in Sagittarius.

In House X

Saturn is strong House X, where its position enhances the desire to succeed while creating serious obstacles to surmount before reaching the desired objectives. Time and patience increase determination and favour ultimate success with long-lasting effects. Position comparable to Saturn in Capricorn.

In House XI

This position indicates a life path marked by setbacks in the human or geographical environment. Wanting to help others is a source of difficulties that hinder potential success. The condition of the elderly may become a professional and social motivation to help. Position comparable to Saturn in Aquarius.

In House XII

This position indicates a karmic tie with the past, especially where difficult events are concerned. The elderly may be a source of responsibilities due to their need of care and attention. Religious beliefs and spirituality are linked to hardship and burden rather than God. Position comparable to Saturn in Pisces.

CHIRON

In House I

Health may be a cause for concern during the early years of life. Later, an interest in medicine or health care may develop and contribute to a career choice. The ability to analyse and need to understand, allow diagnostics in various areas. Position comparable to Chiron in Aries.

In House II

Food may be a source of concern during childhood. Later, the material aspect of earthly life and money may have been considered either as poison or as medicine. Earning a living in therapy may be a way to heal oneself somehow. Position comparable to Chiron in Taurus.

In House III

When the first cry is a cause for concern, later, communicating may require more effort. A profound need to understand, to investigate and to analyse develops. It may be a way to heal oneself from forgotten traumas during childhood. Position comparable to Chiron in Gemini.

In House IV

The first encounter with the mother is essential for the newborn to feel "at home" and safe. If this moment is not right somehow, one may develop an uneasy feeling within or about family life. Health may also play a part in domestic difficulties. Position comparable to Chiron in Cancer.

In House V

Love is essential during childhood. Later it makes private relationships come easy, enhancing creativity and the appreciation of the good and beautiful things of life. There is a strong need, but a tendency to doubt and worry too much. Position comparable to Chiron in Leo.

In House VI

Work, duty, and health are major concerns. There is a karmic need to take up the number of responsibilities imposed daily. Chiron is strong in this House. A tendency to worry, making problems worse than they really are, is observed. Position comparable to Chiron in Virgo.

In House VII

If personal relationships are uneasy or ambiguous, it is perhaps due to the quality of the first encounter with other people shortly after birth. Later, it can make it awkward to relate to others freely as a need to observe and analyse prevails. Position comparable to Chiron in Libra.

In House VIII

From the moment of birth, we know that we are going to die. The concept motivates the way we lead our earthly voyage. If health is a major concern during early childhood, later, it creates a tendency to worry too much about minor issues. Position comparable to Chiron in Scorpio.

In House IX

Learning is an essential part life. The more we know, the more we want to discover. When the potential to study is disrupted during childhood, it creates intellectual awkwardness and an insidious need for knowledge and adventure. Position comparable to Chiron in Sagittarius.

In House X

The father image is a factor of motivation to succeed in life. If adverse circumstances temper the perception of this major influence during childhood, it creates awkwardness and doubts that may alter the ability to climb up the social ladder. Position comparable to Chiron in Capricorn.

In House XI

Friendship and social relationships are important. If adverse circumstances during childhood hinder the natural need to relate to others, later it produces a lack of self-confidence or social interest, favouring tedious rather than joyful ties. Position comparable to Chiron in Aquarius.

In House XII

What happens during the gestation period resonates deeply into the foetus in formation. Cellular memory stores uneasy information that can create strange reactions linked to forgotten events. A strong need to connect with the past ensues. Position comparable to Chiron in Pisces.

URANUS

In House I

This position enhances originality, and the way inner personality is expressed and put forward. It also increases the activity of the nervous system, conferring good reflexes and imagination, as well as a tendency to act and react in an unpredictable manner. Position comparable to Uranus in Aries.

In House II

This position enhances the ability to adapt and to make good use of imagination and originality in finance and other down-to-earth areas. It can also indicate sudden changes that drastically affect the source of income. Food may be a source of interest and innovations. Position comparable to Uranus in Taurus.

In House III

This position enhances intellectual performance and originality. It confers imagination and the faculty to quickly adapt to situations and people. It may, however, create too much mental energy and a state of nervousness that alters the ability to focus and concentrate. Position comparable to Uranus in Gemini.

In House IV

This position indicates an original or unusual family background or home environment. It confers mental creativity to adapt to sudden changes in family life. The mother may be perceived as someone quite exceptional although quite nervous or unstable in some way. Position comparable to Uranus in Cancer.

In House V

This position shows that imagination feeds creativity in arts or in dealing with loved ones. It can, however, indicate sudden turns of fate and the necessity to adapt to them quickly. Unexpected or lucky surprises may suddenly contribute to radically change the way of life. Position comparable to Uranus in Leo.

In House VI

This position enhances imagination and originality at work or while pursuing a career objective. Sudden changes at work may be frequent but quickly dealt with. Success could be favoured in areas such as the audio-visual, aeronautics, or electronics. Health is erratic. Position comparable to Uranus in Virgo.

In House VII

This position indicates originality in marriage or other important relationships. Divorce is not unusual due to a need for variety rather than stability. Adaptability helps preserve harmony. The choice of partners depends on the situation more than the person concerned. Position comparable to Uranus in Libra.

In House VIII

This position enhances natural attraction to occult sciences, finance, and sex. Sudden changes may occur due to unexpected deaths or painful circumstances. There is an ability and possible desire to succeed in astrology, psychology, medicine, or criminology. Position comparable to Uranus in Scorpio.

In House IX

This position confers the ability to adapt to drastic changes with a philosophical approach that enables quick reactions and understanding of the situations. Higher education, foreign countries and cultures, and politics may be a lifelong source of motivation. Position comparable to Uranus in Sagittarius.

In House X

This position indicates potential career success in the media, show business, television, film industry, aeronautics, electronics, or computers. Uranus here also indicates frequent changes of professional position or situation, and places of residence accordingly. Position comparable to Uranus in Capricorn.

In House XI

This is the natural rulership House of Uranus. It enhances adaptability, essentially on the social plan. Spontaneous attraction to people contributes to popularity as much as scandals. Sudden changes may temper the social life, humanely and geographically. Position comparable to Uranus in Aquarius.

In House XII

This position indicates an unstable life path, marked by drastic changes with spiritual and physical consequences. The nervous system can also be a source of concern. Unusual spiritual needs may lead to involvement in sectarian or religious movements. Position comparable to Uranus in Pisces.

NEPTUNE

In House I

Neptune here enhances imagination, sensibility, and artistic qualities. It also confers a degree of confusion in the expression of the inner personality due to a natural ability to perceive life on subtle plans. Sensitivity to the environment may trigger mysterious medical afflictions. Position comparable to Neptune in Aries.

In House II

This position enhances imagination to improve finances, but it can also indicate confusion and uncertainty wherever material values are concerned. A rational diet is a must to preserve physiological balance. Allergic reactions to some foods are occasionally observed. Position similar to Neptune in Taurus.

In House III

This position usually enhances imagination, sixth sense, and the ability to learn by osmosis. An interest in spiritual healing is present. In some cases, extreme sensitivity may induce mental confusion and a tendency to develop psychosomatic disorders. Position comparable to Neptune in Gemini.

In House IV

This position creates a subtle link with the mother and family members. The need to be living near the sea or to convert the home into an artist studio is not uncommon. Health concerns may be of genetic origin, mostly from the mother's side of the family. Position comparable to Neptune in Cancer.

In House V

This position enhances creativity and imagination in art and the expression of love. Success in music, dancing, painting, or writing is favoured. Neptune here may also indicate confusion and uncertainty in sentimental relationships or in dealing with children and loved ones. Position similar to Neptune in Leo.

In House VI

This position indicates uncertainty in the choice of a profession. Any area requiring intuition, creativity, and sensitivity are potential avenues of success. Health and medicine or spiritual healing interests may also contribute to the choice of a career. Psychosomatic tendencies are observed. Position comparable to Neptune in Virgo.

In House VII

This position indicates a natural attraction to spiritually oriented partners. However, confusion and uncertainty prevail until the right person is met. There is an innate need to help others with a tendency to consider it a mission and a karmic earthly duty. Position comparable to Neptune in Libra.

In House VIII

This position often shows an innate ability to communicate with invisible or parallel plans. There is an intuitive approach to spirituality through a profound interest for the mysteries of life and death. Neptune may, however, create confusion in finances and other down-to-earth areas. Position comparable to Neptune in Scorpio.

In House IX

This position enhances the need for a spiritual and philosophical life path. Dealing with administrative or legal matters may, however, be a source of confusion. Morality and knowledge are major aspects of life to ensure personal wellbeing and success. Position comparable to Neptune in Sagittarius.

In House X

This position indicates potential to succeed in a wide range of professional activities including but not limited to religion, philosophy, teaching, politics, welfare, medicine, spiritual healing, chemistry, or ecology. However, there may be confusion in making the right choice. Position comparable to Neptune in Capricorn.

In House XI

This position enhances the ability to perceive humanity spiritually. There is a lofty approach to social issues. Friendships with people of similar philosophical trends are favoured. However, excess receptivity may affect both social and geographical environments. Position comparable to Neptune in Aquarius.

In House XII

Neptune here indicates extreme sensitivity to, and awareness of the spiritual aspect of earthly life. Intuition borders on clairvoyance, together with the ability to subtle perception. This position may also induce a need to withdraw due to both moral and physical vulnerability. Position comparable to Neptune in Scorpio.

PLUTO

PLUTO in House I

Pluto here indicates a greater ability to regenerate from illnesses and other setbacks, together with sustained concentration, determination, and strength. An interest in the mysteries of life and death is observed. A nihilist tendency may, however, deter the joy of being alive. Position comparable to Pluto in Aries.

PLUTO in House II

Pluto here indicates a life path marked by great upheavals and misfortune that may seriously threaten finances and material life. Food may be considered poisonous or health threatening. However, spontaneous regeneration helps solve the harsher upheavals. Position comparable to Pluto in Taurus.

PLUTO in House III

This position indicates an innate interest in psychology, the mysteries of life, occultism, and sexuality. Mental focus and endurance enable long-lasting studies and most intellectual endeavours. Communication may be sarcastic, caustic, or morbid. Position comparable to Pluto in Gemini.

PLUTO in House IV

This position indicates a life path marked with family upheavals. Leaving home early to settle away from the "troubled nest" is often observed. However, Pluto enhances the natural ability to regenerate and recover from the worse suffering and hardship that may be endured. Position comparable to Pluto in Cancer.

PLUTO in House V

This position indicates sentimental difficulties due to a strong and profound, but often dark approach to love and romance. There may be deep moral traumas from hardship endured during childhood. Relationships with loved ones have a deep karmic connotation. Position comparable to Pluto in Leo.

PLUTO in House VI

This position indicates a tendency to strong actions, reactions, and decisions to deal with professional responsibilities. The need to question and transform work conditions is a source of chronic tension. Health may be affected by infections, poisoning, or contamination. Position comparable to Pluto in Virgo.

PLUTO in House VII

This position strongly affects private partnerships and marriage. Pluto confers authenticity and determination to deal with important relations efficiently. It is also responsible for destructive tendencies. Relationship difficulties leave deep scars that may deter personal reconstruction indefinitely. Position comparable to Pluto in Libra.

PLUTO in House VIII

Pluto's influence is strong in this House and essentially linked to the regeneration principle. It confers willpower, determination, and physical endurance. There is a strong sex drive playing a major role in personal relationships. Finances may be a source of chronic disturbance. Position comparable to Pluto in Scorpio.

PLUTO in House IX

This position confers a strong need to contest and revoke the social, religious, educational, political, or legal system. Revolutionary philosophical values may lead to radical decisions with socially detrimental repercussions. Death may occur in a strange or foreign place. Position comparable to Pluto in Sagittarius.

PLUTO in House X

This position confers a "do-or-die" approach to important goals. When ambitions are too far-fetched, they create family disruptions. There is a tendency to question authority to the point of alienation. Determination and regeneration foster great realisation when applied sensibly. Position comparable to Pluto in Capricorn.

PLUTO in House XI

This position confers an overwhelming need to reform or transform the social environment. It enhances the ability to deal with others to change and regenerate their life in various ways and areas. Radicalised positions may become a source of disruption and separation from the conventional. Positions comparable to Pluto in Aquarius.

PLUTO in House XII

This position indicates a life path deeply scarred by unfortunate events that may have taken place as far back as the intrauterine period. It can produce an unrealistic tendency to feel threatened that may lead to paranoid reactions. However, karmic disruptions are a means for spiritual progression. Position comparable to Pluto in Pisces.

Lesson 12

The planets in the Houses

In the previous lesson we learned how the Houses took on different meanings and values according to the signs in which they were found. The importance of a House must always be related to its rulers. Therefore, the signs and Houses in which such rulers are found are essential elements to analyse a birth chart correctly.

The ruler/s of the sign/s in which a House falls must be primarily considered. Then the "natural" ruler/s can be considered, *but only if you think it necessary to improve the analysis.*

EXAMPLE:

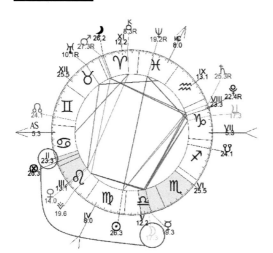

In a Chart we found House II in Cancer, meaning that the money earned is spent to provide for the home and family. Money spent to improve the quality of the home environment is earned working in the place of residence, or in a family business.

To understand the connection between the acquisition of material possessions and other areas of life, the position of the Moon (ruler of Cancer) must be considered.

In this chart we find the Moon, in Libra, in House V. See the explanation provided in the supplementary section called "The planets in the signs".

Once this is done, consider the Moon's influence in the Fifth House. See what it means from the explanation provided in supplementary section called "The planets in the Houses".

We know that House V is the area of creation (artistic) and procreation (children) it also represents the capacity to enjoy the good things of life, the quality of the relations with members of the opposite sex and the good fortune. Any planet positioned in this House enhances its initial influence. The more planets found in any House; the more important such a House becomes. Each planet must be analysed individually and according to other planets or elements around the chart.

In the example chart, we are considering now (the Moon in House V) we must bear in mind the prime quality of the planet (i.e. Feminine principle, sensitivity subconscious, public relations, etc.) and blend it with the signification of House V.

Thus, we can say that the Moon in House V confers an innate need to create and perhaps great artistic sensitivity. Good relationship with women in general, fertility and a genuine interest in children are also products of this Moon Position. However, because of the fluctuating quality of the Moon, the qualities derived from its position in the chart, are subject to intensity variations. New Moons and Full Moon's occurrences may affect or enhance these qualities.

Once we have done this, we must remember that the Moon is the ruler of House II, as seen earlier. Therefore, we may say that the ability to earn money may be influenced by art, creativity, and public or social expression of emotions and feelings.

Here is an example according to someone born with the Moon

in the Fifth House in Libra, ruler of the second House in Cancer.
"The native has strong artistic abilities and enjoys creation and a life of good relationship with women in general. If found in a lady's chart, the feminine and mother instinct is strongly developed. Money is made and spent in relation with the home, children, and family members."

To understand if such artistic talents are used as a hobby or to achieve personal ambitions, other Houses such as the MC (Mid-Heaven) and House VI must be taken into consideration.

Going back to the beginning of the analysis, when the chart had just been drawn, step by step, here is what you need to do.

STEP ONE: Determine Quadruplicities and Triplicities to get a general idea of the person you are about to analyse. (*)

STEP TWO: Examine the planets in the signs and take note of their influence on human nature in general.

STEP THREE: Examine the Ascendant and other Houses in the signs and take note of their general influence.

STEP FOUR: Examine the ruler of the Ascendant and other Houses in the signs and take note of their influence always relating such influence with the House concerned.

STEP FIVE: Examine the rulers of the Houses in relation with their House positions in the Chart.

STEP SIX: Analyse the Aspects (aspects are part of later lessons).

With the help of the supplementary sections included in this lesson, proceed with the analysis of your own Birth Chart from step one to step five. You should get a resembling self-portrait. However, it is an unfinished picture, with blending colours and almost perfect lines. What you will learn to do next is to consider your own qualities and faults according to *the Aspects.*

Before you learn about the aspects, analyse each House and its ruler/s individually, then in relation to the other Houses.

House I or Ascendant placed in a sign is ruled by the ruler/s of that sign. If a House is wide and covers 2 signs, the rulers of such signs become the rulers of such a House. If two Houses fall into the same sign. In the example chart presented on the first page of this lesson, House I and II are in Cancer. They are both ruled by the Moon. Across from the Ascendant, House VII and VIII are in Capricorn. They are both ruled by Saturn, ruler of this sign.

IMPORTANT NOTE

A House belongs to the sign in which it starts, NOT to the following sign. Many beginners tend to systematically associate two signs to each House. A House belongs to two signs, ONLY when the following sign in ENTIRELY included in that House (intercepted).

In this chart, you can see that Houses XII and VI begin in a sign and fully included the following one, ending at the beginning of the next one to which, however, it does not belong.

House XII belong to Taurus and Gemini.

House VI belong to Scorpio and Sagittarius.

The first charts are the most tedious ones to analyse because of the need to refer to the "book" repeatedly. To make it easier and more interesting, choose people you know best, such as your husband, wife, brother, sister, mother, or father. Knowing them will help you understand how astrology works. You will "verify" more than you "discover" but to verify is to learn and to learn is to progress. The more charts you cast, the quicker you will progress.

In the last lessons of this first section of the astrology course, I will show you how to cast your own chart "by hand". There are hundreds of computer programs and Internet websites to do this very accurately and quickly, but I feel that it is important to know and to learn how to do it the old-school way. Like I had to when I began my own study of astrology back in the early seventies.

The time of birth is essential to determine the Ascendant. "Sidereal time" is a time according to the rotation of the Earth around the Sun. The Exact Sidereal Time or E.S.T. (T.S.E. in French) is the result obtained from the addition of Earthly and Sidereal Times of Birth.

Right now, we will go ahead with the study of the **ASPECTS**, an essential chapter. Aspects are the backbone of any chart analysis. Without the aspects, the interpretation is worthless, empty.

THE RULERS OF MY HOUSES
In Signs and Houses

House	Sign	Ruler/s	In Sign/s	In House/s
I (ASC.)				
II				
III				
IV				
V				
VI				
VII				
VIII				
IX				
X (MC)				
XI				
XII				

Use a similar layout for other charts you will analyse

Supplementary section

THE RULERS OF THE HOUSES IN THE SIGNS

NOTE: If a House has more than one ruler because it includes the following sign, each ruler must be considered separately, then blended to obtain the proper meaning of the influence of such a House.

THE RULER OF HOUSE I (ASCENDANT) in:

ARIES: initiative, aggressiveness, ambition, and a sense for leadership. Competitive and assertive behaviour.

TAURUS: taste for material possessions, beautiful things, music, good food, money not for money's sake, more for what it can buy.

GEMINI: intelligent but fidgety nature with a need to communicate and a taste for reading and writing.

CANCER: family-oriented personality, the mother and the home environment are essential values.

LEO: artistic ability, creation is important, pride and egotism, fond of children. Paternalistic and protective.

VIRGO: sense of duty, good working capacity, precision and analysis, critical approach with a tendency to anxiety.

LIBRA: importance of partnership and marriage, friendliness, acting and artistic abilities, sense of justice.

SCORPIO: Deep thinker. Strong sexual needs. Attraction to the occult and the mysteries of life. Determination and endurance.

SAGITTARIUS: Intellectually active. Interest in higher

studies, religion and philosophy, or foreign countries and cultures.

CAPRICORN: Ambition, respect of hierarchy, studious, potential to long-term investments, reserved and old-school manners.

AQUARIUS: Importance of friendship and human relationships, original approach to life, interest in electronics, IT, media.

PISCES: Intuitive with a universal awareness of human nature, poetical, sensitive to music, easily influenced.

THE RULER OF HOUSE II in:

ARIES: Impulsiveness and aggressiveness in financial matters. Impulsive spending tendencies. Fast eater.

TAURUS: Importance of material possessions needs to be surrounded by beautiful and expensive things. Likes good food.

GEMINI: Money spent on books, travels, communication tools and equipment. Ability to quickly adapt to financial changes.

CANCER: Money is spent for comfort and security in the home. Financial stability depends on the quality of family relations.

LEO: The exhibitionist tendencies of the sign can create expensive tastes and much money spent on luxuries.

VIRGO: Financial matters and material life are a source of concern that generates a need to analyse and organise to preserve stability.

LIBRA: Money is shared with others or earned in worthwhile partnerships such as marriage. Art may be a source of income.

SCORPIO: Money is invested or earned in relation to an interest in the mysteries of life, magic, occultism, sex, astrology, or real estate.

SAGITTARIUS: Money spent or earned in education, travel, horse races, court cases, justice, or spiritually oriented activities.

CAPRICORN: Money is spent to realise long-term projects that may in turn become an important source of revenue.

AQUARIUS: Friends, social activities, social causes, and welfare programs, are ways of spending or earning money.

PISCES: Money may be spent or earned in spiritual activities, religion, art, music, holistic medicine, alcohol, or drugs.

THE RULER OF HOUSE III in:

ARIES: The intellect is argumentative and combative, creating difficulties and tensions in social and private relationships.

TAURUS: Intellect turned to materialistic rather than spiritual subjects. Taste for music, art, good food, objects to collect.

GEMINI: Versatile, intelligent, and somewhat unstable and superficial in thoughts and ideas. Strong need to communicate.

CANCER: Strong intellectual attachment to family and home environment. Values family origins and heredity.

LEO. The intellect is creative, artistic, in search of approbation with a tendency to a know-it-all paternalistic attitude.

VIRGO: Attachment to details may thwart objectivity. Conventional thinking with a tendency to polemics and criticising.

LIBRA: Harmony and balance feed the intellect and create a strong need to communicate and share thoughts and ideas.

SCORPIO: Strong interest in the mysteries of life and death, sexuality, finance, astrology, occultism, and scientific research.

SAGITTARIUS: Interest in higher education, foreign countries, and cultures, and long-distance travels, philosophy, and religion.

CAPRICORN: The past or older people influence the intellect and personal or social ambitions. Conservative and pragmatic.

AQUARIUS: Friendship and communication are major values. Interests in electronics, IT, the media, and social work.

PISCES: Interest in religion, spirituality, medicine, music, dance, and other sensitive means of communication. Good intuition.

THE RULER OF HOUSE IV in:

ARIES: Strong-headed mother or tensed family atmosphere. Sudden domestic incidents or conflicts between siblings.

TAURUS: Warm and comfortable home environment. The mother is possessive. Food and nature are major family values.

GEMINI: Many changes of residence or an anti-conformist family environment. Communication between siblings is a major asset.

CANCER: Importance of the mother and family ties. The home is an essential value to preserve. Residence near water.

LEO: Indicates an artistic and creative family atmosphere, and a need for a comfortable home environment to be proud of.

VIRGO: Health plays a prevailing role in the emergence of home and family duties motivated by a strong sense of responsibility.

LIBRA: Equity is a dominant value to share within the home and family environment. Harmony and balance are favoured.

SCORPIO: Mysterious situations and events may influence the development of an unusual family and home environment.

SAGITTARIUS: A strong need for a comfortable and successful home lifestyle motivates a positive approach to family duties.

CAPRICORN: Conventional and rational approach to family values and responsibilities. Hardship is seen a part of the process.

AQUARIUS: Original home environment and family relationships. Intellectual and friendly home atmosphere is needed.

PISCES: Religious beliefs, mysticism or superstition may create a lofty, but at times confused home environment.

THE RULER OF HOUSE V in:

ARIES: Creativity and feelings are expressed intensely and impulsively. Passionate and assertive approach to art and love.

TAURUS: Enhanced fertility favours areas were inspired creativity is a source of personal satisfaction, love, and social success.

GEMINI: Intellectual or mental creativity favours success in areas where communication, affability, and mobility are major assets.

CANCER: The home and family are propitious to the development and expression of creativity. Emotional and affectionate attitude.

LEO: Enhances creativity due to a need for approbation and love. Art, beauty, and pleasures are major existential values.

VIRGO: Creativity is expressed in a more intricate and detailed manner. Love life is subject to a tendency to analyse and worry.

LIBRA: Harmony and balance are the main sources of incentive to enhance creativity and the ability to express loving feelings.

SCORPIO: Sexuality inspires the creative potential. There is a tendency to be possessive and jealous in romantic relations.

SAGITTARIUS: The creative potential has a philosophical or spiritual connotation. Ardent feelings are generously expressed.

CAPRICORN: Creativity is expressed in a constructive, rational manner. Reserved and discreet with personal feelings and love.

AQUARIUS: Creativity, friendships and love tend to blend and become sources of enjoyment as well as romantic confusion.

PISCES: Inspired by spirituality and a sensitive approach to art and love, creativity is a source of inspiration and insightful realisations.

THE RULER OF HOUSE VI in:

ARIES: A sense of leadership favours success in areas where quick decision and risk taking is a must to get the job done.

TAURUS: Work in cooking, decoration, music, or agriculture is preferred. Health is subject to the quality and quantity of food intake.

GEMINI: Writing, travelling, or teaching are preferred choices for work. Health issues concern the nervous system and lungs.

CANCER: Work in a family business or from home, dealing with the public. The digestive system may cause health concerns.

LEO: Good leadership ability. Work may relate to art or beauty. Heart, blood pressure, and vision may cause health concerns.

VIRGO: Health and hygiene may motivate professional choices. A tendency to excessive worry contributes to erratic digestion.

LIBRA: A harmonious and friendly working environment is essential. Kidneys and lower back may cause health concerns.

SCORPIO: Work may involve research, investigation, occultism, or astrology. Colon and sexual organs cause health concerns.

SAGITTARIUS: Work may relate to sports, justice, travel, or higher education. Blood pressure may cause health concerns.

CAPRICORN: Stability and rationale favour durable work positions and realisations. Bones and joints may cause health concerns.

AQUARIUS: Work in a friendly social atmosphere is crucial to avoid sudden changes. Nerves and veins may cause health concerns.

PISCES: Work may involve chemistry, medicine, religion, or spirituality. Feet and hormones may cause health concerns.

THE RULER OF HOUSE VII in:

ARIES: Marriage may be hastily decided and become a source of tension, also possible in social or professional relationships.

TAURUS: Marriage is based on the appreciation of the good and beautiful things of life. Art, music, and nature are essential values.

GEMINI: To avoid boredom, a large array of intelligent exchanges is a must in private, social, and professional relationships alike.

CANCER: Family origins or members motivate the need for concrete realisation of most personal and social relationships.

LEO: Marriage and most relationships are sources of personal interest and social growth. Proud and demanding with partners.

VIRGO: Marriage may be linked to work, making it a potential professional partnership. Interests include health or hygiene.

LIBRA: Harmony and equity are essential values in marriage as well as in most other social and professional partnerships.

SCORPIO: Marriage and other important partnerships have a profound meaning to overcome human relationships difficulties.

SAGITTARIUS: Marriage and other close relationships have a philosophical meaning to favour optimism and positive evolution.

CAPRICORN: Marriage and other important relationships are considered as serious long-term investments and realisations.

AQUARIUS: Originality and sociability influence the choice of marriage partner and other types of important companionship.

PISCES: Marriage and other important partnerships may be linked to religious or spiritual beliefs and customs.

THE RULER OF HOUSE VIII in:

ARIES: Strong sexual drive with a need to dominate partners. Impulsive reactions produce violent conflicts and incidents.

TAURUS: Personal property, money, real estate, and inheritance may become a source of material realisation and social progress.

GEMINI: Financial adaptability is present with a more intellectual than rational approach to money and sex.

CANCER: Family inheritance and heredity may play a major role in the evolution of personal wealth and financial standing

LEO: Money is invested or spent in works of art or to improve social standing and personal appearance. Sexually creative.

VIRGO: Practicality, criticism and analysis improve managerial skills and interest in real estate, corporate money, or inheritance.

LIBRA: The need to preserve harmony and equity enhances the ability to collaborate in favour of financial evolution.

SCORPIO: Strong interest in sex and the mysteries of life. Death may play a role to improve personal finances through inheritance.

SAGITTARIUS: Death is seen as a need for spiritual evolution. Material realisation may be linked to foreign assets and activities.

CAPRICORN: Time, patience, financial logic, saving plans, careful spending, and pragmatism favour material effectiveness.

AQUARIUS: Unusual or unexpected circumstances may favour material growth. Carefree tendencies may alter financial stability.

PISCES: Intuition is useful to improve finances by blending spirituality and money with a non-materialistic ingenuity.

THE RULER OF HOUSE IX in:

ARIES: The leadership quality of the sign is applied to thought patterns and principles. Life is seen as a philosophical battle.

TAURUS: A down-to-earth philosophical approach to life allows for more rational applications and physical satisfactions.

GEMINI: The intellect is bright and versatile. Interest in foreign countries, languages, and cultures. Ability to teach and converse.

CANCER: The philosophical approach to life's circumstances and situations is deeply related to family and home environment.

LEO: A philosophical approach to art, love and creativity improves the potential and skill to succeed socially and morally.

VIRGO: The ability to scrutinise, observe, and analyse enhances objective thinking within the limits of philosophical boundaries.

LIBRA: Personal expression and morality are associated with spirituality and a deep interest in politics and higher education.

SCORPIO: Mystery, occultism, sex, and death may motivate personal philosophy in a profound and melancholic manner.

SAGITTARIUS: Traditions, religion, education, or foreign influences motivate spiritual growth and personal realisation.

CAPRICORN: A conservative and pragmatic appreciation of life produces an efficient philosophical approach to self-realisation.

AQUARIUS: A free-spirited philosophy of life confers an innate ability to adapt and a genuine interest in human behaviour.

PISCES: Religion and mysticism inspire a lofty philosophical approach to earthly life. Intuitive connection with the soul.

THE RULER OF HOUSE X (MC) in:

ARIES: Personal goals and career are motivated by a need for active physical situations where authority, strength, speed, and quick reflexes are essential assets to succeed.

TAURUS: Personal goals and career are influenced by food, art, nature, aesthetics, and other areas where the good and beautiful things of life are the main ingredients to succeed.

GEMINI: Education and culture influence personal ambitions and career. Teaching, travelling, writing and areas where the ability to communicate and quickly adapt are preferred choices to succeed.

CANCER: Family and home environment may be a source of motivation and career orientation with strong emotional concern for the region or country which may lead to political ambitions.

LEO: Personal ambitions are motivated by a need for social consideration and high-level realisation. Creativity is an important factor of success. Good leadership potential.

VIRGO: Personal ambitions and success can be achieved in areas where skill, precision, and attention to details are essential. Careers in business, medicine and science are also possible.

LIBRA: Personal ambitions are inspired by an interest in acting, diplomacy, sharing, justice, and harmony. Architecture, music, politics, comedy, public speaking, are possible choices.

SCORPIO: Career orientation is influenced by an interest in areas where the occult, death, sex, research, and profound understanding of human nature are essential assets to succeed.

SAGITTARIUS: Wealth, spirituality and traditions influence and motivate personal ambitions. Foreign countries, teaching, politics, or religion may participate in successful career choices.

CAPRICORN: Professional goals and personal ambitions are far-fetched. Time, authority, determination, perseverance, and patience condition important projects and career achievements.

AQUARIUS: Original, unusual, and socially oriented career choices. Electronics, IT, communication, media, politics, theatre, and astrology are some of the areas of potential success.

PISCES: Religion and spirituality motivate personal ambitions in areas where intuition, psychology, alternative medicine, ecology, biology, the sea, the air, or the soul is associated.

THE RULER OF HOUSE XI in:

ARIES: There is a need for an active social environment. Sports and other physical activities promote meaningful relations.

TAURUS: Friendship has a strong affective connotation. Art, beauty, and good food are some of the pleasures to share.

GEMINI: Socialising succeeds when it allows sharing thoughts, ideas, or concepts in a spontaneous and dynamic manner.

CANCER: Personal emotions have a strong influence on choice of friends and on behaviour within the social environment.

LEO: Luxury, beauty and wealth share their influence on the evolution of social life, friendship, and role in the community.

VIRGO: Indicates a tendency to be hard to please in friendship and social life with a responsible approach to social interaction.

LIBRA: Friendship and social interactions are based on harmony, balance, and justice, with diplomacy and fair play

SCORPIO: Meaningful friendships and social life are based on the mysteries of life and death, sex, occultism, or hardship.

SAGITTARIUS: Foreign friendship and intellectual social interactions motivate an altruistic approach of human relations.

CAPRICORN: A conservative and stable attitude in friendship and social life favours long-term relationships with wise people.

AQUARIUS: Friendship is a source of renewed inspiration that motivates original and philanthropic social interactions.

PISCES: Spiritual friendships are preferred to more ordinary earthly relations. Social life is inspired by lofty motivations.

THE RULER OF HOUSE XII in:

ARIES: An innate tendency to violent fits of anger is linked to an unconscious karmic memory of brutality and aggression.

TAURUS: An innate taste for the good and beautiful things may be linked to unconscious karmic artistic gifts and situations.

GEMINI: There is an innate need to communicate, move, learn, and be mentally active as if life were too short to waste time.

CANCER: Family and place of residence are important values emanating from an unconscious need to deal with karmic debts.

LEO: Aristocratic and artistic innate tendencies may come from a past life when creativity and status allowed many privileges.

VIRGO: Work and duty, health and hygiene are major values stemming from unconscious links with a laborious past life.

LIBRA: Justice and fair play are essential values that contribute to a spontaneous diplomatic approach to human interactions.

SCORPIO: Sex and supernatural phenomena are a source of renewed interest in the search for a deeper meaning of life and death.

SAGITTARIUS: Learning and teaching, foreign countries, and cultures, are essential to fulfil a major social karmic mission.

CAPRICORN: The notions of respect of authority, hard work and duty come from a karmic need to be strict and disciplined.

AQUARIUS: Social life and friendship are important to come to terms with a karmic need to transform and reform society.

PISCES: A spiritual approach to the realities of life is linked to karmic reminiscences of a religiously complicated existence.

SUPPLEMENTARY SECTION

The rulers of the Houses in the Houses

The position of the RULER OF A HOUSE in another HOUSE determines the areas of life interacting in various ways according to the ASPECTS conferred to such ruler by other elements in the chart.

If the RULER OF A HOUSE is found in "its own house", the areas represented are enhanced and the ASPECTS, if any, determine how the areas concerned are affected.

THE RULER OF HOUSE I or ASCENDANT IN:

HOUSE I: gives a stronger, more determined, and authentic personality in relation with the sign in which it is found, and the aspects formed with other planets.

HOUSE II: it seems that money and the material aspects of life are strongly influenced by the way the inner personality and personal behaviour are expressed and exercised.

HOUSE III: mentally versatile, the intellect has a definite ability to express itself in many ways. Brotherhood is an important aspect of the development and expression of personality.

HOUSE IV: family and home environment are a major source of motivation with a strong influence on the development of personality. The influence of the mother is dominant.

HOUSE V: creativity, art, children, joy, love, and romance are prime interests. There is a strong need for approbation that can greatly influence the development of personality.

HOUSE VI: work, duty, service, and a routine lifestyle may alienate from excitement and adventure. The preferred approach is a well-planned organisation to avoid any surprise.

HOUSE VII: marriage and other associations are most important to ensure personal wellbeing. Companionship is a must to favour success and long-term comfort and care.

HOUSE VIII: the affairs of the dead, material or spiritual, are of prime concern and interest to the point of depending on them for emotional or financial balance and wellbeing.

HOUSE IX: A genuine interest in foreign countries and cultures favours the development of a broader philosophical approach and understanding of human nature.

HOUSE X: ambition can lead to success or failure. The potential to achieve prominence should be backed by authenticity and sincerity. Strong influence of the father.

HOUSE XI: friends and social life are important to favour self-expression and personal achievement. Preconceived values may alter authenticity and personal sincerity.

HOUSE XII: There is a strong interest and tie with the past. A tendency to withdraw is linked to an intense but sometimes confusing spiritual search. Spontaneous ability to astral travel, to ESP and intense oneiric activity are also indicated.

THE RULER OF HOUSE II IN:

HOUSE I: material conditions and financial life have a strong influence on the development of personal expression and inner needs for the food of life.

HOUSE II: accentuates the importance of material possessions to favour personal wellbeing. Creativity, art, or food may be a source of financial success or spending.

HOUSE III: money and the materialistic side of life play an important part on education and the development of communication. Money is spent to travel and for studies.

HOUSE IV: money is spent to care after the home or family members. Work from home or in a family business is possible.

HOUSE V: money is spent to care for loved ones and for the pleasures of life. Gambling or earning money through art or activities involving children are possible.

HOUSE VI: much money may be spent for medical reasons. Working in the food industry, the arts or with children are often remarked with this position.

HOUSE VII: money may be spent to look after and preserve wellbeing in various types of associations and partnerships even if the cost surpasses the outcome of the expenses.

HOUSE VIII: money is meant to be invested wisely. Work involving money (bank, finance companies) is one of the potential areas for professional success.

HOUSE IX: money is spent to travel, to study, and to discover with a philosophical approach to material values. Charity work and community welfare activities are sources of interest.

HOUSE X: money is usually spent to pursue personal ambitions and projects. Success depends on the degree of objectivity and organisation revealed by the sign and planet concerned.

HOUSE XI: money is spent on friends and on social activities. Personal acquaintances and relationships often play a major part in the development of material life.

HOUSE XII: money may be acquired or spent in an unusual or secret manner. The spiritual approach to material life may motivate donations to religious or sectarian organisations.

THE RULER OF HOUSE III IN:

HOUSE I: education plays a crucial part in the development of personality. A brother or sister may have a strong influence on intellectual orientation and interests.

HOUSE II: education is responsible for the way money and the material aspect of life are perceived and care for. A brother or sister may influence the development of personal wealth.

HOUSE III: enhances the need to learn to favour intellectual development and communication ability. Interests in travelling, writing, reading, and human interactions are frequent.

HOUSE IV: education, brotherhood, and communication play an important part in home life. The home may become a place for various intellectual activities.

HOUSE V: education plays an important part in the romantic side of life. Communication with children and the younger generation is important. Interests in gambling or gaming.

HOUSE VI: education has a major influence on the ability and motivation to work. Psychosomatic illnesses or hypochondriac tendencies are sometimes indicated.

HOUSE VII: communication is important in all kinds of partnerships. Education is sometimes responsible for the choice of the partner. A brother or sister may play a part in it too.

HOUSE VIII: the mind and intellectual interests are motivated by sex, death, money, and occultism. Indicates innate abilities in astrology and other occult sciences and subjects.

HOUSE IX: indicates an innate interest in travels, foreign countries, and cultures, with a philosophical approach to life. There is a strong inner need for equity and righteousness.

HOUSE X: education may be a prime interest, leading to a teaching career. Communication and travels are some of the best avenues of social and professional success.

HOUSE XI: shows a rather friendly approach to social relations. Communication is a source of motivation and enjoyment. The intellect is active when it comes to human interaction.

HOUSE XII: the past and the mystical side of life are a source of profound interest that motivates intellectual and educational activities. There is a taste for meditation and spirituality.

THE RULER OF HOUSE IV IN:

HOUSE I: family life and home environment have played an important part in personal development and self-expression. Strong influence of the mother, family background or heredity.

HOUSE II: family life often plays an important part to favour or deter the potential to succeed financially. The mother or mother figure dominates. Work in a family business is often remarked.

HOUSE III: the mother has or had a strong influence on the intellectual and cultural development. Family ties and history are a source of interest. At home, communication is a must.

HOUSE IV: enhances family ties as well as the importance of the mother and of family roots. There is a need for a secure and comfortable home environment. Accrued patriotic tendencies.

HOUSE V: childhood is deeply marked by family life and the presence (or absence) and influence of the mother. In a feminine chart, it accentuates the mother instinct.

HOUSE VI: shows the influence of family life and home environment on the choice of a profession. It may also indicate physical or physiological hereditary resemblance.

HOUSE VII: shows the influence of the mother and family background on the choice of partners for marriage and other important social or professional relationships.

HOUSE VIII: inheritance may play an important part on the level of financial development and realisation. Death or unclear and uneasy circumstances may affect family history.

HOUSE IX: family background strongly influences the potential to intellectual development and social behaviour pattern. Settling overseas or far from the place of birth is also possible.

HOUSE X: family background is often largely responsible for social success and status. Projects and personal ambitions are subject to the influence of the close environment.

HOUSE XI: family background and status influence the choice of friends and social surroundings. It sometimes shows that the mother is considered as a friend more than a parent.

HOUSE XII: family background and origin are a source of motivation for spiritual development and interest in family history. Karmic family situations and events are indicated.

THE RULER OF HOUSE V IN:

HOUSE I: shows a romantic personality, fond of children, playful and interested in gambling. This position also enhances artistic tendencies and natural talents. Creativity is increased.

HOUSE II: luck may play a major role in the evolution of financial status. Children and romance are a source of motivation for material success or failure, depending on the rest of the chart.

HOUSE III: this position is often found in the charts of teachers or educators. The intellect is strongly influenced by romantic life and by personal desires for pleasures and good times.

HOUSE IV: often shows a family life surrounded with children who play an important part in the home environment. The home may become a place for artistic or gaming activities.

HOUSE V: enhances talent and creativity. It is often found in the charts of artists or gamblers. Indicates strong romantic needs and creativity. Children are a source of motivation.

HOUSE VI: romantic activity extends to professional life. Love partners may be met at work. Creativity and natural talents enhance the potential for professional success.

HOUSE VII: marriage is a love affair, not a business deal. Artistic traits are valuable assets to define the choice of the ideal partner. Children are an essential part of marriage.

HOUSE VIII: creativity is influenced or motivated by the interest in the mysteries of life and death. There is a reference or natural penchant for morbid forms of sexual expression.

HOUSE IX: this position is often found in the charts of teachers and educators. Art and intellectual interests in foreign countries and cultures are a source of renewed motivation.

HOUSE X: indicates art-oriented careers and social objectives. Projects involving children, teaching, or gambling. Love is a dominant source of inspiration and motivation to succeed.

HOUSE XI: friendship is essential to enhance the quality of social life. Love and affection enhance popularity among friends and acquaintances in a creative and pleasant way.

HOUSE XII: shows a tendency to secret romantic relationships as well as to unusual love habits. Childhood may be marked by mystery and confusion. Karmic sentimental relationships.

THE RULER OF HOUSE VI IN:

HOUSE I: the state of health, hygiene, an interest in medicine together with a strong sense of responsibility favour the development of a meticulous but anxious personality.

HOUSE II: medicine may be the main source of earnings. Finances are subject to meticulous organisation. Feeding habits and tastes are considered essential to good health.

HOUSE III: the intellectual development and education are strongly influenced by the idea of work, service, and a strong sense of responsibility. May indicate an interest in medicine.

HOUSE IV: work may involve the family or the place of residence. This position indicates the effect of health in family life. Hereditary pathological tendencies are likely.

HOUSE V: work may involve children or art. Romance and work may cohabit. This position also indicates the impact of daily burdens on the ability to realise artistic or personal objectives.

HOUSE VI: enhances the sense of duty and responsibility with an interest in health or medicine to promote career choice. Possible success working with domestic pets or other animals.

HOUSE VII: work is best done in partnership. The native needs others to express his abilities and sense of responsibility. This position sometimes indicates poor health of the native's partner.

HOUSE VIII: indicates a professional life path in areas such as scientific research, police investigation, occult sciences, sex, finance (trader) or death. Favourable to qualified astrologers.

HOUSE IX: work may involve teaching, travelling, social matters or philosophy. Lawyers, secondary teachers, priests, therapists, and travel agents are favoured by this position in their chart.

HOUSE X: work in health or medical areas is often indicated. Easy success is not favoured due to a tendency to worry and to take on difficult tasks that tend to deter the realisation process.

HOUSE XI: work is best done in a friendly atmosphere and with much human interaction. It often leads to professional interests in social causes, community work, politics, or entertainment.

HOUSE XII: work is often linked to medicine and natural therapies. Some difficulties are indicated to find the perfect job due to health disorders or uncertainty about the best path to follow.

THE RULER OF HOUSE VII IN:

HOUSE I: the expression of the inner personality is strongly influenced by close relationships. There may be a dependency on others to collaborate efficiently rather than succeed alone.

HOUSE II: relationships play an important part on the financial and overall material plans. Marriage and other important personal or social partnerships have a materialistic connotation.

HOUSE III: partnerships are a source of motivation to communicate and progress on the intellectual level. Without mental interaction, collaboration is neither fruitful nor useful.

HOUSE IV: the partner plays an important part in the home and often has a predominant influence on various choices made about various family projects and the place of residence.

HOUSE V: shows the importance of the partner's childhood in personal relationships. Art may also be a major aspect of social and private interactions. Sharing the joys of life is essential.

HOUSE VI: working in partnership seems essential and a source of inspiration. The importance of the other person affects and motivates common professional or personal pursuits.

HOUSE VII: enhances the need for partnership and influence of the other person on the development of personal or professional life. There is a profound need for fusion in common interaction.

HOUSE VIII: the influence of the other person is a source of motivation to pursue financial growth or to share interests for the mysteries of life and death, and sexual practices.

HOUSE IX: there may be a link between personal relationship and a foreign country. Strong spiritual influence of the partner usually contributes to spiritual or philosophical development.

HOUSE X: partnerships play a major role in the development of personal ambitions, career, and other social objectives. The partner's influence may tend to control most interactions.

HOUSE XI: the partner is considered more a friend than a lover. The influence of the other person determines the development and organisation of the social environment and activities.

HOUSE XII: secret partnerships may be indicated together with a strong karmic bond with partners, both personal and social or professional. The past plays a subtle part in such relations.

THE RULER OF HOUSE VIII IN:

HOUSE I: death seems to have played an important part on the development and expression of the inner personality. Position showing strong sexual needs and a deep interest in occultism.

HOUSE II: strong position for matters pertaining to finance and related subjects. There is an innate interest in money and a feel for wise investments. Inheritance is a factor of enrichment.

HOUSE III: the idea of death, the mysteries of life, sex and money are important factors in the development of the intellect and communication. Position often found in astrologers' charts.

HOUSE IV: shows the importance of family inheritances on personal enrichment. There is an innate interest in real estate and other types of unprofitable investments.

HOUSE V: enhances the sexual drive and the attraction to gambling. Childhood may be marked by unfortunate events, such as death, symbolic or real, with strong affective outcome.

HOUSE VI: work may involve matters relating to money (the bank), death (undertaking) or sex (nightclub, sex shop, etc.). Occult sciences and astrology are potential choices too.

HOUSE VII: shows that inheritance may come from the partner or from a favourable marriage. Sex and money are major aspects to determine success or failure of the relationship.

HOUSE VIII: enhances the sexual drive and the interest in subjects pertaining to the mysteries of life, death, and money. Position found in the charts of occultists and astrologers.

HOUSE IX: death is viewed as a spiritual means of evolution. It may occur in a foreign country or far from the place of birth. Money, legality, and morality are important ethical subjects.

HOUSE X: a profession dealing with death, sex, money, or occultism is often observed. This position can indicate a strong influence of the father or father figure on the choice of a career.

HOUSE XI: friends may become sexual partners. Sex, money and occultism motivate human and social interaction. There is a strong need to question and transform society.

HOUSE XII: karmic position showing great dispositions for matters such as death, occultism, mysticism, and similar topics. Unusual sexual practices are sometimes also indicated.

THE RULER OF HOUSE IX IN:

HOUSE I: indicates a strong educational background, the influence of a foreign country and a genuine interest in spirituality, the law, social activities, and long distant travels.

HOUSE II: there is a link between money and social regulations. Involvement in charity organisation is often remarked. Money is spent for education, studies, travels, or to maintain social status.

HOUSE III: this position enhances intellectual development and the attraction to a high-level of education. Teaching, learning, long-distance travels are renewed sources of interest.

HOUSE IV: shows a rather good social background or indicates that the family (particularly the mother) is issued from a foreign country or from an upper-class, bourgeois, or noble descent.

HOUSE V: romantic partners may be met in or originate from a foreign country. It sometimes indicates an interest in the social cause of children, and involvement in charitable organisations.

HOUSE VI: work may involve legal matters, foreign countries, secondary teaching, spiritual matters and long-distant travels. Health may also be an important source of learning motivation.

HOUSE VII: marriage may be contracted in a foreign country or with a foreign partner. Relations are built on spiritual, social, and ethical values. Sharing is a major source of positive motivation.

HOUSE VIII: money may be earned in or from a foreign country. There may be an interest in earning and teaching spiritual and occult subjects. Sexuality and morality need to be closely linked.

HOUSE IX: intensifies the role of this House in the chart. The influence of a foreign country and education on the intellectual and philosophical development is strong and often essential.

HOUSE X: career and professional achievement depend on education, studies, and social equity. Politics, teaching, foreign travels, and charity work are potential areas of success.

HOUSE XI: friends may come from foreign countries or cultures. Interests for social matters, social and humanitarian activities are often a strong source of motivation and realisation.

HOUSE XII: difficulties to integrate the system and comply with laws and regulations may prove disruptive and a source of disappointment. Past events are responsible for such confusion.

THE RULER OF HOUSE X IN:

HOUSE I: the influence of the father or father figure is a source of motivation or conflict, depending on the rest of the chart. Personal ambition and a strong drive feed the need to succeed.

HOUSE II: there is a strong need for financial realisation. The influence of the father or father figure motivates the growth of materialistic interests. Work may involve money or food.

HOUSE III: strong influence of the father or father figure on the intellectual development. Communication may be a major asset to professional success. Work in education, teaching, or short travel.

HOUSE IV: strong influence of the father or father figure on the development of family life. Work may involve family members or the place of residence. Mother and father roles may be inverted.

HOUSE V: strong influence of the father or father figure during childhood. Creativity, art, children, games, gambling, and personal affectivity may contribute to professional success or failure.

HOUSE VI: strong influence of the father or father figure on the energy and motivation to work and to carry out daily duties. Professional interests in medicine or domestic animals.

HOUSE VII: strong influence of the father or father figure on the choice of personal or professional partners. Success is favoured by harmonious partnerships rather than individual involvement.

HOUSE VIII: can indicate the father's premature death and its consequences on the evolution of behaviour. Interest in the occult, astrology, and finance can be paths to professional success.

HOUSE IX: strong influence of the father's background on education. Potential career success in politics, justice, government, philosophy, religion, teaching, or travels.

HOUSE X: enhances the natural drive to succeed. Ambitions, however, are influenced by the father or father figure and may be essentially led by his style of education and aspirations.

HOUSE XI: the father may be considered like a friend more than a parent. Social work is a valuable option. The need to feel useful to others leads to community involvement.

HOUSE XII: the father or father figure is linked to major experiences of karmic connotations. Spirituality, medicine, and humanitarian work are potential successful career options.

THE RULER OF HOUSE XI IN:

HOUSE I: friendship motivates interests in group activities that promise personal wellbeing. However, success or failure depends on the quality of social relationships and interactions.

HOUSE II: friendship influence the development of finance and materialistic realisations. Money borrowed, lent, or spent for community welfare programs or activities is also indicated.

HOUSE III: friendship and the quality of the social environment influence the intellectual development. The mind is turned to others with an innate sense for communication and portage.

HOUSE IV: friends are considered like members of the family. Friendship influences the evolution of home life, making the residence a place to convey, entertain, and socialise.

HOUSE V: friends are warmly considered. There is a tendency to friend-lover relationships. Friends may be a source of inspiration or detriment depending on the rest of the chart.

HOUSE VI: friends and social surroundings influence the choice of a profession There is a need to be useful to others and a desire to satisfy co-workers by positively carrying out daily duties.

HOUSE VII: partnerships depend on social relations and friends. Depending on the rest of the chart, the influence of others can improve or deter the ability to share and collaborate.

HOUSE VIII: finances depend on the influence of the social surroundings to evolve. Friendship is a source of positive motivation to engage in major experiences and projects.

HOUSE IX: involvement in community welfare, social work, justice, foreign countries, and cultures are indicated. Friendship is an important factor of spiritual and philosophical evolution.

HOUSE X: strong influence of social surroundings and friends on the motivation and ability to succeed. Career opportunities in welfare, IT, communication, the media, or entertainment.

HOUSE XI: enhances the importance of friendship and the influence of social status on the evolution of personality as a member of the community. Strong need to be useful to others.

HOUSE XII: hidden or unusual friendships are indicated. Karmic friendships may become a real burden. Disappointment to realise that best friends one day can become worst enemies.

THE RULER OF HOUSE XII IN:

HOUSE I: the past plays a major role in the development of the inner personality. Events and situation of karmic nature are indicated. There is a need to follow a spiritual path of evolution.

HOUSE II: money, food and the material/physical meaning of life, are closely linked to karma. The past is a source of information that may be useful to deal with existential confusion.

HOUSE III: strong karmic links with a brother or a sister is indicated. There is a fascination for mysteries coupled with good investigating abilities. Interest in psychology and research.

HOUSE IV: Karmic ties with the mother and family origin is strong and a source of questioning and confusion. Problems about or because of the mother. Search for the ideal place of residence.

HOUSE V: karmic romantic relationships motivate unconscious needs and the search for answers to confusing questions. Creativity and lofty artistic expression are indicated.

HOUSE VI: innate karmic taste or distaste for medicine. Difficulties or confusion to find the ideal profession is frequent. Early years of life may have been marked by disturbing events.

HOUSE VII: karmic links with the partner. Difficulties in partnerships have a strong spiritual connotation. The past deeply influences the development of personal relationships.

HOUSE VIII: there is a karmic need to search for answers about the mysteries of life and death. Finances may be a source of chronic setbacks. Sexuality is strong but often repressed.

HOUSE IX: a karmic tie may exist with a foreign country. Difficulties to accept laws and rules. Moral, ethical, or spiritual confusion may have disturbing effects on the ability to succeed.

HOUSE X: karmic ties with the father or father figure. Work involving medicine, spirituality or welfare is favoured. The past plays a major part in career and social or personal realisations.

HOUSE XI: friends may become enemies. Confusion may overshadow important friendships. Karmic ties are indicated. Involvement in community welfare, charity, or spiritual groups.

HOUSE XII: this position enhances intuition and the interest in philosophy and spirituality. Life may be a karmic burden, but difficulties do not deter the desire to progress in all situations.

LESSON 13

THE ASPECTS
(Part one)

In previous lessons you learned that an aspect is the accumulation and concentration of the influences of two or more planets or other elements around a chart. An aspect can be harmonious (beneficial) or discordant (difficult).

A beneficial aspect is a link- between two or more planets harmoniously sharing and blending their individual influence. A difficult aspect creates tension because the influence of each planet concerned antagonises the other.

The study of the aspects by astrologers goes back to the Egyptians, Chaldeans, etc. That is to say that more than five thousand years ago it was already understood that the influence of a planet is not enough to motivate and explain human reactions. The basic positive influence of any planet in a sign (such as Jupiter in Sagittarius for example) can be altered by the presence of another planet, positioned in such manner that its influence will affect and afflict the positive influence of Jupiter in Sagittarius.

Some of you may have already noticed, when analysing their birth chart that the positions of the planets in the signs did not fit what they know of their own personality. Here is an example: "someone was born with the Moon in Gemini. He should be outgoing, quick-witted, talkative, socialising, fond of travelling, writing, reading, etc. **This is so if NO OTHER PLANET distorts or alters the influence of the Moon in that sign**. If Saturn is in Sagittarius, opposite the Moon, this will restrict the influence of the luminary. So much that the individual may show opposite tendencies to that of the Moon in Gemini, appearing shy, secretive, pessimistic, melancholy, sedentary, etc. Deep inside, however, the urge of behaving according to the unaffected position of the Moon in Gemini will be present and may occasionally show up, according to certain transits of important planets around the birth chart[11].

When analysing a birth chart, the aspects must be very seriously taken into consideration. They are the key to the analysis which would be vague, superficial, and wrong without them.

Imagine the influence of a planet like a magnet and its magnetic field. The closer you bring it to a piece of metal, the stronger the attraction becomes. The same applies to the position of a planet in its sign of rulership. Does this mean that the more planets are found in signs of rulership, the stronger the personality of the individual becomes? Not necessarily so. Why?

Because the influence of a planet in its sign of rulership may come in conflict with another planet with an influence just as strong as the first one. This may produce excessive traits in various areas of life in discordance with one another. For example, the Moon in Cancer opposite Saturn in Capricorn is an aspect involving two elements in signs of rulership. An opposition creates an alternance between tendencies that are in contact confrontation until "the middle way" is found to make the best out of both energies.

The opposition is an interesting aspect. The planets do not have to be in their sign of rulership to create tension or

---

[11] A TRANSIT is the constant revolution of a planet around the zodiac, in aspect with the positions of the planets around the birth chart. The TRANSITS are used to make astrological forecasts.

retention. However, the opposition (when it is a "true aspect") concerns complementary signs. Fire/Air, Earth/Water and vice versa. The same relationship applies in sextile aspects (60°) which are said to be beneficial or harmonious. Hence, the opposition may be considered as potentially beneficial once both "parties" come to some sort of tacit agreement. This can be compared to a government with the ruling party and the opposition. Both are necessary to ensure democratic rulership, rather than dictatorship... Nevertheless, although useful, the coordination between the ruling party and the opposition is never a sinecure! Therefore, the opposition aspect remains a source of tension or retention until a compromise is found to bring both planetary influences to the "table of negotiations" ...

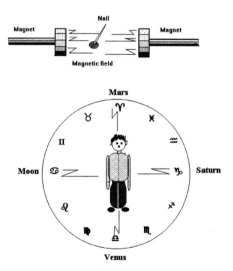

The first rule to remember before we begin the study of the aspects, is that the positions of the planets in the signs and in tho houses are NOT ENOUGH to comprehensively analyse a birth chart. Due to the aspects, any one of the elements concerned may receive a biased, distorted, or supportive influence from other elements.

The aspects are traditionally known as **beneficial** and **difficult**, and as **major** and **minor**.

I prefer the terms: **"harmonious"** and **"discordant".**

The **major aspects** seem to have the strongest and more obvious influence.

The **minor aspects** are those showing a more subtle influence.

There are five (5) MAJOR ASPECTS

1 - THE CONJUNCTION	00
2 - THE SEXTILE	60°
3 - THE SQUARE	90°
4- THE TRINE	120°
5 - THE INCONJUNCT	150°
5 - THE OPPOSITION	180°

There are two commonly used MINOR ASPECTS

1 - THE HALF-SEXTILE	30°
2 - THE HALF-SQUARE	45°

There are many other minor aspects. They are commonly used by "humanist astrologers". In this course, we will mainly work with the major aspects.

To understand what an aspect is, you must refer to the zodiac circle as being 360°, like all circles.

In geometry an angle is determined by two straight lines starting from the centre of a circle and progressively separating as they leave their starting point. The angle is NOT the distance in inches or centimetres from one point to another around the circle, but he evaluation in degrees when compared to the complete circle of 360°.

Since a circle corresponds to 360°, each 360th part of it is called "one degree" (1°). Each degree is then (like the hour in minutes) dividable into 60 parts, each one of it being called "minute" (1').

Furthermore, one minute is dividable into 60 parts, each one of which is called "one second" (1"). Then, of course, each second can be divided into tenth of seconds, hundreds of seconds, etc.

In the present section of this astrology course, you only have to worry about degrees and minutes to determine the positions of the planets in a chart. In the last lessons (13 to 16) you will learn how to do this, using the "ephemeris", your date of birth, and your time of birth.

Memorise this:

An aspect is an angle separating two or more planets or elements around the chart. Such angle is calculated by subtracting the position of one planet from the other.

Example: Venus is at 10° in Virgo and Mercury at 28° in Virgo. The angle separating these planets is: **28° - 18° = 18°**

The angle separating two or more elements around a chart is not necessarily an aspect. The angle is called an aspect and analysed as such when the number of degrees between them reaches that of an aspect, according to the accepted figures.

The CONJUNCTION is an easy aspect to recognise. The elements concerned are standing at the **"same degree"** or **"so close together"** that their respective magnetic fields are said to blend or to conjunct.

The Orb

You have just read that a conjunction is determined when two or more elements are standing at the "same degree" in a sign, or "***very close***" to one another. This "***very close***" is known to be the "***orb***". A "true conjunction" would imply that the planets involved stand at precisely the same degree in a sign. But it happens very rarely.

Instead, you will often find in your future analyses that many elements stand "***very close***" to one another but not necessarily "***on top***" of one another.

When the Sun and the Moon are concerned, this "very close" notion (the orb) applies until both Sun and Moon are ten degrees (10°) apart. For all other planets, an orb of 5° to 7° applies when they are in conjunction between themselves and up to 10° when they conjunct the Sun or the Moon.

Here are some examples...

Sun at 12° in Virgo - Moon at 22° in Virgo	10°
Jupiter at 9° in Libra - Uranus at 14° in Libra	5°
Mars at 22° in Cancer - Sun at 29° in Cancer	7°

These angles may be called "**conjunctions**", but their level of influence depends on the **orb**. In the examples above, the conjunction Jupiter-Uranus is stronger than the conjunction Sun-Moon or Sun-Mars because the orb is wider in the case of the Sun-Moon conjunction.

However, the width of an aspect is left to the astrologer's good judgment. Daily practice allows to gradually be more flexible about the orbs, widening some and narrowing others. There are many reasons for that. Some will be discussed in this course, others you will decide yourself as you progress and become accustomed to the treatment of the aspects.

Quite often, because of the orb applied, a conjunction involves two signs. This occurs when the elements concerned stand within the last degrees of a sign and within the first degrees of the following one. This is called a "**hidden aspect**". Some call it a "*false aspect*".

Any aspect can be a hidden aspect.

In that case, the influence is different. Here is how…

The term **hidden** is not coincidental. It means that whatever is hidden is not seen, or at least, not fully seen. An aspect represents a potentially harmonious or discordant influence with important repercussions at various levels and in various areas of life. A hidden aspect runs the risk of not being fully recognised or accepted as such.

HOW TO RECOGNISE ASPECTS IN A CHART

The beginner is struggling to recognise aspects in a chart. I remember that my first steps were particularly difficult and rather boring... Now, of course, it doesn't take me long to sum up a complete chart, but I must say that unless you take your time (or use a computer program...) to do it carefully from the start, there is no better way to get accustomed to "seeing" the aspects than personal practice.

THE CONJUNCTION

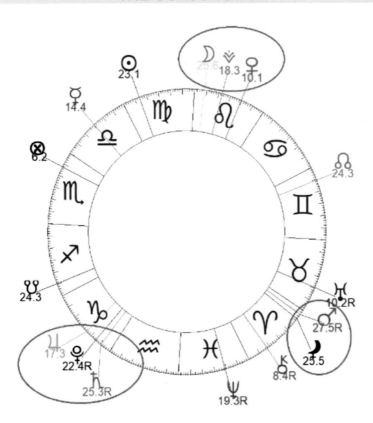

The conjunction is simple to recognise because it is easy to spot two or more elements close to one another somewhere around the chart. See the conjunctions in the chart on the left.

The conjunction is usually considered **harmonious** because the influences of the planets involved tend to blend and complement one another.

In some cases, however, the influence of a conjunction is not so harmonious, it can even become **discordant**. This is so when planets like Mars, Saturn, Uranus, and Pluto are involved, either between themselves or with other elements in the chart.

Mars creates tension; Saturn produces restriction; Uranus increases nervousness; Pluto renders quite radical or destructive.

However, this is not an absolute rule. There are modulations. Do not be too rigid to analyse conjunctions involving these four planets. In fact, all conjunctions may become a source of excess. You will gradually learn to differentiate "problem conjunctions" from "beneficial conjunctions".

THE SEXTILE

The sextile is an angle of around 60°. It involves two or more elements separated by one full sign around the chart. *

Example: Venus at 14° in Capricorn and Mars at 14° in Pisces.

16° to reach 30° from 14° in Capricorn (there are 30° in each sign)
+   30° in Aquarius (the following and separating sign)
+   14° in Pisces

_____

=   60°

When you notice that two planets are separated by one complete sign, check to see if they form a sextile. However, note that in the case of a "hidden sextile" two full signs may be involved. See the sextile Neptune-Pluto in the drawing below. It is "almost" a hidden aspect.

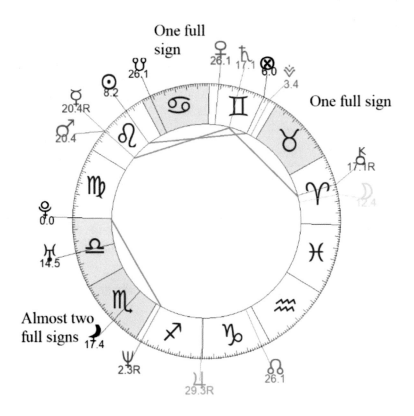

The **sextile** is traditionally known as a **beneficial aspect**, producing a harmonious influence in the areas represented by the planets concerned.

Signs in sextile complement one another. They are:

Aries and Gemini

Taurus and Cancer

Gemini and Leo

Cancer and Virgo

Leo and Libra

Virgo and Scorpio

Libra and Sagittarius

Scorpio and Capricorn

Sagittarius and Aquarius

Capricorn and Pisces.

See the list below. It concerns the major aspects and their commonly accepted orbs.

Remember that they are only indicative and should not be considered rigidly.

☌	⚹	□	△	⚻	☍
Conjunction	Sextile	Square	Trine	Inconjunct	opposition
0° to 10° Variable	56° to 64° Variable	83 to 97° Variable	113° to 127° Variable	145° to 155° Variable	170 to 190° Variable
Beneficial or Difficult Depends on planets involved	Beneficial	Difficult	Beneficial	Ambiguous	Difficult

Take note of the symbols. They are commonly used in astrology.

THE SQUARE

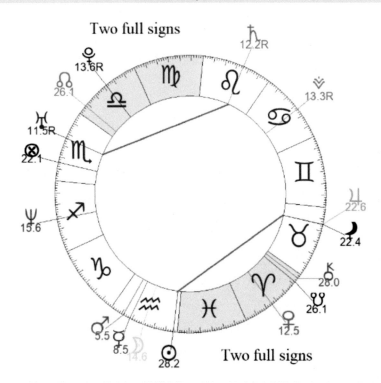

Two full signs

Two full signs

The square is an angle of about 90° separating two or more elements around the chart. It involves two or more planets separated from one another by 2 complete signs, and parts of the signs in which they stand.

In the above chart, the Sun is at 28° in Aquarius and Jupiter at almost 23° in Taurus. They form a square.

There are missing squares in this chart. Can you find them?

The square is said to be a discordant aspect because the planets or elements concerned are in "incompatible' signs. They tend to antagonise one another, creating tension or restriction, according on the planets involved.

Signs separated by a square are considered incompatible.

Aries and Cancer
Taurus and Leo
Gemini and Virgo
Cancer and Libra
Leo and Scorpio
Virgo and Sagittarius
Libra and Capricorn
Scorpio and Aquarius
Sagittarius and Pisces

These combinations are known as incompatible, but that is to be understood according to their respective element. Fire and water, earth and fire, air and earth do not seem to mix easily...

As you know, it is not possible easy to mix fire with water. It produces a thermic reaction that either turns the fire off or evaporates the water.

In the same manner, it is not easy to mix earth with fire...

Likely, mixing earth and air does not provide anything more than earth, due to the inconsistency and invisibility of air.

Lastly, air and water, although molecules and similar atoms are found in both, are not providing more than "bubbly water' when mixed.

Bear in mind that the above theory does not mean that people born under "incompatible signs" cannot make a wonderful couple or partnership. It is only meant to help you visualise the way aspects work and thus, enrich your future astrology readings.

THE TRINE

Three full signs

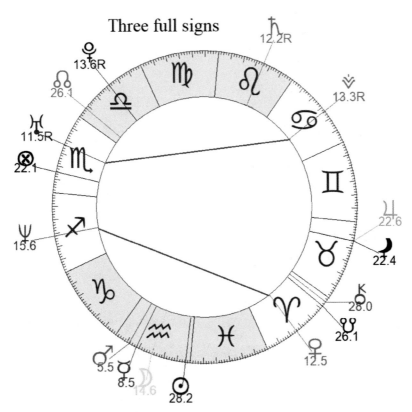

Three full signs

The trine involves two or more elements separated by three complete signs plus part of the signs in which they stand.

In the chart above, Venus is at 12.5° in Aries and Neptune is at 15.6° in Sagittarius. They form a trine.

There are 3 fire signs, 3 earth signs, 3 air signs and 3 water signs. Each one of them, in its own category, is separated from the other by an angle of 120°, the full circle being 120° x 3 = 360°.

Signs of the same category always blend in harmoniously and tend to complement one another. Therefore, the trine is a known as harmonious or beneficial.

Signs in trine are
Aries and Leo
Taurus and Virgo
Gemini and Libra
Cancer and Scorpio
Leo and Sagittarius
Virgo and Capricorn
Libra and Aquarius
Scorpio and Pisces.

There are missing trines in the chart on the previous page. Can you find them?

THE INCONJUCT or QUINCUNX

The inconjunct involves two or more elements positioned on either side of the opposite sign. See the drawing above.

Inconjuncts link signs from contradictory elements, like the squares. That is why they should belong to the discordant category of aspects.

In the chart on the left, Cancer inconjuncts Sagittarius and Aquarius. The elements involved are Water (Cancer) Fire (Sagittarius) and Air (Aquarius).
The angle formed between the objects (planets or other elements) are separated by an angle of around 150°.

The ambiguity of the inconjunct is that it is almost, but not quite, an opposition. Hence, its influence is less flagrant. It represents imperfections that look like qualities. It may also represent events that have left an unclear memory or a biased consideration.

Inconjuncts have voluntarily not been drawn in your birth chart.

Here is the list of signs linked by inconjuncts to help you find them in your chart and any other chart.

Aries/Virgo

Aries/Scorpio

Taurus/Libra

Taurus/Sagittarius

Gemini/Scorpio

Gemini/Capricorn

Cancer/Sagittarius

Cancer/Aquarius

Leo/Capricorn

Leo Pisces

Virgo/Aquarius

Virgo/Aries

Libra/Pisces

Libra/Taurus

Scorpio/Aries

Scorpio Gemini

Sagittarius/Taurus

Sagittarius/Cancer

Capricorn/Gemini

Capricorn Leo

Aquarius/Cancer

Aquarius/Virgo

Pisces Leo

Pisces Libra

Practice: *Find the inconjuncts, if any, in the chart on the next page.*

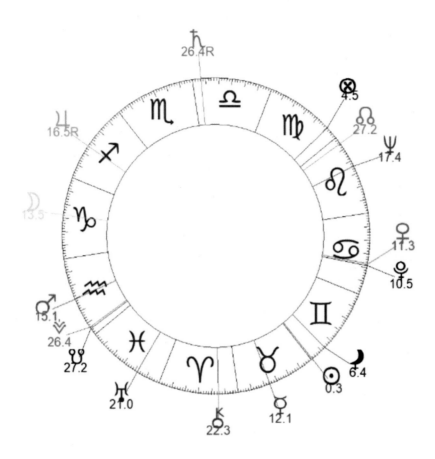

THE OPPOSITION

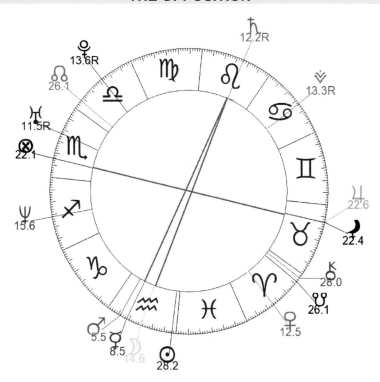

The opposition involves two or more elements situated almost directly opposite one another, therefore in opposite signs.

Example: Saturn at 12° in Leo and the Moon at 15° in Aquarius.

The opposition is easy to spot in a chart. It is known as a difficult aspect because the influences of the planets concerned are directly antagonising one another. This results in conflicts between at least two opposite tendencies creating tension or retention depending on the planets or elements concerned.

As mentioned earlier in this lesson, I personally believe that an opposition is not so "discordant" than the astrology intelligentsia considers it. It should be seen as a means to reach a sort of "inner agreement" that allows positive and constructive use of the energies involved in the areas represented by the celestial bodies[12] concerned.

There are missing oppositions in the chart on the previous page. Can you find them?

MORE ABOUT THE ORB

It is commonly accepted, in the case of major aspects, to allow an orb of 5° either way from the "perfect aspect". Sextiles, however, are usually considered up to an orb of 2° or 3° or even 4° when involving the "luminaries" (Sun and Moon).

When drawing the aspect lines, if a larger orb is found between what may be called "strong planets" in the chart (ruler of the ascendant or MC, planet in sign of rulership, etc.), draw a broken aspect line (- - - -). It is always advisable to keep an eye on "larger" or "smaller" orbs of aspects and consider them for further (and finer) information if necessary.

In fact, after decades of daily practice, I have verified how much the notion of aspects is not only limited to the planets and other elements involved, but more to the quality of the links between the signs where they stand. For example, a sextile Sun-Moon respectively positioned in Leo and Libra is active whether the accepted number of degrees is respected or not. This notion is important when considering hidden aspects about which I will provide more information later.

---

[12] Celestial bodies include planets, asteroids, natural satellites, stars, and other cosmic elements.

Here is a list of major aspects and traditionally accepted orbs...

CONJUNCTION:

0° to 10° either way between Sun and Moon
0° to 5° either way between other planets
0° to 7° either way between Sun, Moon, and other planets

SEXTILE:

58° to 62° between all planets
56° to 64° between Sun and Moon

SQUARE:

85° to 95° between all planets
83° to 97° between Sun and Moon

TRINE:

115° to 125° between all planets
113° to 127° between Sun and Moon

INCONJUNCTS:

145° to 155° between all planets
142° to 158° between Sun and Moon
143° to 157° between Sun, Moon, and other planets.

OPPOSITION:

175° to 185° between all planets
170° to 190° between Sun and Moon
173° to 187° between Sun, Moon, and other planets

Sun and Moon are allowed wider orbs:

> 1) Because of the Sun's obvious importance as the giver of life on Earth.

> 2) Because of the proximity of the Moon and of its speed of rotation around the Earth and around the zodiac (365 times faster than Saturn).

The symbols used for the aspects are:

CONJUNCTION	☌
SEXTILE	✳
SQUARE	☐
TRINE	△
OPPOSITION	☍
INCONJUNCT	⚻

To end this lesson, look at your chart and try to identify the different major aspects.

PRACTICE

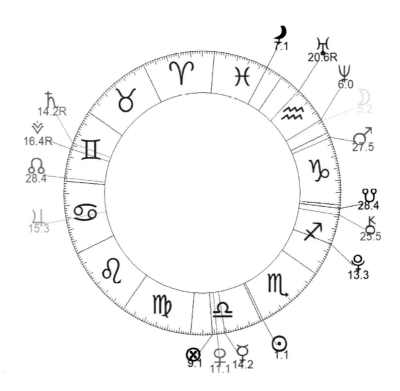

Draw the aspect lines including Inconjuncts.
Don't worry about minor aspects.

Lesson 14

THE ASPECTS

(Part2)

When analysing aspects, it is not enough to consider the planets as such.

You know that:

The SUN is the MASCULINE PRINCIPLE of life
The MOON is the FEMININE PRINCIPLE of life
MERCURY is the INTELLECTUAL PRINCIPLE of life
VENUS is the LOVE PRINCIPLE or life
MARS is the COMBATIVE PRINCIPLE of life
VESTA is the HARMONY PRINCIPLE of life
JUPITER is the EXPANSION PRINCIPLE of life
SATURN is the RESTRICTION PRINCIPLE of life
CHIRON is the OBSERVATION PRINCIPLE of life
URANUS is the TRANSFORMATION PRINCIPLE of life
NEPTUNE is the DREAM PRINCIPLE of life
PLUTO is the REGENERATION PRINCIPLE of life

A beneficial aspect between the Sun and the Moon creates harmony between the masculine and feminine principles. Vitality, authority, willpower, and physical energy are in harmony with the emotions, feelings, and the subconscious mind. It can also be said that, when the baby was born, at least, both parents were enjoying their relationship. Such a beneficial aspect between the luminaries helps preserve a good state of health, and balance between the outer self and inner self.

From then we need to consider the sun and the moon according to their **sign positions**. The Sun in any one sign of the zodiac confers different energy fields, influencing Aries, Taurus, Gemini, Cancer, and the other signs in a manner explained in the first lesson module of the present course. (See the *sun sign potentials* in Lesson 2.)

Once the SUN SIGN has been considered, we know more about the masculine principle and how it is outwardly expressed.

From then on, the position of the Moon in the sign must be considered. (See lesson N° 3.)

Blending both masculine and feminine principles individualises the chart.

In the case of the beneficial aspect, such blending is harmonious.

In the case of a discordant aspect, a certain tension or restriction between these principles emanates.

To analyse aspects between planets, you must:

- **First** consider the **principles** represented by such planets.

- Then you must consider each planet according to its **sign position**.

- Then, according to the type of **aspect**, the energy created can be analysed from a "**primary influence**" point of view. That is **from the point of view of the planets**, <u>not yet according to the individual concerned</u>.

Here is a simple example... (See chart next page.)

In a birth chart, we find:

- MERCURY 13° CAPRICORN
- VENUS 10° PISCES
- MOON 9° VIRGO, etc.

- MERCURY SEXTILE VENUS
- MOON TRINE MERCURY
- MOON OPPOSITION VENUS

What are the principles involved ?

- MOON = feminine principle
- MERCURY = intellectual principle
- VENUS = love principle

The aspects give:

1) Harmony between feminine and intellectual principles (Moon and Mercury)
2) Harmony between love and intellectual principles (Venus and Mercury)
3) Clash between feminine and love principles (Moon and Venus)

The astrologer may begin the analysis as follows...

"The emotions, feelings, internal life and imagination are well balanced and supporting mental expression, intelligence and communication (Moon trine Mercury). Sensuality, affection, loving, and artistic abilities are also effectively supporting the intellectual principle in favour of good communication and relationship with people in general. This is derived from a natural ability to use words (Mercury) with charm and elegance (Venus) (Mercury sextile Venus). However, the ability to love and reactions to affective stimuli are somehow tempered by the emotions, imagination, or from memory of some difficult moments in the early years of life (Moon opposition Venus)."

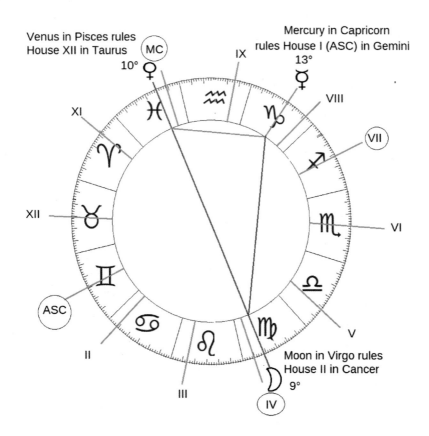

Venus in Pisces rules House XII in Taurus — MC — 10°

Mercury in Capricorn rules House I (ASC) in Gemini — 13°

Moon in Virgo rules House II in Cancer — 9°

While treating the above, it is necessary to simultaneously take note of the influences of the planets in the signs (Mercury in Capricorn, Venus in Pisces, and Moon in Virgo).

- The Moon in Virgo confers the ability to mentalise the emotions, a detailed memory, and a well-structured imagination. The emotions, however, tend to become a source of discomfort and anxiety.

- Mercury in Capricorn gives a down-to-earth, conservative, ambitious, rational, and somewhat fatalistic view of life.

- Venus in Pisces confers an over-sensitive nature, prone to confused or irrational sentimental needs and relationships. However, it confers a universal understanding of love on a spiritual level.

With that added information, the analysis could now read...

"The native has excellent intellectual abilities and memory, and a well-structured imagination supporting a down-to-earth, conservative ambitious mind. (Moon in Virgo Trine Mercury in Capricorn.) A sensitive nature makes this person prone to a rather uneven romantic behaviour pattern while conferring a universal understanding of the love principle, backing up communication abilities regarding personal ambitions and intellectual needs (Mercury in Capricorn sextile Venus in Pisces). However, the emotional pattern is erratic due to a latent conflict between objectivity and the need for love and understanding. Past events, such as a difficult relationship with the mother, may have made it uneasy to remain emotionally stable (Moon in Virgo opposition Venus in Pisces)."

To complement the analysis about personal and social life, we must complement with the Houses involved in relation with the planets concerned in the aspects, as well as the Houses ruled by such planets.

REFER TO THE EXAMPLE CHART ONCE MORE

The Moon, in our example, is positioned in **House IV** Venus is positioned in **House X** or MC. Mercury is positioned in **House VIII.**

The Moon being the ruler of Cancer, it therefore rules **House II** which begins in this sign.

Mercury being the ruler of Gemini, it therefore rules the Ascendant or **House I** which begin in this sign.

Venus being the ruler of Taurus, it therefore rules **House XII** which begin in this sign.

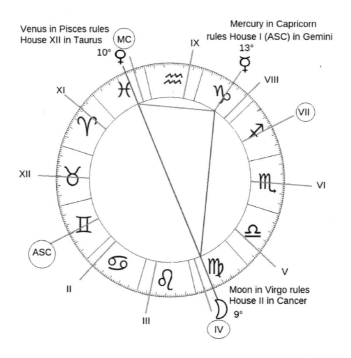

Venus in Pisces rules House XII in Taurus (MC) 10°

Mercury in Capricorn rules House I (ASC) in Gemini 13°

Moon in Virgo rules House II in Cancer 9°

In all, the three planets in aspects influence several areas represented by the Houses concerned: **Houses I, II, IV, VIII, X and XII**…

We find that:

The **TRINE MOON - MERCURY** involves:

- House I (Ascendant) which Mercury rules

- House VIII where Mercury is found –

- House II which is ruled by the Moon.

The **SEXTILE MERCURY - VENUS** involves:

- The Houses concerned by Mercury (See above) I and VIII

- House X or MC where Venus is found

- House XIII which Venus rules.

The **OPPOSITION MOON - VENUS** involves:

- The Houses concerned by Venus (see above) X and XII

- House IV where the Moon is found

- House II which the Moon rules.

What does it mean?

It means that the areas of life represented by the Houses concerned are influenced by the aspects which need to be blended and analysed accordingly.

I will not go into the complete analysis of this example but rather ask you to turn to your own chart and to your notebook...

Using the principle just explained, choose three planets in aspect with one another in your chart. **They do not have to be Moon, Mercury, and Venus. Any other three planets will do**. Then, draw up a list of the Houses concerned using the same method as above.

Then, from your list of Houses concerned, try to understand how it is done and what the influences are according to your own birth chart.

Remember that...
HOUSE I is personality
HOUSE II is money
HOUSE III is intellect
HOUSE IV is family
HOUSE V is love and children

HOUSE VI is health and work
HOUSE VII is marriage HOUSE VIII is death, etc.
HOUSE IX is travels, philosophy, etc.
HOUSE X is ambitions HOUSE XI is friends
HOUSE XII is hidden motivations, etc.

Refer to all supplementary sections included in this course as much as you want to help you along.

You will use the supplementary sections often and for quite a while, so take good care of them ☺...

A word on the aspects

The CONJUNCTION is often considered as a BENEFICIAL ASPECT. However, when Mars, Saturn, Uranus, or Pluto is part of the aspect, the result is known to create tension or restriction. Tension with Mars and Uranus, and restriction with Saturn and Pluto.

A conjunction Mars-Saturn creates tension and restriction. Each one can balance one the other out or lean toward the effect of the "stronger" planet. Mars in Aries, for example, is stronger than Saturn in this sign. But Saturn in Capricorn is stronger than Mars in this sign.

The sign in which the conjunction occurs is a major factor to consider when analysing the effect of a conjunction. The same applies to all other aspects and planets.

In this third module of four lessons, you will find supplementary sections to help you along analyse astrological charts. They deal with the aspects between planets as such and between planets considered as rulers of the houses. Use them extensively and without any reserve but always remember that **YOUR OWN WORDS** are always better than simply copy from the book.

Lesson 15

THE ASPECTS

(part 3)

Let us begin the third of four lessons about the aspects, hoping that they will be enough to cover the essentials and that they will help you understand how they work and what their roles are in an astrological chart. Aspects are the skeleton of the chart. Without a skeleton, what would we be? 😊

The major aspects are invaluable sources of precious information. As mentioned earlier, minor aspects are not treated in this course. See the list and symbols of the aspects in the previous lesson.

MAJOR ASPECTS

THE CONJUNCTION:

The CONJUNCTION unites or blends two or more principles of life together "for better or worse", depending on the planets involved. For example, Sun conjunct Jupiter implies that the masculine principle and the expansion principle are sharing their respective energy to enhance each one in a way that may be beneficial or discordant. The Sun gives vitality and life to the expansion principle of Jupiter. Jupiter confers its material and spiritual growing energy to the life force represented by the Sun.

Thus, such a conjunction confers definite positive willpower to succeed and usually a rather jovial (Jupiter) and sunny (Sun) personality.

However, a conjunction is the addition of two or more energy fields.

Imagine a heater. You turn it on to get warm in winter. Compare it to the Sun. It shines and dispenses heat and helps you get warm or hot, depending on the season…

When the Sun is in Leo, it is summer in the northern hemisphere of the Earth. The sun is strong. Many people tend to flee the sun in summer.

When the Sun is in Capricorn, it is winter in the northern hemisphere of the Earth. The sun is weak. We tend to look for some nice sunrays to warm ourselves just enough to feel warmer.

Jupiter has a physical constitution similar to that of the Sun. Hydrogen and helium constitute the main composition for both and in comparable proportions. When they are conjunct, it is like having two heaters next to, or on top of one another.

A conjunction means that the generated energy field emanating from the conjunction is almost twice as powerful.

When Jupiter transits in Leo, the heat of the sun in summer is usually much stronger. Observe the chart on the following page. Some of the configurations are quite significant of the heat wave that swept over Europe in 2003.

15/08/2003 12:00

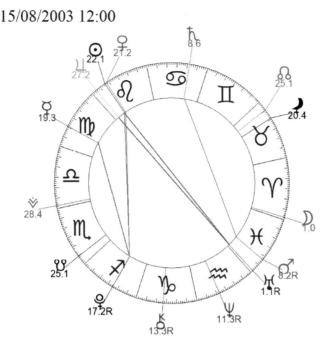

It appears that in some cases, the conjunction produces disturbance, rather than harmony. In the chart on the left, Venus is also forming a triple conjunction with the Sun and Jupiter. Venus is a very hot planet too. The temperature of the side facing the Sun exceeds 400° Celsius… Venus is never far from the Sun. The same applies for Mercury.

When considering a conjunction, then, keep in mind the notion of "addition" that can lead to excessive energy and the difficulty to control it.

Note also that the strength of a conjunction depends on the planets concerned and on the sign in which it is found. Obviously, the conjunction Sun/Jupiter of August 2004 in Virgo, did not produce a historical heatwave. However, in astrology, a conjunction is always a source of interrogation.

The conjunction between the Sun and Jupiter indicates an over-optimistic personality. Enthusiasm, opportunism, charisma, and magnetism are usually greatly enhanced.

Other planets in conjunction create different reactions.

In the case of Mars and Saturn, the conjunction tends to create **tension and retention**. The combative principle of Mars seems to be incompatible with any other principle of life. A

conjunction Sun-Mars, for example, brings the masculine and combative principles together, conferring too much reactivity, authoritarian tendencies, impulsiveness, and a defensive attitude. Although useful if some situations, such tendencies lead to various incidents or accidents. So perhaps, the conjunction Mars/Saturn is better controlled than most other conjunctions involving Mars. However, comparing Mars to the accelerator in a car and Saturn to the brakes, when both are operating simultaneously, the vehicle is impossible to drive…

The conjunction Sun/Mars

In the signs…

The sign in which a conjunction occurs tells much about the quality of its influence.

Found in Aries, a conjunction Sun/Mars, for example, indicates authoritarian and aggressive tendencies, impulsiveness, and intense reactivity. Physical violence may ensue because of an inability to control anger and its outcomes.

In Taurus, the combative and masculine principles control physical and sentimental needs leading to excessive sexuality, passionate feelings, sentimental breakups, overeating and an attraction to exuberant materialistic goals.

 In Gemini, the conjunction Sun-Mars operates on a mental and intellectual level. There is a tendency to excessive talking, chattering, with strong cerebral activity. Nervousness and precipitation may lead to various diplomatic incidents or worse, to accidents.

In the Houses…

Just like the position of a planet in a sign is not sufficient to understand its influence, the position of a conjunction in a sign should also be analysed in relation its **House position**.

Our first example concerned the conjunction Sun-Mars in Aries. The analysis revealed *authoritarian and aggressive tendencies, impulsiveness, and intense reactivity. Physical violence may ensue because of an inability to control anger and its outcomes.*

Such tendencies may be expressed in many ways and in **many areas of life**. **The House position shows how.**

An example…

 **Placed in House IV** this conjunction Sun-Mars in Aries directs its influence into the home and family life, creating tensions and potential conflicts and family breakups. However, it can also confer more determination and combativeness to look after the home and family. This is more so if the

conjunction Sun-Mars is *in harmonious aspect* with other planets in the chart…

Another example…

Placed in House X or MC, personal ambitions have a martial connotation, derived from Aries, the sign in which it is found. Authority and determination may favour careers related to fighting, war, weapons, sharp tools and utensils, sports, adventure, and most areas where action is the keyword to success. There is a tendency to rebel against authority and hierarchy. The father image is a dominant influence. This conjunction indicates good leadership ability, but lack of diplomacy that may contribute to chronic conflicts…

Placed in any other House, this conjunction Sun-Mars in Aries will influence different areas of the native's life.

THE RULERS OF THE HOUSES…

We have seen in a previous lesson that the planets must be analysed as such and as RULERS OF HOUSES according to their sign positions. The same applies to the analysis of the aspects. Masculine, feminine, intellectual principles and all other principles represented by the planets always have a HOUSE-RELATIONSHIP.

Our example above concerned the conjunction Sun-Mars in Aries.

Mars is the ruler of Aries. **It therefore rules the house beginning in this sign**.

The Sun rules Leo. **It therefore rules the House beginning**

in this sign.
Using the sample chart on the following page, in which the conjunction SUN-MARS appears in ARIES, imagine that HOUSE IV begins there…

- Print the page

- With a pencil, write "IV" next to the word "HOUSE" near the SUN-MARS conjunction…

- Now write: "V, VI, VII, etc." in the next house spaces (V in Taurus, VI in Gemini, VII in Cancer, etc.).

Using this example, you will find that Mars, ruler of Aries, also rule House IV beginning in Aries. The Sun, ruler of Leo, also rules House VIII because it begins in this sign.

From this example we see that **House IV is doubly concerned** because of the rulership of Mars and of this House position in conjunction with the Sun. House IV becomes the "sensitive spot" of the conjunction which also involves House VIII ruled by the Sun.

The "starting point" of the analysis (House IV) is the home and family life. Relationship with a severe mother and a difficult early family life are the main sources of perturbation. House VIII could imply that death has had a profound influence on the development of morbid tendencies. It may also indicate the untimely death of the mother. In this case it could have been produced by an accident (Mars) or a medical operation (Mars again). Family heritage may also be responsible for various conflicts or disruptions.

THE CONJUNCTION SUN-MARS IN ARIES

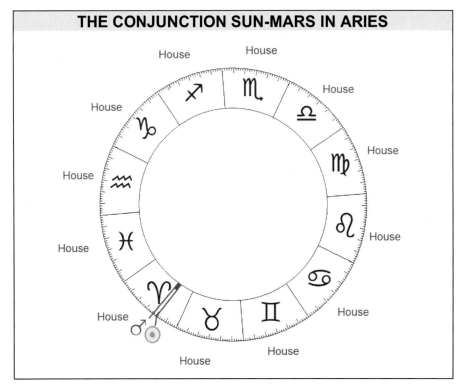

Taking the Houses into consideration allows a much more comprehensive approach of one single aspect than the simple analysis of the conjunction Sun-Mars on a purely planetary point of view. The **SIGN-AND-HOUSE-POSITION** procedure is the **KEY** to a correct and more accurate interpretation.

What applies to the **CONJUNCTION** applies to **ALL OTHER ASPECTS** which must be analysed in the same manner. This process individualises the reading of a birth chart.

Each planet rules one House or more. Therefore, each planet represents certain areas of life. However, each planet retains what it "purely" represents, regardless of sign or house position and rulership.

WHAT, HOW, WHERE and WHY

Mercury represents the communication potential. Its sign position indicates **HOW** this communication potential is expressed. Its house position shows us **WHERE** (in what area/s) this potential is applied. The aspects help understand **WHY** the potential is creating specific consequences that often differ greatly from one birth chart to another.

A planet is the **WHAT**

The sign position is the **HOW**

The house position is the **WHERE**

The aspect is the **WHY**

Lesson 16

More About the Aspects

In this fourth lesson on the aspects, let us review them TO broaden your approach and your analysing potential of such important configurations.

The aspect between two or more elements in the chart is an essential factor to determine why life is what is in the areas concerned. They are what you must rely on PRIMARILY to analyse a chart. Harmonious and discordant aspects cohabit to make up the complete portrait. Without them the interpretation is inconsistent and shallow. Aspects are the ties or connections between the planets so that they can share their energies to form other energies that are more complex and subtle.

Aspects are used just like artists using colours, mixing them to come as close as possible to what their creation. It is extremely rare to use a colour straight from the tube. A colour is a certain vision of things caused by a vibration produced by a wavelength captured by the eye and transformed into what is seen to be a colour. No one can say for sure that the colour red that I see is the same as the one you see. It goes for all other colours and colour ranges. They are infinite. The present computer programs allow a mix of up to sixty million colours and shades from only three essential ones called primary colours: red, green, and blue. A printer reproduces colours in a surprising way from four essentials: black, blue, yellow and red. More than sixty million colours can emerge from mixing four primary ones...

Aspects function in the same manner. They allow mixing the "colours" of the planets to create various shades of their respective influences. Aspects allow us to discover how the basic (primary) energy of a planet reacts or expresses itself. There are also important variations within the aspects themselves. A conjunction, sextile, square, trine, inconjunct or opposition can be much more than just that aspect. The subtleties cannot all be unveiled in the context of the present course. They would make it too complex and confusing. Nuances will emerge through your own practice. To give you an example of the complexity of an aspect, let us return to the conjunction for a moment.

INFERIOR AND SUPERIOR CONJUNCTIONS

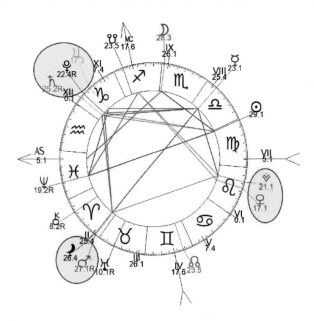

The closer, the stronger, but that is not all.

There is another way to differentiate between conjunctions: I call them "***superior***" and "***inferior***" conjunctions.

As you know (see lessons 1 to 4) the planets evolve within the limit of the "zodiac band" north or south of the ecliptic.

The superior conjunction occurs when the planets are on different latitudes. They are above and under one another. See the drawing below. The superior conjunction seems much stronger than the inferior one.

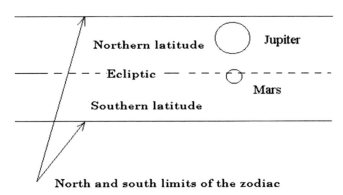

In this example, Mars being smaller than Jupiter, its energy is strongly submitted to the influence of the giant planet during a conjunction. The superposition of energies makes the conjunction much stronger during a superior conjunction because Mars is less "imprisoned" by Jupiter's energy field than during an inferior conjunction as shown by the drawing on the following page.

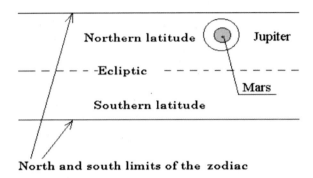

North and south limits of the zodiac

The "inferior" conjunction occurs when the planets concerned are travelling at a similar north or south latitude. Viewed from the Earth, they virtually hide one another.

This is especially true in the case of the conjunctions of the Sun with the lower planets, Venus, and Mercury. They rotate around the Sun on closer orbits than the Earth does. Therefore, when Venus or Mercury is "behind" the Sun at the time of a lower conjunction, its influence is overpowered by the solar energy. In this case we say that the planet is "combust" but, in my opinion, it could also be called a "hidden" conjunction. The lower conjunction implies a loss of energy for Mercury or Venus, hidden and absorbed by the Sun's own energy on which all planets of the system depend.

The same principle applies to conjunctions involving the Sun with any one of the other planets. Pluto, for example, is ten times smaller than the Earth. When it forms a superior or lower conjunction with the Sun, the energy of Pluto is absorbed, diluted into that of the Sun.

Yet, the astrological interpretation functions (with some nuances) whatever the type of conjunction. Why? Because I think that the global energies are not the main factors of influence. I believe that the global configurations are like a kind of roadmap proposed by "destiny" to guide us through the maze of our life. Therefore, it may be necessary to interpret the lower conjunction like a sign, a message, or a warning. "Beware of what is hiding behind apparent reality…" The influence of the "hidden" planet would therefore represent an important element not obvious at first glance.

Imagine a lower conjunction between Jupiter and Pluto. The energy of Pluto would be quite overpowered by Jupiter and would be rendered "invisible" or, at least, "hidden" by the giant planet. Looking at the chart, however, we can easily see both planets. The chart indicates, like a "spy satellite", that something hides behind appearances to produce a modification of such appearances.

Imagine that Jupiter represents House VII and Pluto House VI. Pluto rules Scorpio and Jupiter Sagittarius. Both signs follow one another. Therefore, the houses they represent also follow one another. In this type of conjunction, the message concerns private or professional partnerships. It may be about health or profession (house VI). The energy of Jupiter gives every reason to feel confident, while the presence of Pluto shows potential disruption, or even destruction. Such "message" must be considered very seriously.

The superior conjunction is more explicit. It puts forward the risk of being misled by appearances. It enhances the problems engendered by the presence of Pluto. In the case of the lower conjunction, on the contrary, the danger is not seen or not spontaneously accepted as such. Analysing such a conjunction necessitates a more subtle approach to avoid misunderstandings.

JOUR	☉		☽		☿		♀		♂		♃		♄		♅		♆		♇	
DÉCLINAISON @ 0H TU																				
D 1	22 N 02		4 N 34		14 N 17		24 N 10		3 N 37		14 S 55		4 N 41		18 S 44		19 S 48		8 S 14	
L 2	22	10	8	42	14	47	24	14	3	28	14	55	4	43	18	44	19	48	8	13
Ma 3	22	17	12	19	15	18	24	17	3	18	14	55	4	44	18	45	19	48	8	13
Me 4	22	24	15	13	15	49	24	20	3	09	14	54	4	46	18	45	19	48	8	13
J 5	22	31	17	15	16	21	24	22	2	59	14	54	4	48	18	45	19	48	8	13
V 6	22	38	18	17	16	52	24	23	2	49	14	54	4	50	18	45	19	49	8	13
S 7	22	44	18	21	17	24	24	23	2	38	14	54	4	52	18	46	19	49	8	13
D 8	22	50	17	29	17	56	24	23	2	28	14	54	4	53	18	46	19	49	8	13
L 9	22	55	15	48	18	28	24	22	2	18	14	54	4	55	18	46	19	49	8	13
Ma10	23	00	13	26	19	00	24	20	2	07	14	55	4	57	18	47	19	50	8	13
Me11	23	04	10	32	19	31	24	18	1	56	14	55	4	58	18	47	19	50	8	12
J 12	23	08	7	14	20	02	24	15	1	45	14	55	5	00	18	48	19	50	8	12
V 13	23	12	3	39	20	32	24	11	1	34	14	56	5	01	18	48	19	50	8	12
S 14	23	15	0 S 05		21	01	24	06	1	23	14	56	5	03	18	48	19	51	8	12
D 15	23	18	3	52	21	30	24	01	1	12	14	57	5	04	18	49	19	51	8	12
L 16	23	20	7	33	21	56	23	55	1	01	14	57	5	06	18	49	19	51	8	12
Ma17	23	22	11	00	22	22	23	49	0	50	14	58	5	07	18	50	19	51	8	12
Me18	23	24	14	01	22	45	23	41	0	38	14	59	5	09	18	50	19	52	8	12
J 19	23	25	16	24	23	07	23	33	0	26	14	59	5	10	18	50	19	52	8	12
V 20	23	26	17	57	23	27	23	24	0	15	15	00	5	12	18	51	19	52	8	12
S 21	23	26	18	28	23	45	23	15	0	03	15	01	5	13	18	51	19	52	8	12
D 22	23	26	17	50	24	00	23	05	0 S 09		15	02	5	14	18	52	19	53	8	12

Where or how do we find the latitudes of the planets? In some ephemeris or in some computer programs. Below is an extract from the "Vega Ephemeris 1950 to 2050" available in PDF format on the "astroquick" French website. If you cannot read French with Google Chrome, you can translate the page. Order the book for only 12€ (price in September 2020). The ephemerides are essential to all astrologers. They are used to forecast planetary transits and much more.

https://www.astroquick.fr/astrologie/30_astrologie_ephemerides-1950-2050-0h.php

The position of a planet is shown in degrees around the zodiac circle. This is called the "longitude" of a planet. That same position is also shown in degrees north or south of the ecliptic. This is called the "latitude" of a planet.

The same applies to geographical positions on Earth. It is always given in degrees of longitude and latitude.

The longitude is the position around the Earth according to its rotation around its axis, from degree zero, a line that runs through the town of Greenwich, in England. This first meridian passes through the North Pole to the South Pole and comes back on the other side, from the South Pole to the North Pole, where it becomes meridian 180. There are 360 meridians around the Earth, just as there are 360 degrees around a circle.

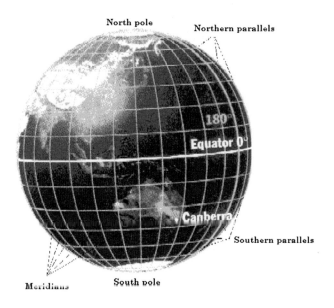

The latitude of a particular place on Earth is its position, in degrees, north or south of the equator (comparable to the ecliptic). There are 90 degrees north of the equator to the North Pole and 90 degrees south of the equator to the South Pole. Each degree is called a parallel, which is a circle around the Earth, parallel to the equator, from the south to the North Pole. See the picture on the left to familiarise yourself with these notions or to refresh your memory.

In a chart, for example, we find a conjunction Moon–Mars with an orb of 2° (two degrees) showing a strong aspect. According to the ephemeris, the latitude of the Moon would be 1° 29' north and 0° 01' south for Mars, meaning that this planet stands right on the celestial equator (ecliptic). The Moon being also remarkably close to it (only 1° 29' north) it tends to "hide" Mars, since it is situated "in front" of it according to our point of view on Earth.

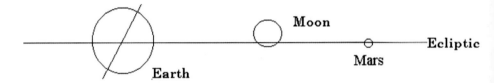

This conjunction could therefore indicate a "hidden problem", given the nature of Mars, especially if it rules house VIII or XII…

THE SEXTILE

The sextile separates two planets by an angle of about 60° around the chart. This aspect is said to be harmonious. It indicates a potential that can be developed into a concrete skill or talent.

The sextile needs to be accounted for and used accordingly. It associates planets or elements positioned in complementary signs: Fire–Air, Earth–Water or vice versa.

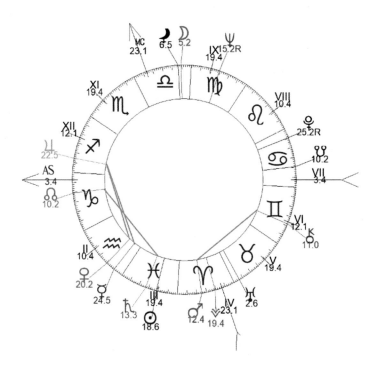

The ensuing energy depends on the homogeneity of the "mixture" between the two elements. Too much air boosts fire, but too little can kill it. Too much fire overheats the air, but too little makes it too cold and uncomfortable. Similarly, too much earth absorbs water, but too little produces a swamp. Too much water absorbs the earth, but too little makes it hard and dry. The assets represented by a sextile need a voluntary effort to reap the rewards it represents. That is perhaps why sextiles do not seem significant. Hence, the sextile must be put forward to stimulate action that may benefit certain areas of life. Under such conditions the positive energy expresses itself more clearly and much more convincingly!

THE TRINE

The trine is an angle of about 120° between two or more elements around the chart. Stronger than the sextile, the trine is known as the best beneficial aspect there is.

It represents a positive potential to succeed without having much effort or determination. The trine may also indicate laxism and a tendency to rely on the lucky star to prosper. Consequently, it can encourage laziness or idleness. The trine can also decrease the "immune system", be it moral, physical, intellectual, emotional or of any other kind, depending on the planets and houses concerned. In conclusion, the most popular of all aspect is perhaps not as beneficial as it seems…

Although it probably represents a kind of protection linked to a positive karma (a "divine credit"), it essentially depends on personal action rather than on sheer good fortune to honour its name. The trine can also represent other people whose "earthly mission" is to either protect or guide in various favouring ways.

The trine also represents above-average capacities or gifts in areas represented by the planets and houses concerned. It can be about an innate artistic talent, an extraordinary ability, physical advantages, and many other types of "heavenly present". The trine seems to make it easier to progress while rendering life more pleasant and more successful. It also represents a kind of holy protection that allows goals to be reached quicker and easier. It favours potential evolution and summits that can be reached with little or no effort.

I compare beneficial aspects to good quality tools, remembering that they depend on the user to do the job. Left on the workbench, the most expensive and sophisticated tool is useless…

THE SQUARE

The square has the reputation to be less virulent than the opposition. It represents an obstacle to overcome, which often produces an incentive to act accordingly. It therefore represents stimulation to use its energy in view of solving the problem represented by the square. It can also represent a trait of character, a difficult situation or an unpleasant event. There again, Houses and planets concerned inform on the nature of the unrest.

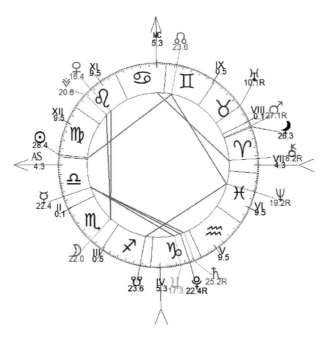

The square is "half the angle of the opposition" but it seems to act more spontaneously. It represents a defect, a flaw in the person's rhythm leading to atypical action or reaction. It indicates the necessity to remain fully awake and aware to avoid incidents (or accidents) or to deal with difficult situations…

The square is a source of stimulating energy because it represents a friction between two "incompatible" elements: fire with water, earth with fire, air with earth and water with air. The energy derived is unstable, disorganised, and often inconsistent. The blend between water and fire (or vice-versa) is impossible in a natural way without and earthly medium (such as a pot for example). The same remark applies to a blend of air and earth (or vice-versa). Nothing concrete will ensue in the way of mortar or clay, as the mixture of earth and water creates through a sextile. Mixing earth and fire is an uneasy task too. As for the mixture of water and air, what can it produce besides "bubbly water" or excessive humidification of the air? Something we know too well in Queensland, Australia, during the summer months…

Introducing these notions at the time of the interpretation of a square, makes it easier to understand how it works. The square needs to be analysed carefully because its energy is flagrant but not always recognised or understood by the person concerned. A square Mercury–Uranus, for example, makes one nervous and fidgety. However, we often note that a person concerned by such an aspect drinks too much coffee, tea, or other stimulating substances. We also note a difficulty to concentrate and to focus. There is a tendency to quickly burn out mental energy, causing rises and falls of nervous tension, and fatigue. An effort to be more moderate is necessary to avoid errors and other unpleasant consequences.

Analysing a chart for someone, it is important to warn of the possible effects of squares and their potential internal or external disruptions. Their repercussions can be a source of chronic disorder if the influence of a square is not taken into consideration. To realise and recognise one's shortcomings or weak points is vital but useless if nothing is done to improve.

In presence of an obstacle, we have three options: move back, move forward, or move around. We often don't have much choice because we must move on with our lives, which it is just as well in fact because when the obstacle is finally overcome, the satisfaction is just as good as the experience acquired…

THE OPPOSITION

The opposition is an ambiguous aspect because it opposes two planets that are in signs belonging to compatible elements. Opposite a fire sign is an air sign; opposite an earth sign is a water sign; opposite an air sign is a fire sign; opposite a water sign is an earth sign. Each of the signs in opposition is also of the same quality: cardinal, fix and mutable… Why then, is the opposition considered to be a difficult aspect? The reason is due to these complementarities…

Two people may decide to get together because they are different but seem to complement one another. They may occasionally separate for the same reasons… Humans are often naturally attracted to their opposite, and that starts with the opposite sex. What we look for in a relationship is unity. Yet, as time goes by, differences impose themselves and often make the relationship more and more difficult. Both parties involve differently, in different directions… Successful long-lasting couples are rare indeed. They understand that sharing protects and nourishes the relationship. Sharing tasks, burdens, joys, hardships, possessions, feelings, tastes, and needs, while admitting and respecting differences.

The middle way is the point of harmony and balance. Once it is reached, the opposition becomes a positive and constructive energy. The opposition is like a seesaw going up and down…

The drawing below symbolises the opposition. It symbolises my personal vision of the aspect. Beyond the problems it can produce, it also allows finding the "blending point" between two opposite tendencies…

We could also picture the influence of the opposition with the image of a rope on which ends two people pull. Their respective strength will determine the winner. Two people of equal strength will create a tension that, if it ends up breaking the rope, will most probably do so halfway its total length…

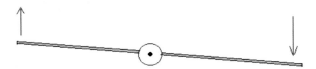

This notion of "equipoise" or "middle way" must be retained when analysing the opposition. Indeed, the principles represented by the planets involved are in "conflict of interest" if I may say, because they both try to rule the other. The result is a continual twinge that sometimes produces extreme contrary reactions. The solution to such a conflict of tendencies depends on the ability to get both sides to collaborate rather than oppose one another. Then, the opposition becomes positive and constructive. Just like a governing party needs an opposition party in a democratic leadership, life is made up of pros and cons that are useful to fight limitations, while accepting qualities and flaws…

THE INCONJUNCT

Earlier on, I mentioned the notion of ambiguity when relating to the opposition. The inconjunct is another example of it, in a subtler and less direct or less "candid" and less obvious manner. With a total of about 150° (accepting an orb of around 5°) the inconjunct is the addition of a sextile (60°) and a square (90°). It is therefore a sort of "ambush" made up by the influence of the sextile moving toward the square, therefore toward difficulty.

The "easiness" offered and represented by the sextile has a sedative effect on the behaviour. On a physiological point of view, the absence of effort does not favour muscular development, it decreases it. A stronger person can effortlessly lift a weight than a weaker person would find straining. However, the weaker person derives greater benefit and personal satisfaction from such effort. Meanwhile, the stronger person, satisfied with the initial performance may end up less combative and efficient.

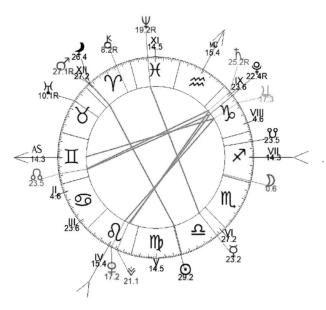

Can the same remark be made about the intellectual capacities, about the famous IQ? How many intelligent individuals waste their good mental energy by leading a more than ordinary and boring life? How many children fail at school despite their mental capacities, often way above average? The reasons why intelligence is so often put to the service of mediocre realisations or sterile projects remains a mystery to me. The same remark applies to innate artistic talents that are not exploited...

Examples of the inability to use talent and other capacities are numerous and I believe that the inconjunct has something to do with this *"wasting of good seeds that will never be sowed"*. The talents represented by the sextile must be exploited. We must use our assets. Why shouldn't we benefit from the heavenly gifts that life has given us at birth? It is essential to consciously realise what we possess. Then, we must learn to use such skills or natural benefits. But we must do so in a constructive, creative, and concrete manner. Simultaneously, we must assess the obstacles and compare them to our goals. Learning to appreciate such obstacles while evaluating their impact on our progression is a fundamental to succeed.

While the square is a direct and "straight forward" aspect, even though it is not always recognised as such, the inconjunct is ambiguous. Being the addition of a square and sextile, it produces an ambivalent tendency to let go rather than fight, or to hesitate rather than decide.

 If the square makes someone lazy or lymphatic, lack of energy and willpower becomes a handicap that makes it harder to benefit from the sextile effect of the inconjunct. One can be very gifted but not motivated to exploit that talent. We need Incentive to fight our natural fear of failure that generates doubt and abandon. To fight doubt is to fight oneself. Doubt is basically linked to the fear of death, the fear of the unknown…

The inconjunct symbolises this deep ambiguity that is, at times, a good enough reason to do nothing of our life. Each of us manages these notions of life and death in a different way, while struggling with the reality of it. Whatever tools we use with incertitude but determination, each one of us must survive in a world where material values prevail. If we cannot control what happens on the larger scale, we can at least try to master what happens within ourselves. It is from there that pure energy springs out to connect us to the spiritual dimension of life.

The importance of interpreting aspects cannot be emphasised enough. It really is the key to the analysis and to understanding human nature.

When harmonious, the conjunction is more powerful than the sextile and trine. Whereas the sextile and trine confer luck, good will, privileges, easiness, skill, talent, and much more, the conjunction indicates personal strength and potential in the areas concerned according to sign and house positions.

A conjunction Sun-Mars, for example, as we have seen earlier, is a rather difficult energy combination to channel and control because it confers too much strength and will power. The influences of both elements do not complement one another, they add-up to one another.

A sextile or trine Sun-Mars, on the contrary, balances the powers of the Sun and Mars. The Earth is situated between such influences, sharing them as harmoniously as possible. Authority and willpower blend in and create a determined personality, without the extremist tendencies engendered by the conjunction.

The trine is probably the "best" of all aspects because it confers natural talents and an innate ability to create the right situation at the right time, according to WHAT, HOW, WHERE, and WHY...

The sextile has a similar effect than the trine but with less intensity. It confers natural talents but not necessarily the instinct to use such talents for the best of results. Someone may have natural artistic talents for painting or music but may not necessarily derive any real success from these.

As far as the square and opposition are concerned, the difference is important to understand to make a good analysis and precise forecasts.

The opposition, much in the same manner as the conjunction, puts "pressure" on the individual. Such pressure, however, does not result from the addition of planetary influences but rather from a conflicting attitude between two or more opposite tendencies. It can be a tendency to save up money as much as possible opposed to a tendency to spend regardless. It can render very talkative, alternating with total silence. The opposition, then, creates extremes, because of a tendency to be pulled from one end to the other, subject to extravagant spending followed by tight budget-oriented policies. In our second example, the tendency is the urge to talk incessantly then to become silent for no obvious reason.

In the case of an opposition, one needs to learn to live with it. There is a centre point between such extremes. Self-discipline is the key to finding the middle way. In most cases, unfortunately, it is difficult to recognise. Major fluctuations may then be triggered by planetary transits. This is quite obvious in the case of alcoholism, for example, when drinking has become a bodily need as much as a psychological support. Drug addiction is another example usually involving the Moon, Neptune and the ruler of the Ascendant, the Sun in Pisces, Scorpio or Aquarius, and Houses III, VI or V.

In more common and "ordinary" cases, the opposition can indicate conflicts between parents, co-workers, or between people in the areas of life represented by the houses concerned (planet position and rulership). Oppositions are part of early life motivations, childhood being a most influential period when major events, although forgotten, remain a source of recurring complications.

On a physical point of view, the opposition can indicate irreversible disabilities such as we have all seen around us in children or adults. Usually, at least a square and conjunction accompany and support the opposition to create physically destructive influences.

The square is not such a "bad" aspect because it gives the opportunity to test out personal skills needed to surmount life's obstacles. The square is an energy field that can distort mental or physical development and expression. The influence, however, is not irreversible. There is a need to overcome intellectual or physical deficiencies despite the difficulties they may represent and trigger.

The square can confer nervousness, skinniness, fatness, shyness, aggressiveness, and many different forms of "handicaps". It is up to us to neutralise the influence of such square. Tendencies to drink too much, to overeat, to over worry, and other excesses are mainly engendered by squares in an individual's chart but are certainly not impossible problems to solve.

To help you along, refer to the supplementary section included in this lesson but USE YOUR OWN WORDS to describe the influences of the aspects you analyse.

Supplementary Section

Aspects Between Planets

CONJUNCTIONS

SUN – MOON: Good as far as energy and sensibility are concerned. However, this conjunction can create serious problems in the early years of life.

SUN – MERCURY: Excellent intellectual and communication abilities. Good, sunny approach to people in general. Fond of travelling.

SUN – VENUS: Strong affective and sentimental needs. Reinforces artistic abilities. There is a tendency to be passionate, possessive, and jealous.

SUN – MARS: Extreme energy creates tension and impulsiveness. Incidents and accidents occurring because of a fiery temper. Usually interested in sports and outdoor activities.

SUN - VESTA: There is a need to preserve or restore harmony on a physical and psychological level. The manners are usually pleasant and the approach sensible and diplomatic.

SUN – JUPITER: Confers generosity, luck, good health, and a tendency to seek spiritual and material expansion.

SUN – SATURN: Gives a strong sense of responsibility, determination, and ambition. The potential to succeed is derived from the ability to concentrate and to have far-fetched ambitions.

SUN – CHIRON: There may be a natural interest for medicine and health derived from early-life illness. A natural ability to heal may motivate a career in medicine. Hypochondriac tendencies may be present.

SUN – URANUS: Renders overactive, and original in many ways. Interests in electronics and in new fields of modern discoveries are indicated. Can give eccentric or bohemian tendencies.

SUN – NEPTUNE: Extreme sensitivity confers excellent artistic tendencies and abilities, especially in music and poetry. The dream principle is highly developed and can give rise to intense inspiration.

SUN – PLUTO: Excellent regenerating ability is indicated. Strong constitution enables to overcome many obstacles that seem impossible to others. The person is difficult to deal with and stubborn.

* * * * * * * * * *

MOON – MERCURY: Gives an intuitive mind capable of good writing and communication abilities. The thought, however, can be overpowered by feelings and emotions especially if the conjunction is found in Cancer or in Pisces.

MOON – VENUS: Emotions and affections are closely linked and constantly interrelating. Artistic tastes and abilities are indicated together with a strong attachment to the mother image. In the chart of a woman, this conjunction enhances the mother instinct and procreation abilities.

MOON – MARS: Extreme sensitivity leads to a defensive attitude for self-protection. Emotional aggressiveness and apparent harshness are indicated. Unexpected emotional reactions.

MOON - VESTA: There is a deep emotional need to preserve balance and harmony. It has a strong influence on the quality of all personal relationships favoured by diplomacy and compassion. ,

MOON – JUPITER: Renders generous and optimistic especially in relationship with women. Emotions tend to have a spiritual bend. Luck is indicated with this conjunction, especially if it is related to House V in the birth chart.

MOON – SATURN: Emotional expression is restricted, which renders rather cold or shy. Relationships with women are rather difficult and may be purposefully avoided.

MOON - CHIRON: Emotions can have a strong influence on physical and psychological wellbeing. A tendency to somatise may have a detrimental effect on health due to overwhelming emotional surges.

MOON – URANUS: Extreme nervousness is indicated, together with moodiness and unpredictable changes of attitude, feelings, and emotions.

MOON – NEPTUNE: Gives daydreaming tendencies that can lead to utopia and unrealistic goals. It indicates excellent artistic abilities and psychic, mystically oriented, or visionary tendencies.

MOON – PLUTO: Renders emotionally resourceful, showing great depth when it comes to personal feelings. There is an ability to draw on hidden sources of energy to regenerate after an illness or other traumas.

MERCURY – VENUS: Renders rather well-mannered and refined, with charming and diplomatic manners. Intellectual creativity is enhanced and a source of punctual satisfaction.

MERCURY – MARS: Manner of expression can be harsh, sharp, and callous. There is little patience with those who do not understand, and a tendency to gossip or to lie.

MERCURY - VESTA: Indicates an innate ability to communicate in a diplomatic manner to preserve the quality of personal and social relationships. The notions of justice and injustice are majors intellectual concepts.

MERCURY – JUPITER: There is an interest in philosophy, higher education, travelling, foreign cultures and in the spiritual side of life. Intellectual generosity and optimism are indicated.

MERCURY – SATURN: This conjunction tends to restrict the communication principle, making one rather shy, austere, pessimistic, and prone to solitude and to old-fashioned intellectual views.

MERCURY - CHIRON: Indicates an interest in medicine and health. Body and mind influence one another. Psychosomatic tendencies are frequent and an above-average intellectual capacity.

MERCURY – URANUS: Gives originality and sometimes eccentricity or even genius to the thought pattern. Extreme nervousness, talking and driving fast and an interest in electronic forms of communication such as radio, TV, telephone, etc. are also indicated.

MERCURY – NEPTUNE: A poetical mind, fond of music and finding it hard to communicate on a down-to-earth basis is indicated. It also indicates great sensitivity and natural artistic talents.

MERCURY-PLUTO: The mind is profound and extremely resourceful. Excellent concentration power is also indicated, together with an interest in the mysteries of life and occultism.

* * * * * * * * * *

VENUS – MARS: Sex and general feelings are usually closely linked. Tension and difficulties are indicated because of a tendency to aggressiveness and jealousy wherever love and romance are concerned.

VENUS - VESTA: Love, compassion, and an innate ability to harmonise, are a source of positive and protecting energy. This conjunction, present in the charts of artists and diplomats, is an asset to greatly improve the quality of life.

VENUS – JUPITER: This is an excellent aspect conferring luck, optimism, beauty of feelings, and generosity. Sentiments are spiritualised and become a source of inspiration, artistic or otherwise.

VENUS – SATURN: The ability to love and general feelings are restricted because of the influence of Saturn. Therefore, the appearance may be cold because of excessive shyness that makes it difficult to relate to the opposite sex.

VENUS - CHIRON: Indicates a protection to preserve health and wellbeing. Love plays a major role psychologically and physiologically. This configuration is often found in the chart of medical practitioners who have a lofty approach of their work.

VENUS – URANUS: Feelings and affections are subject to sudden and drastic changes. The ability to love is unusual because of an attraction to unusual romantic partners. Love at first sight is common with this conjunction.

VENUS – NEPTUNE: Artistic abilities are greatly enhanced. There is a strong love of beauty and an excellent musical ear. However, idealism may lead to utopia and romantic disillusions.

VENUS – PLUTO: Strong and deep feelings can lead to a "love or die" attitude, to jealousy and to extremely passionate romantic relationships. However hard can the heart be hurt, the need to love and to be loved never dies.

* * * * * * * * *

MARS - VESTA: Indicates potential to control reactions to obtain better results with diplomacy than with authority. There is a strong need to protect others by defending their rights. A useful configuration for lawyers or social workers.

MARS – JUPITER: Impulsive generosity can lead to unwise speculation and extravagant taste for luxury. A tendency to force personal opinions and ideas onto others is also indicated.

MARS – SATURN: This conjunction may have a beneficial influence in the sense that it confers the ability to balance out tension and restriction, favouring more concrete results. It can also indicate repressed anger.

MARS - CHIRON: Indicates accrued risks of health incidents due to excessive reactivity, impatience, and impulsiveness. Well controlled, however, this configuration enhances accuracy and efficiency. Useful for surgeons and other precision work.

MARS – URANUS: Extreme nervousness, irritability and impulsiveness are indicated, making one prone to accidents, arguments, fights, nervous fits, etc. Great care should be taken when handling electrical devices. Erratic sexuality.

MARS – NEPTUNE: Can give an excessive lean for medicine, drugs, alcohol, tobacco, etc. A tendency to overdo it one way or another can lead to addiction and dependency or to total rejection of all "unnatural" food and other elementary needs.

MARS – PLUTO: This powerful aspect can lead to be either a hero or a murderer… Extreme courage to the point of temerity, recklessness, and foolhardiness, together with a violent nature, prone to memorable fits of anger.

* * * * * * * * * *

VESTA - JUPITER: Indicates an above-average generosity and an innate sense of justice and harmony. There seems to a divine protection that helps achieve great heights, both socially and personally.

VESTA - SATURN: Seems to restrict the potential as much as the desire to be in harmony within and without. However, patience and determination may prove an excellent asset to overcome obstacles without losing balance and temper.

VESTA - CHIRON: This configuration seems to protect and preserve physiological balance and harmony with happy repercussions on health condition. Favours medical practitioners and health-related professions.

VESTA - URANUS: This is the "acrobat" configuration. It confers the ability to quickly adapt to changes and restore or preserve balance and harmony. Imagination and originality complement one another to favour success.

VESTA - NEPTUNE: This configuration favours intuition and inspiration so useful to the creative person, sensitive to vibration, sound, and movement. Ideal for musicians, dancers, or holistic therapists. It confers a spiritual approach to universal harmony and wellbeing.

VESTA - PLUTO: There is an innate ability to regenerate and preserve harmony and balance despite occasional upheavals. A tendency to question the notion of justice and equity may lead to radical actions contrary to the wellbeing expected.

JUPITER – SATURN: The expansion principle is restricted with this conjunction. Therefore, one is pulled between optimism and pessimism. This conjunction also creates financial ups and downs. However, when balance is achieved it leads to success, often remarked in the second part of life.

JUPITER - CHIRON: Confers a greater ability to observe and analyse, useful qualities for therapists and anyone interested in studies, research, and teaching. Jupiter may, however, produce hypochondriac tendencies by exaggerating occasional health disorders.

JUPITER – URANUS: Unusual and sometimes extravagant ideas and principles make one unexpectedly generous and sometimes too optimistic. It appears that the expansion principle is forever changing. The mind is inventive and innovative.

JUPITER – NEPTUNE: This is a good aspect as far as the artistic potential is concerned because it confers good expanding power and desire to progress and succeed according to the most intense dreams and desires. An instinctive well-minded attitude toward mankind is also indicated.

JUPITER – PLUTO: This is a powerful aspect because it deals with expansion and regeneration. It confers strength and good health, together with the ability to deal with obstacles and difficulties in the most vivacious and determined manner.

* * * * * * * * * *

SATURN - CHIRON: Although Saturn may tend to limit the capacity to analyse and diagnose, it confers patience and determination to deal with the realities of life in a rational and efficient manner. Honesty and humility are also produced by this conjunction.

SATURN – URANUS: The transformation principle is restricted by the presence of Saturn. The attitude is conservative. However, this conjunction must be analysed in relation to the rest of the chart because it influences a large number of people due to the planets' slow speed of revolution around the zodiac.

SATURN – NEPTUNE: This conjunction tends to restrict the ability to dream and to "feel", especially in artistic areas such as music and painting. However, in some cases, Saturn can give the capacity to realise the greatest dreams by means of realistic and well-planned management.

SATURN – PLUTO: This is a strong aspect because of the power usually bestowed by Pluto which is well structured and organized constructively in the presence of Saturn. It renders extremely resourceful thanks to the ability to channel inner energy to fuel endurance and determination. It can also act to thwart the body's regenerating natural processes.

* * * * * * * * *

CHIRON - URANUS: Sudden physiological changes produce unexpected health issues that may have a psychological or neuronal origin. Adaptability to unforeseen circumstances is, however, helpful to quickly restore or protect health in the areas represented by the Houses concerned.

CHIRON - NEPTUNE: Indicates an intuitive approach to the rational side of life. This conjunction may, however, create a confused approach to health care with detrimental consequences. Extreme sensitivity to drugs and alcohol can lead to various health disorders and social disturbances.

CHIRON - PLUTO: Favours quick regeneration and healing process. The inner energy is spontaneously acting to restore balance when needed. However, a tendency to infections, or to viral and bacterial contamination requires strict hygiene rules for protection.

* * * * * * * * *

URANUS – NEPTUNE: This conjunction can give extremely intuitive abilities, visions, and artistic genius. It can also have a disturbing effect upon the nervous system, making him strongly and uncontrollably attracted to drugs, alcohol and medicine. The speed at which the mind can divert from one thought to another makes it difficult to control and put ideas into concrete forms.

URANUS – PLUTO: Uranium + Plutonium = Atomic bomb… This type of planetary conjunction influences a large number of people. Transformation and regeneration make for destruction in view of reconstruction. There is a tendency to destroy and to start anew at any time in life.

* * * * * * * * * *

NEPTUNE – PLUTO: This conjunction occurred from 1890 until 1895 and will not happen again until approximately 2178… It has a powerful effect on mankind and is more interesting in world astrology rather than in an individual chart. However, its influence enhances the regenerating capacity issued from a positive partnership between body and mind.

SEXTILES AND TRINES

Even If they are different, as explained earlier, sextiles and trines are both beneficial aspects although a sextile is said to have less intensity than a trine. Keep it in mind when using this supplementary section to analyse birth charts.

SUN - MOON: Protect health and confers good energy flow and harmony between the active and passive principles of life. It usually indicates good relationship between the parents, at least around the moment of the person's birth.

SUN - MERCURY: Only the half-sextile is possible. It gives good intellectual and communication ability. Writing, reading, studying, and travelling are some of the possible areas of success and pleasure.

SUN - VENUS: Only the half-sextile is possible. It enhances the love principle. It indicates sensitivity and creativity, together with an artistic nature. Venus being the second benefactor, in astrology, after Jupiter, luck may have a positive influence in various ways.

SUN - MARS: Enhances natural strength and vitality. There is a liking for sports and a need to use body for personal expression. Tends to protect from illnesses and accidents.

SUN - VESTA: Enhances the ability to preserve balance, harmony, and wellbeing in the areas of life represented by the Houses concerned by the aspect. It also seems to confer more luck due to a positive approach of most situations and events.

SUN - JUPITER: Is an excellent aspect, especially the trine. It shows excellent dispositions to succeed in today's world. Generous and optimistic, one attracts sympathies and feels at ease in most situations. Excellent health protection.

SUN - SATURN: Indicates a serious and well-minded attitude. There is an ability to undertake long and fastidious tasks with determination. This kind of aspect is a factor of long life due to above average physical endurance.

SUN - CHIRON: Sextile or trine have a positive influence on the state of health and physiological energy and strength. There is an innate ability to diagnose and treat problems quickly and efficiently.

SUN - URANUS: Enhances natural abilities, giving easiness in most areas of life. The mind is interested in everything, willing to learn and to investigate in all areas of life. Excellent communication ability.

SUN - NEPTUNE: Intensify the dream principle, allowing to live up to expectations. Enhances artistic ability also giving a warmer and more positive view of life in general.

SUN - PLUTO: Enhances vitality and regenerating ability. It renders resistant and well minded, eager to test everything in life in a sane and sensible way. Determination and concentration favour long-lasting success.

* * * * * * * * * *

MOON - MERCURY: Excellent aspect conferring great communication ability. There is a natural ability to enjoy being in harmony in any kind of relationship. Enhances diplomacy and adaptability.

MOON - VENUS: Enhances artistic ability and natural talents. There is a strong need to love and to be loved. Enhances optimism, positivity, and creativity. Love of children. Close to the mother.

MOON - MARS: Confers energy and willpower as well as a good sense of responsibility when it comes to the goals of life. There is a need to be helpful to others.

MOON - VESTA: Feelings are a source of inspiration that may be useful wherever and whenever creativity is requested. Family wellbeing is important to preserve existential balance and emotional satisfaction.

MOON - JUPITER: Protects health and the emotional side of life. Optimism and a positive attitude make for good relationships with other people in general. Shows a certain amount of luck.

MOON - SATURN: Indicates seriousness and a well-balanced emotional stance. This kind of aspect allows better concentration, and emotional strength and stability.

MOON - CHIRON: Emotional balance preserves a healthier mind and body. The ability to feel and diagnose allows more efficient treatments or solutions to solve all sorts of crises.

MOON - URANUS: Confers excellent intuitive ability. Renders quick-witted and adaptable. There is a natural ability to derive great mental stimulation form emotions, never running short of new ideas and projects.

MOON - NEPTUNE: Like Uranus, Neptune here confers excellent intuition. Increases sensitivity to the point of being able to "read" other people's mind to act or react accordingly.

MOON - PLUTO: Enhances the emotions and confers strength and willpower. There is an ability to concentrate and to draw on hidden sources of energy to regenerate in most situations and circumstances.

* * * * * * * * * *

MERCURY - VENUS: (only the sextile is possible) Confers harmony between intellectual and love principles. There is a natural ability to use one's mind in a sensible manner, deriving great pleasure and enrichment from reading, travelling, and communicating.

MERCURY - MARS: Confers mental strength and determination. Usually indicates a strong-headed attitude without the unpleasant consequences. Natural diplomacy and smooth authority favour success.

MERCURY - VESTA: The intellect is favoured by a harmonious flow of positive energy issued from an innate need and ability to communicate with diplomacy and to learn from experiences the best way to preserve and feed uplifting relationships.

MERCURY - JUPITER: Enhances intellectual development and general capacity. There is a natural liking to communicate and interests in all forms of studies, while enjoying travels due to an innate attraction to foreign countries and cultures.

MERCURY - SATURN: Confers excellent stability and seriousness to the overall thought process. Favours concentration and the ability to communicate well with others. It confers an innate ability to listen to the elders to improve in various ways.

MERCURY - CHIRON: The intellect is linked to natural ability to analyse and observe, to learn and progress in the areas represented by the Houses concerned by both planets. Areas and activities requiring precision of thought and communication are favoured.

MERCURY - URANUS: This is an excellent type of aspect as far as intelligence and overall mental resources are concerned. There is an ability to understand quickly and to be inventive, innovative, and original.

MERCURY - NEPTUNE: Enhances intuition and confers an innate ability to rely on the sixth sense to communicate with the environment. This is an excellent aspect for artists, storytellers, comedians, therapists, and other medical professionals.

MERCURY - PLUTO: Confers excellent intellectual ability to concentrate and regenerate whatever the problems may be. Indicates a deep-thinking personality, interested in psychology and in all manners of investigation. The mind can be used in a positive way to support the body when necessary.

VENUS - MARS: Enhances sexual drive that can be diverted into positive actions in other areas of life. There is an innate ability to be firm, yet charming and sensible. Sensuality and strength share a harmonious relationship to favour personal endeavours.

VENUS - VESTA: Compassion and generosity are a source of wellbeing and success. Luck may also play an important role in the evolution of life in the areas represented by the Houses concerned by this type of aspect.

VENUS - JUPITER: Enhances the natural luck factor. The life path seems to be "protected" by some invisible heavenly influence. Optimism and a positive approach to life in general, favour good contacts with other people and harmony in romantic life.

VENUS - SATURN: Good taste and natural balance are blending here to give a sense for simple beauty, rhythm, and long-lasting values. Personal feelings are genuine and deep. Excellent aspects for artists and professions where patience and diplomacy musts.

VENUS - CHIRON: This type of aspect protects health and facilitates general wellbeing due to an innate ability to diagnose and treat occasional issues with ease and efficiency. Therapies and precision work that require creativity are favoured.

VENUS - URANUS: Enhances natural resourcefulness in sentimental life, friendship, and human relationships in general. There is a natural ability to adapt to most situations, keeping cool and efficient in most circumstances.

VENUS - NEPTUNE: Enhances natural artistic talents, especially in music and dancing. Emotiveness is managed constructively. This kind of aspect confers excellent creative ability, in the areas of life represented by the planets in the birth chart.

VENUS - PLUTO: Confers deep feelings making for profoundly meaningful relationships. Enhances natural creative ability as well as the interest for all things pertaining to the supernatural and to the mysteries of life.

* * * * * * * * * *

MARS - VESTA: The ability to act and react quickly is facilitated by this type of aspect that preserves harmony by use of diplomacy rather than force to obtain better results in the areas of life represented by the Houses concerned by Mars and Vesta in the chart.

MARS - JUPITER: Confers determination and willpower favouring success in the areas of life represented by these planets in the birth chart. Love of sport and an adventurous way of life are indicated.

MARS - SATURN: Confers seriousness, precision, and the ability to separate facts from fiction. Mathematics, surgery and military careers are some of the areas for personal success.

MARS - CHIRON: Surgeons and other precision workers are favoured. Quick diagnosis and reactions help solve sudden problems efficiently. There is potential to succeed in activities and situations in the areas represented by the Houses concerned in the chart.

MARS - URANUS: Enhances the natural ability to transform or revolutionise life. Gives excellent adapting capacity in the presence of adversity, favouring early success in life.

MARS - NEPTUNE: Enhances natural intuition and the ability to act instinctively in a positive and constructive manner. Excellent aspect for research work, medicine and in areas where a pioneering attitude is required.

MARS - PLUTO: Confers great physical strength and an excellent regenerating ability, whatever the problems of life may be. Enhances the ability to concentrate and to use inner resources to succeed.

VESTA - JUPITER: Confers a compassionate and generous approach to life and human relationships. It favours success due to an innate ability to recognise the right opportunities. Harmony and balance are enhanced by a positive attitude.

VESTA - SATURN: Allows stability and resilience to achieve the most important goals and succeed durably. A rational approach to the realities of life improves the ability to find pertinent solutions to problems and serenely overcome many obstacles.

VESTA - CHIRON: Harmony and balance are expressed to preserve health both physically and psychologically, as well as in the areas represented by Vesta and Chiron in the chart (Houses in Libra and Virgo, and the Houses where both are positioned).

VESTA - URANUS: Adaptability to unexpected circumstances and events allows to preserve balance and harmony despite occasional difficulties. Inventiveness is an asset to quickly find original solutions to many unforeseen crises.

VESTA - NEPTUNE: Intuition and inspiration are enhanced to become a source of creativity valuable to artists and to anyone embarked on a spiritual journey. Subtle connections with the inner self confer an innate understanding of the loftiest needs of human life.

VESTA - PLUTO: Enhances the regeneration potential to restore and preserve balance and harmony in the areas represented by the Houses concerned in the chart. Health and wellbeing are protected despite occasional crises and disruptions.

* * * * * * * * * *

JUPITER - SATURN: Enhances the ability to learn from life's lessons. What is acquired is used to complement the existing capital to progress and to expand. Long-term schemes and investments are favoured.

JUPITER - CHIRON: The general state of health is protected by a positive approach to occasional crises and ailments. There may be an interest in medicine and therapy motivated by a genuine need to be of service and positively useful to others.

JUPITER - URANUS: Ability to transform life in a positive way, there is great spontaneity to launch new schemes and develop ideas to improve the situation. Mental alertness and optimism are indicated.

JUPITER - NEPTUNE: Confers good will and strong spiritual needs. Great sensitivity and generosity are noticed. Interests in religion and in philosophy favour social success. The sixth sense is a spontaneous source of success.

JUPITER - PLUTO: Confers extreme energy to the expansion principle favouring success despite the occasional difficulties of life. Determination and endurance cohabit with a deeply generous and well-minded approach to human relationship.

* * * * * * * * * *

SATURN - CHIRON: A rational, objective, and serious-minded approach to health has a positive protecting effect. Saturn favours longevity. The value of personal experience is useful to deal with occasional crises in the areas represented by the Houses concerned.

SATURN - URANUS: The ability to transform and change things around is well supported by a conservative attitude allowing for fewer mistakes to be made in the areas represented by these planets.

SATURN - NEPTUNE: Indicates the ability to put ideas into concrete forms to realise the most important objectives. Seriousness and endurance favour far-fetched projects. The ability to mix dreams with realities allows concrete realisations.

SATURN - PLUTO: The power conferred by Pluto is well supported by Saturn, giving it long lasting and sustained qualities. Confers a scientific mind and a more determined attitude in the areas of life represented by these two planets in the birth chart.

* * * * * * * * * *

CHIRON - URANUS: Adaptability and ingenuity to deal with various crises preserve wellbeing. The body has a natural ability to adjust to unforeseen health issues. This process is also useful in the areas represented by the Houses concerned in the chart.

CHIRON - NEPTUNE: Body and soul are connected and communicating to protect physical and psychological health. Intuition helps find lofty solutions to occasional health crises. The aspect is also useful in the areas represented by the Houses concerned in the chart.

CHIRON - PLUTO: This type of aspect represents an innate ability to regenerate and heal. It protects health and enhances the longevity potential. Physical resilience is a source of strength to deal efficiently with crises.

* * * * * * * * * *

URANUS - NEPTUNE: Gives extremely acute intuition and ability to sudden and original inspiration. There is an innate ability in art and in all creative activities. The areas of life represented by both planets in the chart are primarily concerned

URANUS - PLUTO: Confers excellent regenerating ability and adaptability, especially in the areas of life represented by these two planets in the birth chart. Inventiveness and resilience cohabit to favour original solutions to the most challenging crises.

* * * * * * * * * *

NEPTUNE - PLUTO: The beneficial influence of such an aspect is like a lucky charm in today's society. In the present times of lust and power, destruction, wars and conflicts of all sorts, Neptune allows the new generation to combat wickedness and selfishness to improve the world.

* * * * * * * * * *

SQUARES AND OPPOSITIONS

In the context of this supplementary section, squares and oppositions are considered in only one category: "the discordant aspects". Refer to the previous lessons to make the difference between squares, inconjuncts, and oppositions.

SUN - MOON: Can restrict physical development. Indicates some degree of incompatibility between the parents. In a woman's chart that kind of aspect indicates some difficulty to accept and assume femininity or motherhood.

SUN - MERCURY and SUN - VENUS: Squares or oppositions not possible.

SUN - MARS: Tends to render aggressive, impulsive, and prone to arguments and accidents of all sorts. Courage and temerity are also conferred but the outcome of such bravery is often to the detriment of health and safety.

SUN - VESTA: Harmony and balance are challenged by the ego and the inadequate behaviour it occasionally produces. There is a need for more appropriate practices to replace those responsible for chronic crises in the areas represented by the Houses concerned.

SUN - JUPITER: Creates either an overgenerous personality or a rather selfish attitude, depending on sign and house position of these two planets. Too much optimism makes for many mistakes. Health problems may be due to poor blood circulation, liver malfunction and blood pressure.

SUN - SATURN: Confers a rather pessimistic approach to the realities of life in general. Shyness leads to introversion and solitude or melancholia. Saturn here restricts the life principle, slowing down natural growth or producing physical deficiencies.

SUN - CHIRON: Vital energy is essential to remain in good health. This type of aspect indicates physiological fluctuations that can lead to serious issues. There is a need to be more objective and analytical to prevent disturbances in the areas represented by the Houses concerned.

SUN - URANUS: Renders quite nervous and unstable, experiencing physical stress and difficulty to concentrate on anything for long. Accidents of all sorts are possible because of lack of vigilance or carelessness.

SUN - NEPTUNE: Confers a tendency to dream and imagine rather than face up to reality. There may be attraction to drugs or alcohol. It can also render physiologically too weak to overcome the obstacles of life due to a certain vulnerability.

SUN - PLUTO: Two extremes are in confrontation... The Sun, giver of life and Pluto, the outer planet, dark and lonely, so far away from the beneficial sun activity. It confers a tendency to be pulled between the notions of life and death. Construction and destruction cohabit with difficulty...

* * * * * * * * * *

MOON - MERCURY: Difficulties to communicate are indicated due to interferences between emotions and mental processes. Problems may have their root in poor relationship with the mother leading to uneasiness with women in general.

MOON - VENUS: Emotions are strongly influenced by the movements of the heart. Extreme sensitivity is a source of punctual discomfort and confusing relationships. A difficulty to relate to women is also indicated as well as a dependency on emotions and romantic feelings.

MOON - MARS: There are emotional stress and aggressiveness when personal feelings are aroused. This can lead to all sorts of difficulties with members of the opposite sex. The role of the mother may be the cause for inhibitions and inner contradictions.

MOON - VESTA: Emotions destabilise and create uncertainty in the areas represented by the Houses concerned in the chart. They can be a source of ambiguity and worries with undesirable health consequences due to emotional vulnerability.

MOON - JUPITER: Generosity is often considered to deserve a reward in return. Opportunism and apparent optimism serve to hide emotional vulnerability. There may be a strong need to help others to the detriment of personal wellbeing.

MOON - SATURN: Can produce an 'old fashioned' look and attitude due to a restricting education and disturbing events in early life. Fate seems to play an important part in the development and expression of emotiveness.

MOON - CHIRON: Emotions have a detrimental effect on the general state of health. Early life may be marked by family crises or physiological issues that produce a tendency to worry, thus favouring the development of various discomforts.

MOON - URANUS: The emotions are subject to numerous sudden changes. The attitude is unpredictable and moved by memorable fits of temper. The mind is overflowing with thoughts and ideas that are difficult to be transformed into concrete forms.

MOON - NEPTUNE: The unconscious and subconscious minds are in conflict. There is a degree of difficulty to distinguish between dreams and reality. A tendency to psychosomatic illness and subjectivity to drugs or alcohol are indicated.

MOON - PLUTO: The emotions tend to have a self-destructive effect. There seems to be a latent torment for no apparent reasons.

Childhood or motherhood may have been marked by great emotional stress and difficulties.

MERCURY - MARS: Sharp intellectual activity and impulsiveness can become a source of arguments, heated discussions and gossiping. An overpowering tendency to mentalise makes it difficult to relate agreeably to others and communicate pleasantly.

MERCURY - VESTA: There is difficulty to communicate to preserve harmony and balance. The mind is working overtime to find solutions to relationship issues with little or no success. Outside influence alters rationality and intellectual stability.

MERCURY - JUPITER: Indicates great curious and the ability to learn quickly but superficially. Principles of justice, fair play, spiritual progression, and social order are used to achieve prominence, rather than being sincere personal opinions.

MERCURY - SATURN: The learning process is slow and communication at all levels is made difficult because of the restricting influence of Saturn representing education or all other forms of fateful influences.

MERCURY - CHIRON: Mind and body are closely related and interfering with each other to the point of inducing negative thinking which enhances the idea of being sick or threatened by unforeseen health issues. Focusing on details leads to irrational worry.

MERCURY - URANUS: Nervousness and instability are indicated. There is difficulty to concentrate and to focus on any subject for long. In some cases, the influence of Uranus can lead to psychosomatic or even mental disorders.

MERCURY - NEPTUNE: Confers great imagination but some difficulty to relate to realities in a pragmatic and orderly manner. The need for mental stimuli can motivate the use of artificial mediums such as drugs, alcohol, or medicine.

MERCURY - PLUTO: The mind is destructive and morbidly attracted to the mysteries of life and death. The personal perception of the world is rather dark and pessimistic, and occasionally harsh and destructive. Sarcasm or cynicism deter personal relationships.

* * * * * * * * * *

VENUS - MARS: Arguments with romantic partners, a bossy attitude and aggressive manners are likely to make sentimental life complicated. It can also indicate a struggle to accept and assume one's own gender. Love and hate cohabit with great difficulty.

VENUS - VESTA: Indicates some difficulty to control and harmonise romantic needs and relationships. Dependence on love and approbation leads to errors of judgment and moral dissatisfaction in the areas represented by the Houses concerned by this configuration.

VENUS - JUPITER: Excessive generosity, optimism and trust in human goodness lead to moral and sentimental disappointment. The need to love and to be loved is overwhelming and a source of moral and romantic shortcomings.

VENUS - SATURN: Shyness and secretive sensuality are indicated. Late marriage or celibacy may result. The need for love and affection is often disappointing. A fatalistic opinion of personal human relationships may stem from unfortunate childhood events.

VENUS - CHIRON: Love and romance can become a source of health issues when feelings trigger a tendency to worry and doubt sincerity in intimate relationships. The areas represented by the Houses concerned are subject to chronic health crisis.

VENUS - URANUS: Romance is subject to sudden changes. Erratic and unstable feelings seem to last only while curiosity is excited. There is an innate attraction for original, unusual, or eccentric romantic partners and sentimental lifestyles.

VENUS - NEPTUNE: This combination produces some difficulties to realise the ideal romance. To forever wait for a fairy tale type of relationship leads to disappointments and disillusions. Intuition and sensibility cohabit to create sentimental uncertainty.

VENUS - PLUTO: Destructive tendencies are expressed with romantic partners in sentimental involvement. Profoundly distressful events in personal life are often represented by this type of aspect. Sexuality strongly influences intimate relationships.

* * * * * * * * * *

MARS - VESTA: Impulsive reactions are a source of discord that threatens balance and harmony in private and social relationships. Feeling threatened creates a defensive attitude with detrimental consequences in the areas represented by the Houses concerned.

MARS - JUPITER: Eager to succeed and to expand personal wealth and intellectual or spiritual position, creates an aggressive and generous but impulsive or opportunistic attitude. It may lead to disappointment issued from an overwhelming need to please others to gain their recognition and respect.

MARS - SATURN: This is a dangerous kind of influence as far as accidents and physical disorders are concerned. Time and space misevaluations are a source of hesitation and doubt. The effect varies according to the signs and Houses concerned by this configuration.

MARS - CHIRON: This configuration indicates sudden physical incidents with unpleasant health consequences. A tendency to rush into conclusions produces contradicting reactions and chronic tension in the areas represented by the Houses concerned in the chart.

MARS - URANUS: Nervousness and instinctive aggressivity create all sorts of difficulties due to lack of consideration and excessive precipitation. Impatience and temerity become a source of sudden incidents with unpleasant and stressful consequences.

MARS - NEPTUNE: Dreams of power may linger in the mind and influence life greatly. Problems with the nervous system and accidents due to nervousness and fear are likely. There may be adverse medical side effects and a strong dislike of hospitals and confined places.

MARS - PLUTO: Creates a very destructive personality. Whether this tendency is directed toward others or oneself depends on the rest of the birth chart as well as the Houses and sign positions of the planets. Death may happen suddenly and sometimes in violent circumstances.

* * * * * * * * * *

VESTA - JUPITER: Excessive generosity leads to personal loss and disappointment. Balance and harmony in human relationship can become detrimental to personal needs and wellbeing. Deceptive influences affect the areas represented by the Houses concerned.

VESTA - SATURN: Limitations are self-imposed, says the philosopher. The potential to preserve harmony and balance is tempered by doubt and wrong calculation. Restrictions create frustration and lack of confidence in the areas represented by the Houses concerned.

VESTA - CHIRON: It seems difficult to preserve or restore physiological balance and harmony when health issues strike. A tendency to overanalyse and worry damages the efficiency needed to solve problems in the areas represented by the Houses concerned.

VESTA - URANUS: Sudden changes are destabilising. The nervous system is subject to unexpected surges of strong energy that may affect wellbeing with detrimental consequences in the areas represented by the Houses concerned.

VESTA - NEPTUNE: Imagination can become a source of disappointment and regrets due to poor planning and a tendency to nourish dreams more than reality. Inner harmony is tempered by the difficulty to connect with the spiritual dimension of life.

VESTA - PLUTO: The idea of death tempers the need for harmony and wellbeing by making difficulties darker than they really are. A sombre approach to the realities of life affects enthusiasm and the ability to regenerate and restore balance in the areas represented by the Houses concerned in the chart.

* * * * * * * * * *

JUPITER - SATURN: Restriction of the expansion principle creates worries and difficulties of all kinds. Pulled between the tendencies to save and to spend, financial problems can be expected together with melancholia and depression. There is no need to count on luck to succeed. Work, patience, and determination are much better assets.

JUPITER - CHIRON: Health is a source of excessive worry that can lead to hypochondriac tendencies. The digestive system suffers from anxiety with various unpleasant effects. A constant effort to avoid exaggerating is necessary to keep a rational approach of life's challenges.

JUPITER - URANUS: There is a tendency to change from one attitude to another, to suit the situation, thus creating instability of thoughts and actions. Financial ups and downs are also likely due to a lack of proper planning and excessive generosity.

JUPITER - NEPTUNE: A tendency to be intellectually and spiritually influenced can lead to unrealistic schemes and involvement such as in religious organisations, sects, or utopistic and disappointing financial ventures.

JUPITER - PLUTO: Lust for power and great financial success may lead to the use of controversial methods to attain the desired goals. Great care should be taken when dealing with joint resources, corporate money for personal rather than mutual interests.

* * * * * * * * * *

SATURN - CHIRON: A negative approach to personal physical resources may temper health with durable restricting consequences. Pessimism is often mistaken for lucidity to enhance self-limitations and lack of realisation in the areas represented by the Houses concerned.

SATURN - URANUS: Disturbing events can radically and unexpectedly change the course of life. Fate plays a crucial part in the development of personal philosophy. Conservatism and liberalism cohabit to create a paradoxical personality and way of life. The areas represented by the signs and Houses in the chart are also concerned by this controversial aspect.

SATURN - NEPTUNE: The dream principle is restricted by the presence of Saturn. There is a conflict between imagination and reality. Living in a down-to-earth world surrounded by material possessions is uneasy to deal with. Medicine can produce adverse reactions and unpleasant side effects.

SATURN - PLUTO: Poor regeneration power is indicated. It may take longer to recover from illnesses or emotional setbacks. Educational background is mostly responsible for latent fears and existential limitations. Death may have played a crucial part in the development of the personal approach of the mysteries of life.

* * * * * * * * * *

CHIRON - URANUS: Health depends on the ability to preserve it with a stable and rational treatment of what body and soul need to feel well. This configuration produces unforeseen health changes due to a lack of control issued from overactive neuronal activity.

Caution should be exercised to avoid crisis in the areas represented by the Houses concerned.

CHIRON - NEPTUNE: Medicine is used to treat various ailments successfully. However, this configuration warns of possible adverse side effects. Allergic tendencies of psychosomatic origins are indicated. Lack of rationality may become a source of unrealistic health issues. It can also temper the areas represented by the Houses concerned in the chart.

CHIRON - PLUTO: Self-destructing tendencies are not always considered as such. Hence, the negativity of various habits slowly but surely tempers physiological condition with unpleasant consequences. A more optimistic approach of health and hygiene requirements is a source of positive energy to help preserve or restore rather than disturb.

* * * * * * * * * *

URANUS-NEPTUNE: Extremely sensitive and easily influenced into the most extravagant schemes, the mind is perpetually disturbed by uncontrollable thoughts and ideas that can lead to neurologic disorders. However, the influence of such slow planets must be analysed according to House positions to understand its true role in individual life.

URANUS-PLUTO: The same remark applies here. Such an influence touches a whole generation of people. Those born in the 1930s present a Square Uranus-Pluto in their charts. They have all been confronted to wars and drastic political or economic changes in their lives. There has been another square between 2011 and 2018 when nuclear issues were brought about following the Fukushima catastrophe in March 2011.

* * * * * * * * * *

NEPTUNE-PLUTO: No one living today can have this kind of aspect in their birth chart. However, when it occurs the Square or

Opposition Neptune-Pluto will indicate social turmoil and the destruction of religious, mystical, and social beliefs to the profit of a new spiritual order.

Lesson 17

THE ASPECTS
(Part 5)

An aspect between two or more planets is a "primary" energy field that should always be analysed in relation with the signs in which the planets are found. The "principles" of life represented by the planets take on the quality of the signs in which they stand at the time of birth.

The aphorisms contained in the supplementary section at the end of the previous lesson relate to the planets as principles of life, and not according to their sign or house positions which will also need to be taken into consideration. Never use the descriptions in the supplementary sections as a final product. Mix them and reorganise them accordingly to obtain the best possible interpretation of every aspect in the chart.

IMPORTANT RULE

Aspects are always considered FROM the fastest planet TO the slowest one. For example: Mercury conjunct Venus, NOT Venus conjunct Mercury.

The order, Sun, Moon, Mercury, Venus, Mars, Vesta, Jupiter, Saturn, Chiron, Uranus, Neptune, and Pluto is to be kept when Describing the aspects.

The Sun comes first because of its obvious importance upon human nature. Then the aspects from the Moon are considered, followed by those from Mercury, then Venus, Mars, and so on. Therefore, you will not find in Mercury's section, for example, *Mercury conjunct Sun* because such aspect is explained in the sections about the Sun.

Because Mercury and Venus are closer to the Sun than the Earth and that their speed of rotation allows for more retrograde motions, Mercury and Venus will never be found in a chart further apart than a sextile.

The same applies to possible aspects between the Sun and Mercury, the Sun and Venus. The Sun will never be further apart from Mercury or Venus than an angle of 42° which is almost a half-square (45°). The conjunction is therefore quite frequent, as well as the sextile and half-sextile. A sextile Mercury-Venus is the largest possible major aspect to be *found* between the two planets.

That said, remember that **an aspect works both ways**. The chronological order is only meant for convenience of classification. A sextile Mercury-Venus, for example, does not only mean that Mercury benefits from the energy of Venus. It also means that Venus benefits from the energy of Mercury.

You learned in previous lessons that the aspects must be considered according to the planets as such. They are dealt with in the supplementary section called **"ASPECTS BETWEEN PLANETS"** at the end of lesson 16.

You also need to use the aphorisms contained in that same supplementary section to analyse the positions of the planets in the signs **and** in the houses.

An example will certainly make it easier for you to understand than a lengthy explanation... Imagine that in a birth chart we find Mercury square Mars. See the example chart on the following page.

Without taking into consideration the position of the two planets in the signs or in the houses, refer to the supplementary section called **"ASPECTS BETWEEN PLANETS"** in lesson 16, in the chapter relating to "squares and oppositions". About **Mercury - Mars**. It says:

"The ability to communicate and the intellectual principle are aggressive, abrupt and impulsive. There is a tendency to argue, gossip and to be prone to incidents and accidents of all kinds."

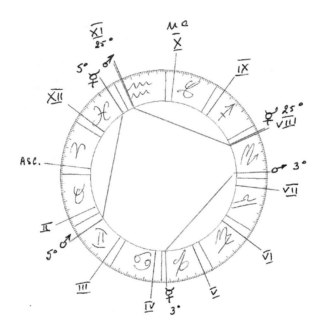

This is a basic analysis of the square Mercury-Mars. The square is a difficult aspect creating tension between the principles represented by the planets involved. This is a fact, as explained in the previous lessons.

On the drawing you see that I have placed 3 possible square aspects between Mercury and Mars. Of course, this cannot happen in a birth chart as there are only one Mercury and one Mars. In this particular and rather unusual chart, you can see three squares between Mercury and Mars.

1) Mercury 5° Pisces   Mars 5° Gemini

2) Mercury 3° Leo   Mars 3° Scorpio

3) Mercury 25° Scorpio   Mars 25° Aquarius

These are "true aspects" (orb 0°) therefore strong aspects. The smaller the orb, the stronger the aspect.

I have chosen 3 different square positions between the same planets so that you understand the importance of considering all aspects according to signs and houses as well as according to the principles represented by such planets.

The square Mercury-Mars is a ***"fixed feature"***, if I may say, as far as the principles of life are concerned. That never changes. The intellectual and aggressive principles are experiencing a ***"tensed"*** relationship. That tension, however, can have a different ***"intensity"*** from one square to another. That ***"intensity"*** depends upon the **sign positions** of the planets involved. In the first instance, Mercury is in Pisces and Mars in Gemini. Referring to the list *of **planets in signs*** included in the first lessons of this course, see what information Mercury in Pisces and Mars in Gemini give to the analysis of that square.

Mercury in Pisces: *Logic and understanding processes are rather weak but intuition and sensibility are excellent, etc.*

Mars in *Gemini:* *gives an aggressive and "cheeky" manner of expression... Willpower is more abundant in words and ideas than in action.*

In this case, the tension created by the square Mercury-Mars may be analysed as follows:

"Because of a certain lack of logic and understanding, the mind is defensively aggressive, and a rude manner of speech is used to protect the native's inner uncertainty and confusion ."

In a way, Mars here supports the native's intellectual difficulties by showing apparent character strength and determination. Unfortunately, the effect of such "support" is to distort objectivity and create a defensive and possibly blind and self-centred intellectual attitude.

In the next instance, Mercury is found in Leo and Mars in Scorpio. Even before we look up what the positions of these planets in signs mean, we notice that Mars is very strong in that aspect because it is the ruler of Scorpio, the sign where it is found. We know, therefore, that Mars creates more tension than in the previous case.

Under Mercury in Leo, we read: *"Pride and an overwhelming manner of speech can create communication difficulties because of a tendency to think too much of oneself. Generosity, enthusiasm, honesty, and stability of thoughts and ideas are also indicated."*

We notice that this position of Mercury is also strong and can already create some tension without any aspect's involvement.

Mars in Scorpio tells: *"inner strength and powerful emotions and desires. The native is resourceful and courageous, capable of achieving anything he puts his mind and will to. The influence of Mars in Scorpio, however, can lead to the greatest heights as well as to the lowest degradation, depending on the rest of the chart."*

Blending could be done as follows:

"Pride, powerful emotions and desires create communication difficulties. The native is not ready to compromise and is prone to arguments of all kinds. The mind tends to be drawn to the lowest aspects of life: treachery, lies, and gossips."

However strong the above analysis may appear to be, it is not enough in itself to give a definite and proper opinion on the square Mercury-Mars . We will elaborate in a moment...

Right now, and this is part of your first-degree exam, analyse the square aspect between Mercury at 25^0 in Scorpio and Mars at 25^0 in Aquarius. Click on the link at the end of this lesson to reach the assignment form.

The position of each planet concerned in a particular sign is not enough to conduct a proper analysis of an aspect. We must consider these planets according to their **House positions** and to their **House(s) of rulership**, as explained in previous lessons.

From the example chart showing three different squares between Mercury and Mars, we need to determine what houses are concerned according to our two chosen examples.

In the first instance, Mercury in Pisces is found in House XI (friends and social life) and Mars in Gemini is in house II (money and material possessions).

That alone tends to indicate that arguments are likely with friends and social relationships based on money and personal possessions.

Furthermore, Mercury rules Gemini. In the chart we find that house III begins in Gemini. Therefore, Mercury rules that House. Referring to lesson 5, we find that House III represents the mind, the intellect, the ability to learn and to communicate. It also represents movement, short distance travel, siblings, and brotherhood.

These areas of life are therefore concerned by the square Mercury-Mars...

As for Mars, we know that it rules Aries, and we find House I in Aries. The inner personality is therefore affected by the square Mercury-Mars. All in all, Houses II and XI are primarily related to the aspect (Mercury in XI - Mars in II- friends and money). Then, according to their rulership, Houses III and I (communication and personality) are also concerned.

Going back to what we said about Mercury in Pisces square Mars in Gemini, earlier on (see previous pages) we wrote: **"Because of a certain lack of logic and understanding, the mind is defensively aggressive and a cheeky manner of speech is used to protect the native from inner uncertainty and confusion ."**

This analysis can now be complemented because we know in what areas of the native's life the influence of the square is likely to intervene. Thus, the aspect between Mercury and Mars can be extended and individualised as follows:

"Because of weakness with friends, the native tends to adopt a defensive attitude for protection, as a person, as well as for financial and material interests. Relationships are usually tensed and mainly based on the principles of money and other material possessions. The notion of death seems to strongly influence the native's mind. Relationships at work are also difficult. Health can fluctuate unexpectedly due to sudden illnesses, accidents at work or disturbing circumstances in social relationships. "

You see that we have come a long way since our first step analysis concerning the primary influence of Mercury square Mars solely on a planetary point of view. Every aspect in a chart must be analysed this way. Then, all the aspects must be blended. Linking planets with signs and Houses is essential and it must be done simultaneously.

Looking at Mars in the exercise chart with three Mars and three Mercury, one is in Aquarius in House XI, it rules House I (ASC in Aries). Mercury is in Scorpio, in House VIII. It rules House

III. To analyse the aspect, you must simultaneously take note of all the areas concerned and apply what you know of such Houses to the interpretation of the aspect.

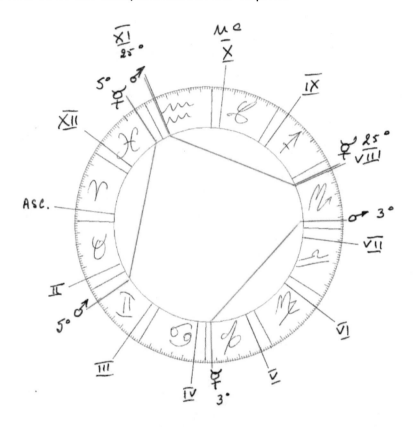

The same principle of analysing a square applies to all other aspects. Conjunctions, sextiles, trines, and oppositions must all be treated similarly. Then, they all need to be blended. Just like colours create a painting, each portion of the puzzle contributes to the final picture. But it's only when all the portions are correctly put together that the picture appears, and the work is finished.

Lesson 18

The aspects to the angular Houses

In this seventeenth lesson, you will learn to analyse the aspects between the planets and the four "crucial" points of the chart; **the Ascendant, Descendant, Nadir, and Mid-Heaven (MC).** Houses I and VII, IV and X.

As you know, these Houses, called **Angular Houses**, play major roles in the analysis of a birth chart. Therefore, astrologers consider their cusps as planets and the angles formed with other planets of the chart are called "**aspects**".

We will start with the basic effect of an aspect to the Ascendant without first considering the zodiac sign in which it is found. We know that there are harmonious and discordant aspects. It implies that any harmonious influence on the Ascendant brings strength and positive energy to the personality of the inner self which is fundamentally represented by his Ascendant.

On the contrary, a discordant aspect, creates tension or restrictions to the expression of the inner personality, in relation to the sectors of life represented by the planet/s involved in this type of aspect.

Use the example chart included in this lesson to follow, step by step what follows. First, we need to determine the aspects involving the Ascendant and make a list of them.

OPPOSITION SUN - ASCENDANT

TRINE VENUS - ASCENDANT

TRINE MARS - ASCENDANT

EXAMPLE CHART

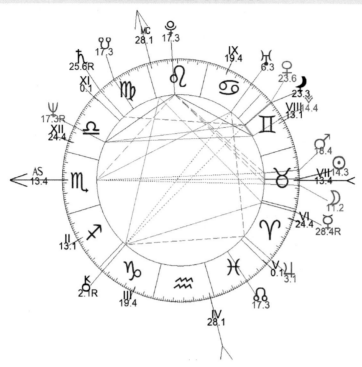

We now need to define the **planets-signs and planets-Houses** relationships.

Let us begin with the Sun.

The Sun is in Taurus, in House VII (Descendant).

What House is this Planet in control of?

The Sun rules Leo, therefore House X or Midheaven (MC) which begins in Leo in this example chart.

The opposition Sun-Ascendant being a discordant aspect, it indicates that the inner personality (represented by the Ascendant) conflicts with the outer personality represented by the Sun. In addition to various health concerns, It may create potential conflicts in partnerships (DESCENDANT or HOUSE VII) and difficulties linked to personal ambitions and career (represented by House X, Midheaven - MC).

The Sun-Moon-Mars conjunction in Taurus is opposed to the **Ascendant**, therefore conjunct to the cusp of **House VII**. This major configuration indicates a difficult birth and a life path marked by some underlying anger issued from the moment of birth. It may be responsible for many incidents, breakups, and other tensions within the family environment, with the parents, and with society in general as soon as an annoyance alters the relations with those around.

The Moon is ruler of House IX

Mars is ruler of House VI

The Sun is ruler of House X

Such aspects cannot be sources of ease, harmony, and relational wellbeing. They rather indicate excess by increasing the influence of Taurus, where these planets are found.

Next, we must check the rising sign and its ruler, Pluto.

We observe, in this example chart again, that Pluto forms a square with the Ascendant. This aspect affects House VII which is diametrically opposed to the Ascendant. This results in a destructive and self-defeating tendency through the sign of Leo, whose ruler is the Sun, which is found in Taurus. The conjunction of this star with the Moon and Mars in this sign illustrates well the enjoyable aspect and gargantuan limit of the needs of this person to the point of becoming a source of various health problems over the years (Venus, ruler of Taurus, the square of Saturn and the trine of Neptune...) The life path is hampered by many obstacles, one of which being a certain idleness and lack of ambition (square Venus-Saturn) despite an obvious taste and ability in music and musicology ((Venus-Neptune trine).

IMPORTANT RULE!
An aspect involving the ruler of the Ascendant with the cusp of the Ascendant is stronger than any other aspect from other planets in the chart.

The same rule applies to the aspects involving the cusps of the angular, cadent, and succedent Houses.

In our example, Mars Opposition Ascendant confers a lot of energy and will, together with a difficulty to control and channel inner strength. Determination to succeed, but lack of sustained stamina to complete personal projects. Impatience is indicated. The energy of Mars is also expressed in relationships or partnerships (Mars in House VII) where tensions and conflicts may arise suddenly.

The Moon in conjunction with the Sun indicates a fluctuating energy pattern. Health may be a source of chronic concern. Overeating (Taurus) does not help. The Moon is in House VI, the Sun is in House VII. They indicate a potential to work in the food industry, in restaurants, or in agriculture. *This person is married to a Taurus. They managed many restaurants and clubs in Australia together quite successfully.*

THE Opposition Sun-Ascendant indicates a state of perpetual conflict between the principle of life, represented by the Sun in Taurus, and the inner self, represented by the Ascendant in Scorpio. Such an aspect may be a source of health problems during the early years of life, due to a kind of "short-circuit" action between the primordial poles represented by the Sun and the Ascendant.

We must take many points into consideration when we analyse aspects between a planet and the cusp of an angular House.

The list of aphorisms in the supplementary section at the end of this lesson will guide your first analyses. However, remember once more that it is not a final product on which you can rely blindly. On the contrary and like what has been explained before in this book, consider **all aspects simultaneously**. As you know by now, the signs involved also have a decisive role to play in the analysis.

Let us progress a little further now.

We note that Mercury forms a trine with the MC, therefore a sextile with the NADIR. Mercury is the ruler of House VIII in Gemini.

These configurations make it easier to communicate with superiors and clientele at work, and the family, promoting success in these areas of life. Sectors of activity where writing, teaching, and travelling are valuable assets are greatly favoured.

Moreover, Uranus forms a trine with the Ascendant, but not a sextile with the Descendant (the orb is too wide). This planet confers originality and adaptability to changes. Uranus being the ruler of House IV means that the place of residence is also original and subject to many changes. Yet the square aspect from Jupiter shows that these changes have far-fetched ambitions that may be disappointing.

How to balance out contradictory influences?

In this example we can suggest that money is earned through personal expression and creation as well as hard work. This is because Jupiter is the ruler of House II (money earned from work) in Sagittarius and is found in House VI (professional life and health).

Although its influence is strong in Aries, we must consider the square with Uranus and the square with Chiron. Family life and health are represented by these planets. They indicate that many changes, especially during early life, were imposed by unfortunate circumstances rather than happily chosen. Chiron is the second ruler of House X, indicating difficulties at work due to various health issues.

IN YOUR OWN CHART NOW

See if there are any aspects involving the Angular Houses.

Using the principle described in this lesson and the list of aphorisms at the end of the lesson, try to analyse the aspects you find with the angular Houses in your chart.

HERE I WHAT YOU NEED TO DO

1) Take note of all aspects,

2) Take note of all Houses concerned,

3) See where the ruling planets of the angular Houses are and if they form aspects with the cuspids of these angular Houses.

Then proceed "in a circle", like a police investigation. You need to find as many clues as possible before reaching a conclusion. Aspects ARE the clues.

No conclusion can be made from a single aspect!

The problem with beginners is that they depend too much on what is written in the book.

If you want to become a good astrologer, *you must use your personal approach from the start*.

Feed your analysis with your own feeling, then compare your conclusions with the book to make sure your reading is correct.

HERE'S HOW YOU CAN PROCEED.

1 - Consider the aspect as being the centre of the spiral that you are about to analyse.

2 - Then turn to the planet forming this aspect.

3 - Then check the rulers of the angular Houses according to their positions in signs and in Houses.

4 - Then see if there are other aspects involving the planets mentioned in this list.

5 - Finally, examine all the possible aspects involving the rulers of the angular Houses and other planets in the chart.

* * * * * *

In relation to our example chart, here is what to consider when analysing the aspects involving the Ascendant.

- ASCENDANT IN SCORPIO.

- ASPECTS:

OPPOSITION MOON

OPPOSITION MARS

OPPOSITION SUN

- THE RULES OF THE ASCENDANT: PLUTO

PLUTO in LEO in HOUSE IX

- THE SUN IN HOUSE VII

- THE MOON IN HOUSE VI

THE SUN IS THE RULER OF THE MIDHEAVEN (MC)

THE MOON IS THE RULER OF HOUSE IX

The work becomes more complex as the list of aspects grows,

especially when aspects %between planets are plotted in addition to aspects between planets and angular Houses! ...

However, each section of such a list must be analysed separately before connecting it to the rest of the list.

The same process should be used for aspects involving the MIDHEAVEN, the NADIR and the DESCENDANT. The same could also be done for aspects involving PLANETS and CUSPIDS OF CADENT AND SUCCEDENT HOUSES (II - III - V - VI - VIII - IX - XI and XII).

* * * * * * * * * *

A WORD ON ASPECTS...

The **conjunction** necessarily involves an opposition with the cusp of the **opposite House**.

The **square** automatically results in a **square** with the **opposite** House cusp and sometimes a conjunction with the cusp of the House where the planet is found, and of course, an opposition with the cusp of the opposite House.

The sextile systematically results in a trine with the opposite House, but the trine does not necessarily result in a sextile with the opposite House. **The orb of the sextile is smaller than the orb of the trine.**

The conjunction is not always beneficial because it creates an opposition with the cusp of the opposite House and sometimes a square with the other two angular Houses. Also, because some planets create tension rather than comfort. Conflicting planets are Mars, Saturn, Uranus, and Pluto, then secondarily (but perhaps that is why we need to be more "cautious" about them) all the others, from the Sun to Chiron.

WHAT NEXT?

In the next lesson, we will study the importance of planetary concentrations in either of these angular houses.

To illustrate this lesson, we will analyse the birth chart of Elvis Presley, famous American singer. His lifestyle, sudden fame, and untimely death are clearly shown in his birth chart.

Before continuing to the next lesson, practice what has been explained in this one. Practice is the keyword to success. Learning an art requires regular practice to master the technique. Do so in a playful manner to make astrology a friend rather than a boring teacher.

SUPPLEMENTARY SECTION

Aspects with the cusps of the Angular Houses

Remember that one aspect rarely acts on its own. It is therefore necessary to consider what may otherwise intervene on a given aspect before drawing any conclusion.

Harmonic aspects between the Ascendant and:

The Sun:

Good balance between the inner self and the active expression of the personality. Ability to succeed and carry out life projects. Promotes good relationship with the father.

The Moon:

Good balance between personality and emotions allowing the development of warmth and understanding that benefit most relationships.

Mercury:

Promotes intellectual development and human relationships as well as a fondness for travels, reading, writing, and all forms of communication. A positive relationship with a brother or brother-like figure is also indicated.

Venus:

This type of aspect brings charm and good manners to the expression of the personality. Diplomacy and tact are also indicated. Emphasises physical beauty, kindness, and empathy with others. A positive influence from a sister or sister-life figure is also indicated.

Mars:

Energy and willpower favour success. The personality is strong and determined. This is a born-leader position of Mars. Good reflexes and physical strength with athletic potential are also conferred.

Vesta:

This type of aspect usually confers a harmonious and well-balanced personality attracting empathy and success in personal and social relationships. Artistic tendencies are also indicated.

Jupiter:

Promotes personality growth, producing a jovial, optimistic, and confident temperament. Often indicates generosity and luck, while increasing moral qualities conducive to personal and social success.

Saturn:

Seriousness and respect of authority and traditions characterise personality and make it endearing and stable. The depth of judgment, realism, and patience (unless contrary aspects) promote success.

Chiron:

The analytical approach to the different aspects of life, objectivity, and the sense of responsibility in human relationships promotes success and social and professional advancement.

Uranus:

Active intellect allows the personality to impose itself in various and most unexpected situations and areas of life. Quick reaction is often the source of success also favoured by surprising strokes of luck.

Neptune:

Thoughtfulness, intuition, and artistic tendencies are indicated. Great sensitivity and a spiritual approach to life's events favour their management and the development of personal potentials.

Pluto:

Enhances the power of regeneration. Depth and interest in the occult and the mysteries of life and death are often present. Inner physical strength, resilience, and endurance promote personal success.

Discordant aspects between the Ascendant and:

The Sun:

There is a contradiction between the inner personality and the expression of the outer self. Health may be a source of concern during childhood and in the later years of life. Difficulties with the father.

The Moon:

Indicates much emotiveness and some problems with or about the mother. Health depends on the emotional state. Self-expression undergoes fluctuations, often linked to the phases of the Moon.

Mercury:

Difficulties in expressing the inner personality. Problems with studies often related to difficult relations with teachers. Nervousness and intellectual instability. Siblings are sources of confusion or discord.

Venus:

The personality is sometimes too imbued with romanticism or, on the contrary, lacking empathy. Romantic experiences are disappointing. Ambiguity in the expression of personal feelings and sentiments.

Mars:

Plenty of energy but little diplomacy and patience create relationship tensions and conflicts. Arrogance and excessive authority harm personal relationships. Painful breakups leave deep moral scars.

Vesta:

The expression of the inner self fluctuates between brightness and melancholy. It requires a constant effort to preserve balance and harmony in important personal relationships.

Jupiter:

Optimism, self-confidence, and generosity share the expression of personality with their opposites. Jupiter promotes the appearance and aggravation of health and personal relations, or social disorders.

Saturn:

Austerity, melancholia, and pessimism temper the positive expression of the inner self. Celibacy or a feeling of loneliness comes from lack of self-confidence. Excessive moral rigour and rigidity.

Chiron:

Socio-professional difficulties and their repercussions in personal life are often the result of a lack of objectivity or practicality. Health can also affect the ability to succeed by altering personal performance.

Uranus:

Nervousness, instability, and impatience are responsible for errors of judgment and strategy. They affect the potential to realise projects and to achieve social, professional, or personal goals.

Neptune:

Extreme impressionability is indicated. Erratic hormonal system. Respiratory and sleep disorders. Great intuition and inspiration but lack of realism and perseverance to make dreams come true.

Pluto:

Self-destructive tendency. Domineering temperament. Strong

sexual needs. Health issues may affect sexual organs and the natural elimination function. Dark or morbid approach to personal relations.

Harmonic aspects between the Midheaven and:

The Sun:

Promotes good relations with the father and with hierarchy in general unless contrary aspects are found in the chart. Success is due to a positive approach and management of situations and issues.

The Moon:

Promotes success in public careers and in professions related to children, art, or femininity. The mother or mother figure plays an important role in the achievement of important personal projects.

Mercury:

Success is favoured by the intellectual efficiency and communication skills. The father or father figure may play a major role in the choice of a career. Success leans on sharing ideas and concepts with others.

Venus:

Luck often plays a determining and positive role in increasing the potential to succeed. Optimism enhances the skill and quality of work. A gentle and creative approach favour success and popularity.

Mars:

Willpower, strength, speed, and efficiency of action are major assets to succeed in most personal projects. Can indicate the help or support of the father. Success is favoured in areas where physical energy is an asset.

Vesta:

Relations with professional hierarchy are favoured by the

stabilising and harmonising energy of Vesta. This type of aspect indicates a more serene management of constraints and other responsibilities.

Jupiter:

Luck, efficiency, and positivity promote social and professional success. Positive influence of the father regardless of the quality of the relationship. The trine is found in the chart of many prominent personalities in the entertainment industry, business, and politics.

Saturn:

Seriousness, depth, endurance, and patience are the basis for success. Long-term projects are particularly favoured. Respect of hierarchy, authority, and traditions. Time is a major asset to succeed.

Chiron:

Increases analytical skills essential to realise important projects. Positive relationships favour the evolution of professional life. An interest in health can lead to a career in medicine or pharmacy.

Uranus:

Originality, speed of adaptation, intelligence and inventiveness contribute to social and professional success and to the achievement of personal projects. Friendly relations with parents and siblings.

Neptune:

Intuition, imagination, and sixth sense favour personal or professional success. The role of the family is noticed in social life and career. Projects are fostered by a positive holistic approach.

Pluto:

Depth, tenacity, and courage are the keys to social success and personal ambitions. Inheritance or heredity plays an important role on the social status and the development or choice of a career.

Discordant aspects between Midheaven and:

The Sun:

Personal behaviour and expression are sometimes detrimental to the realisation of projects and to the career. Relations with the father may be at the root of difficulties with authority and hierarchy.

The Moon:

Emotionality or relationships with women seem to affect the chances of success. The mother may or may have had an ambiguous influence on the potential for social or professional realisation.

Mercury:

Lack of self-discipline and dispersal of intellectual capacities do not promote success. The attitude toward the father and the intellectual relations with him are valuable to understand the motivations.

Venus:

Often indicates frustrated artistic aspirations and the impact of romantic life on social behaviour with their influence on the realisation of personal ambitions. Ambiguity with or about the father.

Mars:

There is a tendency to rebel against authority and hierarchy. Hastiness and aggressiveness increase tensions and unrest. Anger and resentment may colour the relationship with both parents.

Vesta:

Problems arise from the difficulty to preserve balance and

harmony in relationships with hierarchy or authority. A chronic tendency to procrastinate enhances an feeling of incompetence.

Jupiter:

Ambitions fly high, hence are difficult to achieve. Excessive optimism, enthusiasm and opportunism are detrimental to efficiency. Social life rather than personal convictions influences the desire to succeed.

Saturn:

Delays, frustrations, and other obstacles slow down the progression and realisation of the career. Indicates the restrictive influence of the father and difficulties relating to authority in most forms.

Chiron:

This type of aspect seems to interfere with the recognition of hierarchy. Analytical skills and critical thinking interfere with the realisation of important projects. Errors in judgment are likely.

Uranus:

Dispersion, lack of coordination, extreme independence, and the desire for freedom hinder success by causing sudden and drastic setbacks. Father-child relationships are original and often troubling.

Neptune:

Idealism and unrealism push toward irrational and utopian goals. Sixth sense does not seem to work to the advantage of projects and goals. Failures are due to errors in judgment and in risk assessments.

Pluto:

The approach is often totalitarian and radical, resulting in professional and social setbacks. Career progression is punctuated by deep questioning and reassessment of projects and ambitions.

Harmonic aspects between Nadir and ...

The Sun:

The intensity of family relationships and the home play a major role in the achievement of social and professional objectives. A positive relationship with the parents is a source of strong incentive.

The Moon:

Indicates a profound attachment to family and home. The search for harmony with loved ones promotes positive human relationships. Women seem to play a constructive role in various ways and areas.

Mercury:

Intelligent relationships with loved ones promote a friendly atmosphere in the home with parents and siblings. There is a positive influence of a brother on the development of intellectual pursuits.

Venus:

Love and harmony characterise family relationships, except with contrary planetary aspects. Venus increases emotional attachment to family values which promote social and sentimental achievement.

Mars:

Much energy and activity deployed for family causes and the protection of the home and residence. Relationships with loved ones are a source of motivation with positive professional consequences.

Vesta:

The need for harmony and wellbeing is expressed in the home and in family relationships. This can have a positive influence on the socio-professional level. Success stems from a positive image of the self.

Jupiter:

Philosophy, religion, aristocracy, and bourgeoisie are part of family heredity and ancestral heritage. Help from the parents, especially the mother, is an important factor of positive motivation and success.

Saturn:

Strong material and moral values are the dominant elements in family relationships. They are often responsible for lasting social and professional success. Inheritance may facilitate personal ambitions.

Chiron:

The positive energy of Chiron acts like a "medicine" when a family concern or problem arises. A sense of observation and analytical skills preserve or restore wellbeing at home, with parents and siblings.

Uranus:

An original and fraternal family environment promotes social relationships and professional success. Originality and the notions of freedom and independence are part of the positive moral heritage.

Neptune:

Often indicates an artistic or religious family background and a home where social concepts have a philosophical and holistic perspective. They promote social success and harmony with loved ones.

Pluto:

Intensity, depth, and authenticity produce a strong attachment to family values. Socio-professional success is favoured by ancestry and heredity. Important material or moral inheritances are likely.

Discordant aspects between Nadir and ...

The Sun:

Family problems and breakups due to certain differences with parents are responsible for many setbacks. The ego seems to play a preponderant role to trigger conflicts in family relationships.

The Moon:

The influence of the family on the emotional behaviour is noticeable. The role of the mother is preponderant. The emergence of problems in personal or social relations is linked to unpleasant family situations.

Mercury:

Indicates difficulties to communicate with family members and to interact with loved ones. Ethnic origin or heredity may also be a source of social, intellectual, cultural, and professional incapability.

Venus:

Indicates awkward family relations triggering emotional uneasiness with parents. Romantic life or marriage may become dependent on family influence for its development, fulfilment, or stagnation.

Mars:

Indicates tensions in relations with parents leading to family conflicts, breakups, and accidents. Serious events can strongly alter the quality of personal life, with repercussions in various social areas.

Vesta:

Peace in the home and family depends on the ability to

preserve harmony in relationships with siblings. Problems with or about the parents may be a source of destabilisation and affective dependence.

Jupiter:

The ambition is great, and extreme generosity with loved ones may be a source of disappointment despite the costly effort to be appreciated. Ambitious family plans generate financial strife.

Saturn:

Indicates an underprivileged family background, difficulties, and limitations due to origins or heredity. Projects take more time to complete. Education is a source of frustration and dissatisfaction.

Chiron:

A loved one's health may be or has been the source of family hardship and limitations. There may be a tendency to somatise due to a feeling of inability to manage home life effectively or constructively.

Uranus:

Sudden or frequent changes of residence are indicated. Instability in family relationships may be due to original or marginalised parents due to their manner of managing home-life and family values.

Neptune:

Indicates a confused or inconsistent family background. Uncertainty about the place of residence, heredity or ethnic origins makes it awkward to engage constructively into realistic home-life projects.

Pluto:

Can indicate destruction of family environment. Real or symbolic "death" of a parent is possible. Authoritarian and intolerant attitude is a source of profound dissatisfaction and loss of interest in siblings.

Harmonic aspects between the Descendant and ...

The Sun:

Associations or marriage often contribute to social success and the development of life in the sector represented by the Sun (House in Leo). There is an interest in group activities and projects.

The Moon:

This type of aspect promotes human relationships that depend on the emotional. Marital relationships are important, as are family values. The mother may play a positive role in the evolution of life.

Mercury:

Intellectual interactions are important in marriage and partnerships in general. Travel and communication are a source of common enrichment. The need to share with others is crucial and motivating.

Venus:

This type of aspect improves the quality of human relationships in general. There is a strong need for harmony and wellbeing in human interaction. This tendency is a source of personal and social success.

Mars:

Active energy, combativeness, and strength enhance the potential to succeed in social and personal relationships. Sports and other physical activities are often essential in most human interactions.

Vesta:

The quest for harmony favours human relationships of all

kinds. Personal and professional partnership are sources of wellbeing and positive realisations. Sharing is essential to positive interaction.

Jupiter:

Indicates generosity and open-mindedness to others. Success is often linked to a positive partnership in which enthusiasm and optimism feed constructive interaction. The need to be good to others is great.

Saturn:

Indicates the ability to collaborate with competent and experienced people with whom relationships are rational and effective on a long-term basis. Social, professional, or personal success is favoured.

Chiron:

Relationships are a source of "healing" positive energy. Sharing important ideas is an important aspect of personal and social relationships. Interaction is intelligent and rationally constructive.

Uranus:

Originality and independence characterise private or social relationships imbued with humanism and creativity. The need to surprise others pleasantly helps counteract occasional discord.

Neptune:

Art, philosophy, religion, and dreams contribute to the success of personal and social relationships. Intuitive interaction plays a positive and constructive role in the development of important partnerships.

Pluto:

Increases the regeneration potential in personal and social relationships. It helps strengthen bonds to survive major issues. Depth of feelings and compassion favour constructive interaction.

Dissonant aspects between the Descendant and

The Sun:

Relational difficulties and character incompatibility do not favour harmonious relationships. The father may have a strong influence on the choice of personal, professional, or social partners.

The Moon:

Emotional dependence on others increase moral vulnerability. The mother may play a role in the development of unsatisfying human relationships. Difficulty to manage emotional stimuli.

Mercury:

Communication in human relationships is a source of discontent. An effort is necessary to be spontaneous and clear. Misunderstandings and intellectual differences make most partnerships unpleasant.

Venus:

Sentimental disappointments are common with this kind of aspect. Dependence on love and approbation in human relations is a source of displeasure. Celibacy may thus be viewed as a better option.

Mars:

Excessive authority and aggressiveness create conflicts in most types of human relationships. Lack of tolerance and patience makes it difficult to relate to others harmoniously and peacefully.

Vesta:

Although the quest for relationship harmony is present, it is a source of disappointment. There is an overzealous tendency that often produces unsatisfying results and much disappointment.

Jupiter:

Career, personal ambitions, and family environment are often responsible for growing difficulties in personal, professional, or social partnerships. Excessive enthusiasm and trust are deceived.

Saturn:

Partnerships are a source of setbacks and dissatisfaction. Celibacy or late marriage is often noticed. Mistrust, pessimism, and reluctance increase the "better-alone" preference to a fruitless relationship.

Chiron:

Human relationships are a source of moral or physical health concern. Worry emanates from a tendency to dissect, analyse, or criticise others that leads to a gradual degradation of relational wellbeing.

Uranus:

Difficulty in managing human interaction comes from an innate need for originality and nonconformism. Boredom is a source of frequent changes in partners or behaviour within the same relationship.

Neptune:

Lack of realism and confusion do not promote the development of stable relationships or lasting associations. Idealism is a source of disillusion due to an unrealistic approach to human interaction.

Pluto:

Constant questioning and a nihilistic approach to relationships create a latent tendency to dramatise negatively rather than consider the brighter side of human interaction. Painful breakups may result.

Lesson 19

Elvis Presley

Aspects to the birth chart's angular Houses

Born Tuesday, January 8, 1935 at 4:35 AM

Place: Tupelo (MS) USA

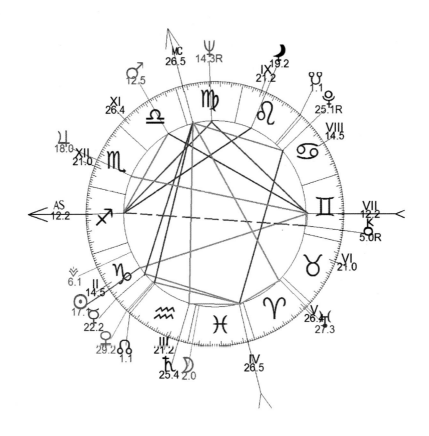

For this last lesson, I chose Elvis Presley's birth chart because I find it to be a good example to illustrate the importance of planetary influences when they are in aspect with the angular Houses. Everyone knows this man, his career, and his unusual lifestyle that led to his ill health and untimely death. His chart is very revealing on these subjects. Studying it will help you understand the importance of **the aspects to the angular Houses**.

For the moment, we will only deal with the planets involved with angular Houses and the links with other Houses in the chart. The Houses they rule and those where they are found.

First, we make a list of the aspects found in the chart between the planets and the angular Houses.

In this chart presented on the first page of this lesson, I have only drawn the aspects to the cusps of the angular Houses to make it easier for you to recognise them. However, they are usually found mingled with all the other aspects and should be analysed simultaneously. Not an easy task, but with time, perseverance, and regular practice, anyone can master the technique.

Below is a list of aspects organised in a chart to make them clearer to assess. Another chart regroups the links with various Houses represented by the planets involved in the aspects with the cusps of the angular Houses.

Then we will analyse such aspect, progressively taking more elements in consideration. You will realise how much one simple aspect can mean in terms of important repercussions in multiple areas of life. That is why it is crucial to proceed in this way.

List of aspects in Elvis Presley's birth chart.

	Ascendant	Descendant	Nadir	Mid-Heaven
Conjunction		Chiron		
Sextile	Mars		Mercury Venus	Pluto
Square	Neptune	Neptune		
Trine	Lilith	Mars	Pluto	Mercury Venus
Inconjunct		Sun Jupiter		Saturn Uranus
Opposition	Chiron			
Semi sextile			Saturn Uranus	

The planets involved are:

The Sun = ruler of House IX in House II
Mercury = ruler of House VII (Desc) in House II
Venus = ruler of House VI in House II
Mars = ruler of House V in House X (Mid Heaven)
Jupiter = ruler of House I (Asc) in House XI
Saturn = ruler of House II in House III
Chiron = ruler of House X (Mid Heaven) in House VI
Uranus = ruler of House III in House V
Pluto = ruler of House XII in House VIII

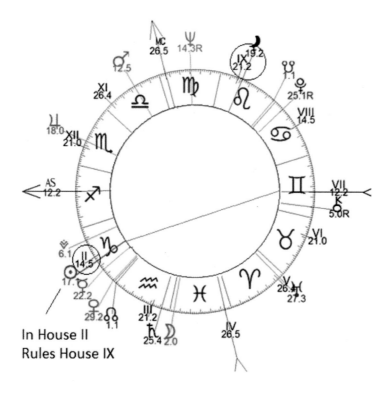

In House II
Rules House IX

Sun inconjunct House VII (Descendant). It indicates a life path marked by karmic difficulties (inconjunct) in relationships (House VII). Being the ruler of House IX positioned in House II, it is revealing of the importance of money in human relations. The legal side of a binding document made it often difficult for "the King" who was over generous with others to the point of absurdity. The aspect also coincides with his financial ordeals due to his dependency on money to preserve relationships without which he would ironically have been better without…

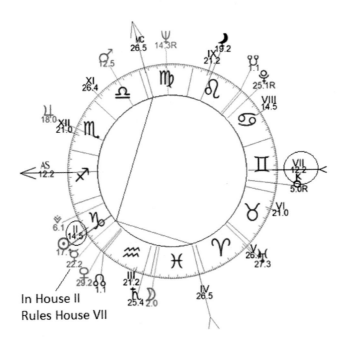

In House II
Rules House VII

Mercury sextile House IV (Nadir) and trine House X (Mid Heaven). These aspects show how well Elvis communicated with both his parents. His mother was the love of his life, while his father remained by his side until the end. Mercury rules House VII, confirming the potential alliance with his parents. His mother's untimely death put an end to her collaboration, but she was the backbone of Elvis's drive to succeed. Mercury in House shows the importance of money and its positive influence in his parents' lives.

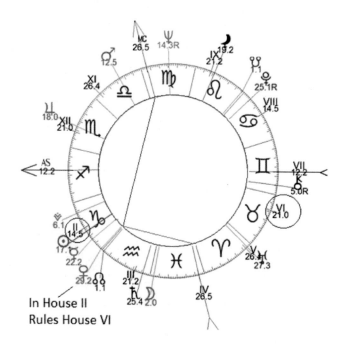

In House II
Rules House VI

Venus sextile House IV (Nadir) and trine House X (Mid Heaven). Love was the motor and the fuel to Elvis Presley's prolific talent. Both parents were a source of positive energy that made it a must for Elvis to express his affection to them and later to the whole world. His first, "It's Alright Mama" illustrates these beautiful configurations. Venus rules House VI and is found in House II, showing how much creativity, love and money cohabited to make him a household must in millions of families around the world and a true investment for those who depended on his talent and success for their financial ambition. Note the number of elements in House II, symbolically linked to Taurus, the second sign of the zodiac. Taurus, the voice, House II, the money. The North Lunar Node conjuncts Venus, the natural ruler of House II, ruling the sixth House in Elvis's chart. The trine to the MC describes the natural attraction and talent that made this extraordinary man a world legend.

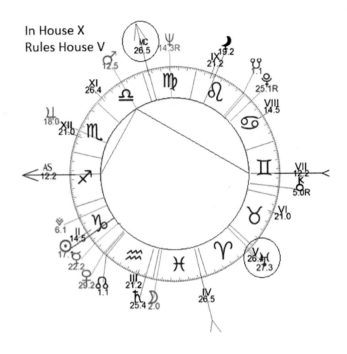

In House X
Rules House V

Mars sextile House I (Ascendant) and trine House VII (Descendant). Lots of energy was put to the service of personal pursuits and to all forms of relationships. Elvis was convincing and enthusiastic. Always on the go and eager to work with his musicians and other collaborators and associates. He felt responsible for those around and must have been a great source of motivation for many. Mars rules House V linked to creativity, love, and children that Elvis valued highly throughout his life, especially in his career, represented by House X, where Mars is found in his chart.

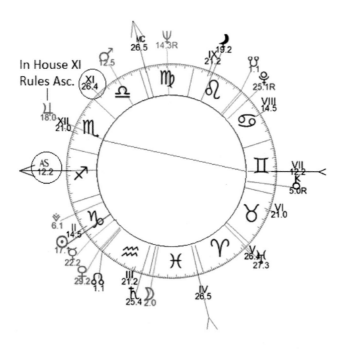

Jupiter inconjunct House VII (Descendant). Generosity was probably a way of trying to pay off some karmic debts. Extreme generosity, however, proved a source of profound moral disappointment. Jupiter rules the Ascendant and is found in House XI. How much his friends depended on Elvis's generosity and largess goes most certainly much further than what has been said, written and remembered. The "King's" excessive need for approbation made him a star as much as prey for the many vultures that revolved around him until his death.

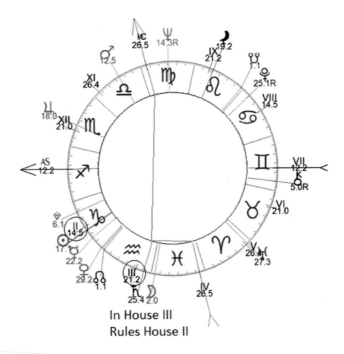

In House III
Rules House II

Saturn is inconjunct House X (Mid Heaven). It rules House II and is found in House III. There is a karmic reason to Elvis's ambition to succeed. Note that this inconjunct implies a semi-sextile with the Nadir. The difficulties he was confronted to in his early life, the loss of his twin brother (House III) and the financial strife (House II) derived from the Great Depression that hit the US in the thirties, became strong motivations to reach the highest level of social achievement. Success, however, became a source of ambiguity (inconjunct) and disillusions.

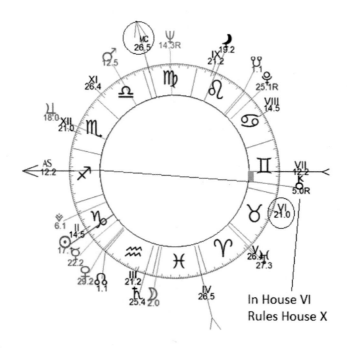

In House VI
Rules House X

Chiron is opposed to the Ascendant. Although a rather "light" aspect due to the orb of over 7°, it tells about health and the necessity to observe certain rules to preserve an optimum physiological state. Chiron is in House VI (work and health) conjunct the Descendant. The aspect shows that Elvis probably attached more importance to the wellbeing of those around (Descendant) than to his own (Ascendant). He was a workaholic with a critical and self-critical eye. He was a master in his own field, but he spent his lifetime doubting and always questioning the reason for his enormous success (Chiron rules the Mid-Heaven) to the point of damaging his health.

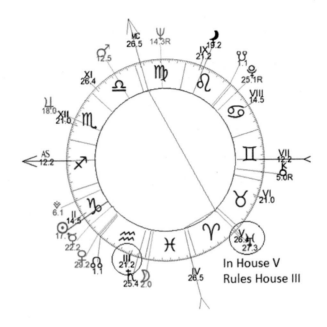

In House V
Rules House III

Uranus inconjunct Mid-Heaven forms a semi-sextile with the Nadir. Perhaps Elvis succeeded too early. Uranus indicates a sudden and unexpected success (Mid-Heaven) to the detriment of a stable home (Nadir). There was a karmic need to come to terms with poverty that triggered his originality. Uranus still in House IV (family) is conjunct the cusp of House V (creativity). The half-sextile, in my opinion, is not as beneficial as it is known to be. The elements representing the signs involved are not compatible. In this example, Uranus is in Aries (Fire sign) and the Nadir in Pisces (Water sign). Fire and water do not spontaneously combine happily. Hence, the difficulties met by Elvis to preserve a stable home environmont, to have a family and a place to really call home. Uranus rules House III (brothers and sisters) indicating that he may have been grieving his dead twin brother, and later his mum. His originally creative (House V) manner of expression (House III) may have very well been induced by the loss of his twin brother (House III) while he was a child (House V).

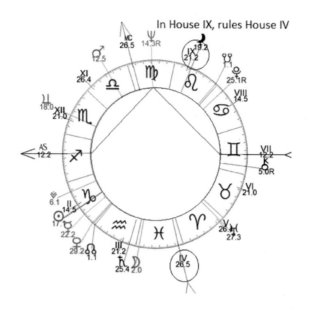

In House IX, rules House IV

Neptune square Ascendant, square Descendant. Neptune rules House IV and is found in House IX. This configuration shows how confused the "King" was about himself and his entourage. It shows the influence of spiritual beliefs that did little to help him concretely. They are relevant of the drugs he would take to keep up with the pace. Medication to sleep and medication to wake up and stay awake. Elvis was not the type to get drunk on alcohol. He did not take illegal drugs. On the contrary, he openly stood up and even financed anti-drug campaigns. However, his doctor never hesitated to prescribe medicine that was said to have contributed to the man's death. Elvis loved lollies. He could eat enormous amounts of these daily. He was a dreamer, an idealist. As such he ran the risk of being profoundly disappointed. He did on several occasions. Those around him took advantage of his generosity and naivety. His philosophy of life and moral principles (House IX) were greatly influenced by his origin, his family background, and his mum (House IV).

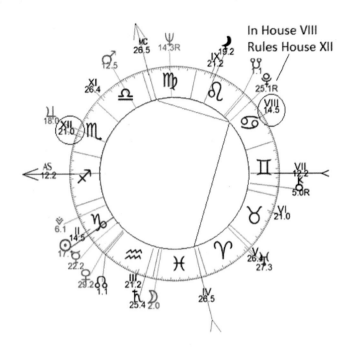

In House VIII
Rules House XII

Last, but not least, Pluto is trine Nadir and sextile Mid Heaven. It rules House XII and is found in House VIII. The strong bond with his parents was an immense source of inspiration and motivation. There was a spiritual quest to succeed to offer his parents the wealth they were deprived of when Elvis was a child. He was fascinated by death (House VIII) and attracted to religious beliefs that made him more determined. Death killed the man, but not the myth. Almost half a century after passing, Elvis is still selling records and DVDs of the movies he made, documentaries about his life, and live shows. Some say that ho is still alive somewhere under another name. Pluto is death and death means resurrection...

Note that the planets mentioned should also be linked to the rulers of the signs where they are found. Mars in Libra is "ruled" by Vesta. Vesta in Capricorn is ruled by Saturn. Saturn in Aquarius is ruled by Uranus. Uranus in Leo is ruled by Mars. This planetary chain shows the directions Elvis needed to take to deal with the energy of Mars more efficiently. However, Mars is forming squares with the elements in Capricorn: Vesta, the Sun, Mercury, Venus, and the North Node. It is also forming a large opposition with Uranus found in Aries, Mars's sign…

In the lives of more "ordinary" people, the aspects described above might not have so obvious consequences. However, when a person decides to lead an adventurous existence, striving for success, for the spotlight, for the front of the social stage, the aspects in the chart become more expressive and revealing. Destiny and personality cohabit to provide the necessary sustained energy to climb to the summit envisioned.

The aspects between planets and cusps of angular Houses are crucial factors to consider. They perfect the analysis of a birth chart, linking planets to the sectors of life represented by the angular Houses and by the Houses where the planets are found and those ruled by such planets. Larger orbs can be applied. They often allow a deeper and more accurate analysis.

* * * * * * * * * *

Epilogue

Many more elements are necessary to perfect the analysis of a birth chart. This book only reveals the tip of the iceberg and some of its submerged part. I hope it has motivated your desire to discover more of this fascinating subject.

To me, astrology is an art. As such, I need to practise every day, like musicians do with their instruments. Mastering an art is a lifetime mission. I was 25 years old when I fell into the celestial void of astrology. It quickly captivated me to the point of obsession. Almost five decades later, I am still like a child discovering Disney Land!

They say that the best way to learn is to do so in a playful way. This is true for children but also for adults. How many of us can remember a funny joke they heard years ago? How many of us can remember the boring lessons they had to learn at school despite their distaste of the subject?

Nowadays, when I watch a talk show on TV, I try to determine the zodiac signs of the guests, or where relevant planets are in their chart. I get the answer on the Internet from sites like astrotheme.com. It is simple, fun, and yet quite a useful exercise. It keeps me in touch with the art even when I relax after a long day's work. It also repeatedly shows how obvious cosmic influences are.

Thank you again for your interest in my work. I wish you success and happiness practising astrology for "a better life"!

Roland Legrand - 4 December 2020

Table of contents

Made in the USA
Middletown, DE
23 October 2021